IN THE RECORD

IN THE RECORD

The *Simeon Stylites* Columns of William A. Caldwell

Selected and with an Introduction by Mark A. Stuart

DISCARD

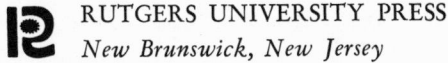

RUTGERS UNIVERSITY PRESS
New Brunswick, New Jersey

I pray Thee make my column read,
And give me thus my daily bread.
Endow me, if Thou grant me wit,
Likewise with sense to mellow it.
                                    Don Marquis

CONTENTS

INTRODUCTION

INTRODUCTION

William A. Caldwell is the most complete reporter and the most self-effacing legend I know. When reporters who've never worked with him are told only half the truth about this man, they don't believe it. The sheer amount of work of which he is capable is staggering. Every morning, five days a week, he writes two or more editorials. They are cogent, logical, parse perfectly, and sometimes irresistibly move the immovable. They may be in turn indignant, humorous, biting, sad, but never scolding.

Caldwell writes these editorials on odd sheets. Sometimes they come on long rolls of teletype paper he cribs from the wire room. Sometimes they are on ruled sheets torn from a looseleaf composition book such as is carried by a sixth grade student. Always the words are set down without an excision, a deletion, without an eraser's mark or an x-ing out, without a single overprint. The copy is as clean as if it had been retyped by an excellent secretary. No secretary would consent to type on such sheets.

Always these editorials talk directly to the reader. They explain, counsel, point an accusing finger, peel the layers of cant from a problem, and always they offer solutions. That is important.

"It isn't enough," he tells colleagues, "to state the problem. You must propose a solution."

Bill Caldwell's solutions are forthright, compounded of old-fashioned common sense, a deep Christian ethic, a profound understanding of the human heart and mind, and a currency with affairs in New Jersey, the United States, the world.

Sometimes Caldwell, say his few critics, can be too fair. He

3

never suffers fools gladly but scoundrels are often treated with scrupulous correctness until they are judged in a court of law. Sins are enumerated, never judged until a jury has its say. Once judged, however, a fraud is fair game. Few can flail as deftly as Bill Caldwell. His innate sense of order and decency offended, he tears into a depredator with the quiet efficiency of a piranha.

All this is in the morning. The afternoon is for other things, mainly the column. It is called "Simeon Stylites" after a fifth-century Syrian hermit who spent thirty-five years in meditation perched atop a pillar in the desert. It is this column for which the 1971 Pulitzer Prize in commentary was awarded.

Simeon Stylites has been preaching from the editorial pages of *The Record,* Bergen County's only daily newspaper, for forty years, six days a week. That's 12,000 columns, give or take a dozen, or 10,200,000 words.

Like the editorials, each is typed faultlessly and always on the long sheet. Each is exactly eighty-five lines long—not eighty-six or eighty-four. It is these columns of which the *New York Times* said that they urged the conservative community to take a more active role in local affairs. The community is not quite as conservative as the *Times* claims, and much of this is due to the column and the views that Bill Caldwell expresses in it each day.

Each day Caldwell sits at his desk in the fourth floor corner office of *The Record's* ultramodern newsroom (there are some who say it looks more like an insurance office than a newsroom) in Hackensack. Before him on the desk are a container of sharpened pencils, a felt-tipped pen he uses for editing, a huge penknife with which he slices apples and cheese (his favorite lunch), several pipes, tobacco, matches, and a few neatly placed sheets of information.

Looking out the wide window at the county courthouse dome in the distance or the huge parking lot just below, he bends to his machine and begins typing. The words stream out, line after steady line, and the world intrudes on 150 River Street.

Bill Caldwell, his brother Bob is fond of saying, was a sage at seventeen. It was easy. "All he had to do," says Bob, "was learn to write beautifully by the time he was fifteen, and along with it learn that you'll never write as well as you ought to, and at the same time learn to be a crack player in football and baseball, be a pianist, an organist."

Caldwell's favorite exclamation at good news about someone else is "great!", but it's a word the young reporters apply regularly to his work. That's because Caldwell is a great editor who would rather be a beat reporter than anything else.

In Chicago at the Democratic Party convention in 1968, when bystanders were being mauled and gassed by Mayor Daley's police, Bill was on the job as reporter. He had with him two colleagues, each half his age or less. Nightly he left them panting. Ready to drop, they would gaze glassy-eyed at the sixty-one-year-old Caldwell off and running to see for himself just what was happening in the streets and the convention hall. Each day his copy flowed into the newsroom crisp, complete, colorful, on time—always on time—and full of insights it took other observers days to arrive at, if ever.

In addition Simeon kept preaching. Each day there was commentary adding to the understanding of the news.

They say all this talent is self-taught. He taught himself to play the piano and the organ, to read music, to cook like Escoffier, to play a major-league brand of baseball and football.

Caldwell can't remember if he ever got his diploma from Hasbrouck Heights High School. He went to work part time in his junior year when his father, a newspaperman, died. But Caldwell never ceased being educated. He reads everything, including Dr. Eliot's famous five-foot shelf. He leads a group of home-grown philosophers who call themselves "The Wranglers"; their diet is the Great Books, or Ovid, or the Mets, or the Eurodollar, or anything anyone that week has decided he'd like to become a nut on.

Bill Caldwell is sixty-five now, but he's tuned in. Young people would rather spend time in his company than with most of their contemporaries. He appreciates. He encourages. He always has time for them. After those two editorials, the column —and more—and the editing of the op ed page, and the layout, and the assigning of think pieces, there's always time for a chat, a pat on the back, an idea-swapping session, a story, some advice to a younger colleague.

It began in Butler, Pa. (that's the home of Miss U.S.A. of 1971) on Dec. 5, 1906. Bill Caldwell grew up in Titusville where his father was managing editor of the Titusville *Herald*.

Bill Caldwell was eleven when the family moved to New Jersey. The elder Caldwell had gone to work for the Associated Press in New York, where eventually he became cable news editor. The father died in 1922 at forty-four, leaving a widow with five minor children. This was a trying time, and fifteen-year-old Bill, a sophomore at Hasbrouck Heights High, took odd jobs to eke out a family living. He was the eldest son and the breadwinner, along with his mother, who went back to school-teaching. One job was pumping the organ at a local church, and this is where he taught himself to play as well as pump. Eventually he worked his way up to paid organist.

One of the odd jobs in which Caldwell had apprenticed was as copy boy at the AP. Young Bill approached the *Bergen Evening Record* and asked for a job. He was tossed out by a singularly unperceptive managing editor. That worthy had the sense, however, to offer young Bill space rates for sports copy covering local high school events. That was 1924.

The Record was a sponge for young Caldwell's talent. He turned in so much copy, all of it good, that two years later the managing editor figured out it would be cheaper to put him on the payroll full time.

In 1929 Caldwell left the sports beat. Sent to the city beat with Caldwell was Donald G. Borg, then the publisher's green young son, now editor and chairman of the board of *The Record*.

"When they transferred us," Caldwell recalls, "from sports to general assignment I guess we still dealt with politics the way a sportswriter would, as if it were a game the name of which is Who Gets What?"

Caldwell remembers: "We tried to seem interested when stuffy dullards talked about .22-caliber patronage, and we wrote the kind of copy that appeared to be expected about the worm-can writhings of titans whose names I don't remember, and we began to suspect, as young people periodically do, that our elders didn't know what was going on.

"The world came to pieces that winter of 1929. In an icy cellar in Garfield I stood with two policemen beside a man's bed. Someone had heard his groaning. He was thin and blue, and his eyes rolled back until the whites showed, and he died. Starvation.

" 'Good God,' I said, 'can such things be?' It did not occur to me that I had raised a political question."

Then came the Lodi Township sewer scandal. From Bill Caldwell, and those of colleagues Don Borg and Jim Sutphen, came the stories that changed the shape of a county, and the victory and the ouster of the state senator who had engineered it all.

They wanted Caldwell on the copy desk after that. Be an editor, they told him. They ordered, and when he didn't obey, they begged. So he came into the desk and it wasn't enough to sit there, and make others' prose shine, and write headlines. He took to writing editorials and then the column, the Simeons.

The modern Simeon has gone forty years now, and he does more than meditate and preach from the column's top.

Bill Caldwell never did get to college, and that didn't prevent him from becoming chairman of the board of William Paterson College, and didn't stop him from being given an honorary LL.D. by Rutgers University in 1970.

He gives of himself too out of the office. The American Cancer Society membership will attest to that, and the Grand Jurors Association, the Tuberculosis and Health Association, the county medical society, Americans for Democratic Action (he was a founding member of the New Jersey branch), and the American Civil Liberties Union, and others.

Wherever the causes are just, Bill Caldwell gives.

"When Bill came to *The Record*," says his younger brother Bob, "he was the youngest member of the staff. He still is."

This is a personal selection, for William A. Caldwell's "Simeon Stylites" column for which he was awarded the 1971 Pulitzer Prize is a jewel of many facets. Any reader could find others as much to his taste, if he were willing to go through the pages of *The Record* of Bergen County for the past forty years.

Of 12,000-odd columns there must be some I've left out that others of his 360,000 readers remember better. It's inevitable. Bill Caldwell reaches all who read him, and for some there is deep personal meaning. Also inevitable is the enjoyment this personal selection will give to those who've never read Bill Caldwell. This is a random selection. It touches his youth, nostalgia, the lonely whistle of the *Phoebe Snow* as she calls out to the Ramapos, the taste of fresh strawberries.

There is a sweetness in the man in the classical sense, in Horatio's statement of Hamlet. There is also fire, terrible indignation at man's stubborn streak, sadness at his persistent folly, and with all that, a love of humans as beings. There is a streak of ethical Puritanism in Caldwell that defends the rights of the pornographer as vigorously as it protects the innocence of youth.

These columns are timeless, whether they are about liberty, parenthood, music and art, New Jersey, religion, education, or his beloved Martha's Vineyard, where he has spent his vacations since the 1940s and where he hopes to retire.

Here also is the story of why "Simeon Stylites" as a column title, and the eleven columns that the Pulitzer Prize judges studied before awarding him the 1971 prize for commentary.

Read them all at once or one at a time. Read them in snatches. Don't try to study them. They are not texts to be memorized but lessons to be enjoyed.

MARK A. STUART

Hackensack, New Jersey
December, 1971

SIMEON STYLITES

SIMEON STYLITES

The column heading had been there so long that few questioned its meaning. Once in a while a reader would come along who would be a new resident, a new mind captured by the sly wisdom of something he hadn't expected to find in a surburban newspaper, and the question would come:

"Just what is Simeon Stylites, and why that name for a newspaper column?"

The answer was usually private. Bill Caldwell's notes are collectors' items, and the reader lucky enough to get his answer in writing was thrilled with it.

Just once was the rule broken. A sweet reader had written of her enchantment with a particular column. This made her bold.

"The title of the column," she asked, "does it have anything to do with apes, you know, gorillas?"

He had to explain it. June 10, 1970, was the day he told her publicly what and who Simeon Stylites was.

Accounting for Simeon

She had said tactfully that the "Simeon Stylites" column of 2nd inst. had enchanted her, and when she added that she didn't remember what it was about, scatterbrain that she was, I knew she had something else on her mind.

"By the way," she said with the sudden brisk clarity that

11

serves notice the by-the-ways are over and we're getting down to the nitty-gritty—"by the way, that title of the column, does it have anything to do with apes, you know, gorillas?"

No, I said; that homonym is spelled "simian."

There was muffled shouting on the line. She had cupped her hand over the mouthpiece.

"I was just telling Mr. Smarty Pants here he was wrong, as usual," she said. "Now, about 'Simeon Stylites.'"

I told her about Simeon Stylites. It takes 36.9 seconds.

"See here, mister," she said; "there's an awful lot of people in the world that never heard of that cat." An edge of asperity had come into her voice. Evidently it does not please everyone to find he has missed the point of a small joke. "Maybe you better explain it, eh?"

I had just finished explaining it, I said.

"In print, eh?" she said. "So cats like Mr. Smarty Pants here can see for themselves, eh?"

Back in the fifties witty, tender Phyllis McGinley undertook to explain Simeon Stylites. He's the title of a poem in the collected *Times Three* (Viking, New York) that begins:

> On top of a pillar Simeon sat.
> He wore no mantle,
> He had no hat,
> But bare as a bird
> Sat night and day.
> And hardly a word
> Did Simeon say.

She explained Simeon Stylites. She didn't explain "Simeon Stylites."

To go back to the beginning, then, we shall have to go back to the fourth century, when the church was become an establishment governing the lives of millions of men. She had grown tolerant of human frailty. She may indeed have shared in frailties and enjoyed them. In Egypt and the Middle East there was angry dissent.

12

Anchorites and hermits, wedded to the good old austerities, formed communes, refused to wash, lived by weaving mats and baskets. One of these bizarre evangelists was Simeon Stylites (390?–459). It would be vanity to try to improve on Will Durant's synopsis. This is from *The Age of Faith,* the fourth volume of his titanic The Story of Civilization:

> At Kalat Seman, in northern Syria, about 422, Simeon built himself a column six feet high and lived on it. Ashamed of his moderation, he built and lived on ever taller columns, until he made his permanent abode on a pillar sixty feet high. Its circumference at the top was little more than three feet; a railing kept the saint from falling to the ground in his sleep.
>
> On this perch Simeon lived uninterruptedly for thirty years, exposed to rain and sun and cold. A ladder enabled disciples to take him food and remove his waste. . . .
>
> From his high pulpit on the column he preached sermons to the crowds that came to see him, converted barbarians, performed marvelous cures, played ecclesiastical politics, and shamed the money lenders into reducing their interest charges from 12 to 6 per cent.

"His exalted piety," says Will Durant, "created a fashion of pillar hermits which lasted for twelve centuries and, in a thoroughly secularized form, persists today."

Everything clear now? No?

Well, along about January 1930 the present Editor and Publisher of *The Record* thought it might be constructive to have on the editorial page a column of local origin rather than syndicated copy or serialized fiction, which was the usage. It would need a standing headline or title, some symbol of continuity, and people were invited to submit suggestions, with the usual embarrassing results, such as "Bon Mots Politique," which wasn't even grammatical, and "The Last Word," which was copyrighted. Oh, hell, said the Editor, let's call it "Simeon Stylites" until something more useful turns up, and for a few years we ran a legend under the title explaining things adequately, we thought:

"From the Top of a Column He Philosophizes About the Interesting Things of Life."

Simeon was a commentator on a column. "Simeon" would be a commentator in a column. The meaning seemed obvious. People began asking why we didn't eliminate the explanatory legend. We did. People began asking why we didn't explain our meaning more clearly. It occurred to me last Jan. 11 that I'd been mumbling away on this perch ten years longer than the original columnist lasted, but I can't say I've acquired any other of his bad habits: no asceticism, no putrefaction, no worms that I know of. I am not sure that quite everything is clear, nor is Phyllis McGinley:

> And why did Simeon sit like that,
> Without a garment,
> Without a hat,
> In a holy rage
> For the world to see?
> It puzzles the age,
> It puzzles me.
> It puzzled many
> A Desert Father.
> And I think it puzzled the Good Lord, rather.

But at any rate affidavit is taken herewith that the facts hereinabove are correct.

THE PULITZER SUBMISSIONS

THE PULITZER SUBMISSIONS

The collection of Simeon Stylites sent to the 1971 Pulitzer Prize judges was made up of eleven columns. There could have been ten or thirty. But these were the ones selected by his colleagues (Bill Caldwell is too diffident to ever say which he calls his best), and these were the ones admired.

William A. Caldwell's work had been submitted for consideration by the Pulitzer Prize judges before. These are the ones that did the trick. They are as representative of that agile, fertile, kindly, and inquiring mind as any.

December's Castaways

I have no clear recollection of the event, but the first of many unforeseen calamities in my life occurred Dec. 5, 1906, in Butler, Pa. I was born.

The pickle into which a December baby gets by letting that happen to him is peculiar and, I have been persuaded, embittering. Except for a relatively few persons who appear to have been generated in the form of mildew on the walls of damp cellars, everyone gets born. But only 8.333 . . . per cent of us have our birthday so close to Christmas that, instead of being a revenue-producing asset, it is a bleak embarrassment.

For the other 91.666 . . . per cent a birthday is when the family forgathers from miles around to indulge in drink and gluttony and insane laughter. The table is festive. Best clothes are worn. In the living room the birthday celebrant presides over the submission of the loot, piece by glittering piece.

"Oh dear, this is much too much," says the child of March or August or November—correctly, by the way.

"Oh, but birthdays come but once a year," oozes Aunt Molly. "Come over here and let your auntie kiss you."

The December child stands in the doorway examining this repellent scene and understanding how oppressed minorities feel. He knows what will happen on his birthday. Everybody will be too much fatigued by the holiday gadding to come to his party, or will be preparing to be all fagged out, and besides there won't be any party. Since everyone is watching his diet at this time of year, cake is an indulgence that should be resisted, and one does grow so tired of turkey!

The small remembrance is in a small, flat, square box. The other kids get Maseratis and Winchester .22s and motorboats and hip boots. December's child will never run out of handkerchiefs.

As a december child named Love was complaining not long ago in one of the Washington papers, this, like any other discrimination based on the accident of birth, is especially hard to bear. Mr. Love worked himself into a fine lather of indignation. I found myself reading the piece with a curious sense of detachment.

A little while before my birthday the bride had been crayoning holiday engagements into the squares on the kitchen calendar.

"You have a birthday coming up," she said. "Or would you just as soon forget it? For two bits I won't tell anyone."

Forget it? What else, I snarled, have people been doing all my life? I do a passable imitation of my aunt with the adenoids.

"Your birthday does come so close to Christmas, William," I said, "that your uncle and I thought you'd rather we saved a real surprise for you until then."

"I wish to peace I'd known you feel so deeply about it," she

18

said. "But now that I know, we're going to do something about it. What would you like for your birthday?"

"Nothing," I said. "If you must know, I'm down to my last three dozen handkerchiefs."

She handles children sympathetically.

"If you had to wish for something or be sentenced to another year as chairman of the board of trustees," she said, "what would you wish for?"

There have been Decembers when I'd have known what to say: a sled with steel runners, an electric train, a BB gun, a pair of football shoes, a deerskin jacket, counterpoint lessons of all things, ice skates, a basset hound, a sailfish, a bicycle, a little printing press and a font of 12-point italic type . . .

She was waiting.

Abruptly, on the eve of my birthday, I had run out of things to want. The goods and gadgets I had yearned for as a kid and had begrudged not getting were irrelevant. I have clothes enough to last me a lifetime though I live to be 200, and as for things to do there's a piano that could keep me busy practicing cheerfully four hours a day at least, plus, although it is old and its lower-case characters are clogged, a typewriter that works quite well enough to keep pace with my brain.

This is not to imply that my cup runneth over. The world is a mess, a dangerous mess, and the air is fouled and there is all around us an anxiety—a combination of tension and envy and smoldering anger and hate—that is becoming diagnosable illness.

But nobody can knit you or run down to the store and buy in a package the cure for things like these, and no kinfolk can chip in and present to a man that whose name he dares scarcely to say even to himself: that, knowing what he does now, he could go back and be again a kid of twenty-five or thirty or maybe forty-five.

He would like to be wiser, leaner, more patient, less lazy, better read, braver, more honest and at the same time more lenient toward the people around him . . .

She was waiting.

"Look," I said, "my birthday comes so close to Christmas, why don't you save a real surprise for me till then?"

The Day Abe Shot a Sexy Myth

That would have been the most uh week of a very nothing winter except that it produced Honest Abe's Goldurn-U-All self-test kit. Try it. In six seconds it detects whether you're a white racist.

Last Monday, a day that will live in the history of scientific diagnosis, Sen. Abraham Ribicoff of Connecticut made a speech in the Senate explaining why he's supporting legislation to apply guidelines for school desegregation uniformly throughout the country.

The North is guilty of monumental hypocrisy in its treatment of the black man. Without question, Northern communities have been as systematic and as consistent as Southern communities in denying the black man and his children the opportunities that exist for white people.

He hauled out his statistics.

In the South, 70 per cent of black children are sent to schools which to all practical intents and purposes are segregated.

In the North, half of all black students are sent to schools which are 95 to 100 per cent black.

The test is coming up. It is as simple and foolproof as the strip of yellow paper that notifies the diabetic in the morning whether sugar is spilling over from his bloodstream into his urine.

If your response to Abe Ribicoff's reproach is that in their black schools is where blacks belong and be damned to them, you're a white racist and know it. Goodbye.

20

If your response is that segregation de facto in the North is different from segregation de jure, by law, in the South, you're a bore.

But if you protest that our kind of school segregation is less mean and obnoxious than their kind you're the sort of racist—innocent, liberal, and self-righteous—who actually prevents solution of an injustice that's tearing the country to pieces.

Black children are concentrated in ghetto schools because their parents are concentrated in ghettos. Their parents live in the ghetto (a) because they haven't money enough to move out or (b) because the white outside's zoning ordinances, transit patterns, or real estate agents prevent them from going where they'd rather be.

Ribicoff said it better. Let's be honest with ourselves whatever else we do, he said, and then:

> Our problem is not only the dual systems of education which exist 16 years after the Supreme Court struck them down in 1954. The more fundamental problem is the dual society that exists in every metropolitan area—the black society of the central city and the white society of the suburb. Massive school segregation does not exist because we have segregated our schools but because we have segregated our society and our neighborhoods.
>
> That is the source of the inequality, the tension, and the hatred that disfigure our nation.

Some tedious old Southern hypocrites in the Senate were, of course, pleased that Abe the Democrat, Abe the liberal, Abe the one-time HEW secretary, the Abe of that gallant stand against the machine in Chicago, was supporting an amendment sponsored by Stennis of Mississippi. The New York Times study that day finding that racial polarization is producing something like anarchy in the schools couldn't have delighted them more. And some tedious Northern hypocrites were shocked that Mr. Ribicoff had said what everybody knows. Don't hold against him his knack of moving hypocrites. What did he do to you?

Segregation de facto is a local story throughout the North. We know this when a city blows up or the Black Panthers, on the

21

mistaken theory that they have nothing to lose, fight it out with the police. We—that is to say, well-meaning white liberals—tend otherwhiles to shove it out of sight, out of mind, or we say it is a school problem and tell the board of education to put it on a bus and get rid of it.

It is so insidiously easy to sigh that we have done all we could but the problem is so large and diffuse, so remote, that we can't do anything about it.

"As every past generation has had to disenthrall itself from its inheritance of truisms and stereotypes," said President Kennedy at the Yale commencement eight years ago, "so in our time we must move on from the reassuring repetition of stale phrases to a new, difficult, but essential confrontation with reality."

The Northern white liberal has been living by a comfortable myth: that oppression de facto is significantly different from oppression de jure. It is a myth that has enabled him to consent, as the much misunderstood and helpless people of Nazi Germany consented, to a horror.

It will no longer do. Abe Ribicoff disenthralled us. The date was February 9.

The Willing and Unable

What does Spiro T. Agnew have in common with the Weathermen, the postal service strikers, the Communists, student militants, and the ad hoc committee of man-hating women who or which took over the editorial offices of the *Ladies' Home Journal* one day last week?

Corpuscles, you say. Don't be a wise guy.

What they have in common is the delusion that he who controls a nation's communications controls the nation.

All Mr. Agnew wants is to change the tone and content of

newspapers and broadcast news programs that do not genuflect and preserve a reverent silence when the President speaks.

All the Weathermen ask when folk dancing with police or college presidents is exclusive access to the bullhorn. An interesting coincidence is the fact that two of the three latest bombings in New York wrecked the offices of IBM and General Telephone—communication companies.

Seizure of the newspapers and radio stations is the classic first step in any Communist revolution.

Don't be too sure the postal workers can't blackmail the country. The mail is the jugular.

Maybe we'd better not discuss the sit-in at the *Ladies' Home Journal*. Somebody's likely to giggle and get disrupted. If there's one thing these owlish busybodies lack besides It, that thing is a sense of humor.

If the life of a great magazine, a great institution, were not involved, it might be suggested that the men and women who run the *Journal* hand it over to the Feminists, the Media Women, the Redstockings, NOW, and the New York Radical Feminists. They have ideas about how the magazine should be edited. It might be constructive to let them try.

They barged into the office with a dummy cover for the special women's liberation issue which they'd produce. It depicted a pregnant woman holding a placard reading: "Unpaid Labor." Doesn't that grab you? No? But inside the book there'd be articles titled "Prostitution and the Law" and "Can Marriage Survive Women's Liberation?" and a column on a variety of subjects under the general heading "How to Have an Orgasm."

You are not to construe any of this as a criticism of the Fem-Lib movement. It is meant to be a wistful defense of competence. I don't know what the feminists want. If it's freedom, I'm with them. If it's bigamy, abortion, licensure of prostitution, the abolition of pregnancy, or a statute reducing the period of gestation, that's their bag. They're entitled to free choice of things to get damp about.

All I'm here to protest is that a willingness to take charge should not be mistaken for ability to do so.

In his own way that sweet crank Ted Agnew may have planted the pernicious notion that just about anybody could edit a magazine or a newspaper or radio and television news programming if the radical billionaires who control the media weren't so effete, arrogant, supercilious, or intellectual. When he asked who elected the editors and commentators he reduced the process of personnel selection to the level of a contest for county committeeman: no qualifications necessary; just apply for the job, and it's yours.

I've seen magazines like the post-liberation *Journal*. They flourish throughout the country. They are the underground press, and don't knock it. It reports things that nobody else is reporting, and it is doing wonders for hundreds of yearning but frustrated egos.

It is not, by and large, well edited. It is not well written. There's a substantive difference between the clean professionalism of the great magazines' expository or narrative writing and the defiant slovenliness of the amateur self-expression that has suddenly become marketable. The business of editors like Carter of the *Journal* is to make the copy as comprehensible as it can be made. "Here I am," says the op-art writer; "it's up to you to understand me, stupid," and the arrogance of this carriage seems to me offensive.

The experiment would be costly and reckless, but someday after the war is liquidated and we've rebuilt the cities and solved the three dozen problems now having top priority we might finance a test of the folks who are nominating themselves to be commissars in charge of colleges and media and medicine and transportation and urban planning and—well, cetera.

Kicks? Agnew would run the bureau of propaganda and public enlightenment, the Weathermen would run enforcement up to and including the courts and the jails, the girls would run the obstetrical quarterlies, the freshmen would run the universities, the patients would perform the operations, and we'd all issue unbreakable commands which nobody would have to obey.

After a few hours of that we'd invent law, order, leadership, and the virtues of merit and talent. Come that revolution!

The Rake's Progress

This is terribly good-natured of me. A reader inquires why These Young People are so weak-minded and badly reared as to use drugs. It seems to me the answer she wants is packaged in her question. It seems to me also that venerable ignoramuses' ventilation of opinions on things they don't know anything about contributes more to environmental pollution than to knowledge and understanding.

But, being relentlessly good-natured, I can tell That Old Reader how and why addiction occurs.

William C—— underwent his first exposure to a habit-forming drug at the age of seven and a half. He was living on a farm, far from corrupting influences such as pornography salesmen and peer groups, but he was a curious, attentive tad, and he could not help noticing the mysterious behavior of the hired man.

After supper and the chores in the barn were done on summer evenings the hired man would take a cigar out of a cedar box he kept on the dresser in his room downstairs, and would go sit on the porch rocking and looking off across the folded valleys and rolling glacial hills. Carefully he would light the cigar, examine the glowing tip, draw and exhale a cloud of fragrant smoke, close his eyes, and lean back in some utter ecstasy of contentment.

The man was stoned.

William C—— naturally stole one of the hired man's cigars and, after breakfast next morning, strolled up the dusty road a

25

mile or so to a bend alongside which the gully paralleling the road was deep enough to hide in. He lighted the cigar. What I am saying, as forthrightly as possible, is that the example of a respected elder led this innocent child into his first experimentation with addictive drugs.

He took two or three puffs, and, although lung cancer had not been invented at the time, it occurred to him that what he was doing would not be good for his health. He coughed a while, took a fourth puff, and found himself remembering a story he had overheard an uncouth old uncle telling his father.

Whatever that was, two boys had heard there was a house of ill fame in town. Somehow they found the fee was $2. They staked out the place and observed that it was patronized by respectable citizens. The two boys put their savings together, cranked up their nerve, and knocked on the door of the house.

"We'll take a quarter's worth," they piped when management came to the door, and she hauled them inside, boxed their ears, slapped their faces, shook them till their eyeballs rattled, whaled their bottoms with a new, stiff bedroom slipper, and flung them out the door and down the steps into the street.

"Well," said the one boy to the other, "thank goodness we had only a quarter. I don't think I could go two bucks' worth of that."

The cigar slipped from William C——'s nerveless fingers. The world reeled about him. Over the rest of the scene we draw the curtain of charity to the sensitive reader. He was spanked when he staggered, green and reeking, back to the house.

Years passed. William C——, now grown to the full-pimpled repulsiveness of adolescence, was sitting in the village park with a circle of fellow students of experimental delinquency. One of them hauled out a ten-cent cardboard box of Luckies. It went from hand to hand. Everyone took a cigarette except him. He remembered the cigar.

"I think I'll pass," he said.

"What, you yellow?" said Walter S——. "Chicken" as a pejorative had not yet entered the language.

"You don't know what you're missing," said Philip R——.

"Why; what's it like?" said our tragic hero.

"Well," said John McW——, "you can't really describe it, can you, fellas?"

No, they agreed, sputtering and sneezing and blinking back the tears, no; cigarette smoking was a thing you just can't talk about very effectively. Either you did it, or you had missed one of life's great moments. Either you had gone into the world out there beyond the first Lucky, or, frankly, you just were not with it.

It had not happened to him before. For the first time he was being notified, as people like him were accustomed to telling persons who went to different churches or wore skin of a different color: "You are not one of us."

He hesitated. He decided, as a wiser man named Socrates had decided millenniums ago, that exile is the cruelest fate that can befall a man. Socrates took hemlock; a bad trip. William took a Lucky.

It made me sick but not sick enough.

I don't know whether anybody can explain to a whisky-guzzling, cigarette-smoking, pill-swallowing adult generation how and why These Young People acquire their wretched habits. As you say, ma'am, the old American virtues are going out of style.

Redemption in Soybeans

There are times when a man wishes he could be as sure about anything as other people are about everything, and this would be one of the times.

27

A word of prologue is indicated.

The American Society of Newspaper Editors invited me to write for its bulletin a piece developing a theory of mine that the media have become the scapegoat of a troubled and frustrated society.

Their reporting the symptoms of breakdown in the other great institutions is resented.

If they don't report the bad news they are reviled as irresponsible; if they do they're whipped as the village scold.

No matter how they conduct themselves, they cannot in the end make a lazy or corrupt community give a damn.

This is not necessarily the last word on the subject. The inability of radio and television and the newspapers to make 210 million care sufficiently probably defines a problem, their problem, and if so they should take it from there. In any event, that's where the piece stopped: "The media should do a better job of marketing the story. It is not yet within their power to make the consumer give a damn."

O.K., and so the telephone rang at an unlikely time of morning, and here was the dean of a small college in the Middle West to report that he has spent many years of scientific research on the phenomenon I mentioned, the indifference or hostility of the large majority toward news about the world that's too much with them.

This sounded interesting, and it was his nickel. I asked him why people resent, resist, and reject the information they need.

"Protein deficiency," he said.

Ah, I said, in the polite but embarrassed way with which one deals with callers who happen to be the late Hitler or to have discovered their mother-in-law has sicked the FBI on them or to have invented a way of running an internal combustion engine on a cupful of warm water—that is, I said ah. Indeed, I added.

He has written twelve volumes on this subject, the dean said, and he is satisfied—as a scientist, heh-heh—that the protein deficiency in the American diet accounts for the average citizen's immunity to damn-giving.

I thanked him. Evidently he construed this as evidence that I didn't sufficiently care about one of the great issues. Irritably he invited me to drop in the next time I'm in Nebraska or wherever it is and join him in soybean steaks, soybean soufflé, soybean salad. I think he said they even make shoes out of soybeans, which goes a long way toward explaining some of the curiosities we get when we order steaks in New Jersey, and that's about all there was to the conversation.

I had just blown another quarter hour of the springtime of youth on a kook.

Or so I think. I wish I could be sure.

The cause and effect relationship between soybean deficiency and epidemic indifference seems to me elusive. But what does anybody know about cause and effect? You dust your roses, and all the fish in a pond six miles away float to the surface dead. You install a new brazing furnace in your factory, and the paint falls off all the houses in town. You double the output of your corn-field, and the baby comes down with DDT poisoning. The welfare office puts a black family on a diet of carbohydrates, which are notoriously inadequate nutrients, and all the children grow up seven feet tall and strong enough to turn a railroad locomotive inside out.

None of the commonplaces was predictable—television, radar, the voyages to the Moon, nuclear energy, penicillin, smog, LSD, plastics, Agnew. And nothing is unpredictable. In a universe that consists of atoms which consist of particles which consist finally of swirling plus and minus charges, what is certain about anything?

The certainties which I assume, such as that my heart will resume beating after its next pause for rest—now—or that if I start for the door of this room the floor will not give way under my feet, these are no better than an actuary's probabilities. And, despite their impressive support in the physical sciences, such

29

probabilities as the Sun's rising on time tomorrow and the snow's melting when the temperature reaches +32 degrees Fahrenheit are based on experience and hope rather than immutable absolutes.

Still, on a bright spring day a man is compelled to believe in something, and with this principle in mind I took the snow shovels from the garage to the cellar and put the boots and galoshes away and helped the bride stow the heavy winter foul-weather gear in mothballs. That was Saturday.

I know a man who believes with all his heart that a compulsory diet of soybeans would produce in the United States an intellectual flowering that would dwarf the glory that was Greece. I envy that amiable eccentric, and where, by the way, could a fellow buy a soybean steak?

But Why Go to Pot?

After a recent meeting of the Ridgewood commissioners' select committee on drug addiction its chairman, B. Franklin Reinauer II, heard himself characterized by a young man about town as a lousy square.

Mr. Reinauer thought it over.

"Lousy I am not," he reported at last in his revealing speech to the Ridgewood Kiwanis Club last week. "Square I may be."

He identified as fellow squares such elders as Washington, Franklin, Jefferson, Nathan Hale, and Patrick Henry and such contemporaries as Glenn, Schirra, Armstrong, and Gen. Eisenhower, and he added:

"If being a square means striving to emulate the principles evoked by these men, I'll bet that like me you want to be counted in and would help us try to get our sons and daughters to join us."

30

Being called a square wasn't the only shock he suffered during the committee's exploration of drug addiction in the village. He described as horrendous these incidents:

A twelve-year-old boy, arrested for possession of marijuana, said on his arrival at the police department, "I am not answering any questions until my attorney gets here," and when he did, he didn't.

A teen-age girl puts drugs in the cookie batter, and serves the goodies at the weekend parties. She calls them hash brownies.

A girl has been on 200 LSD trips. Somebody asked her whether she was aware that if she had a baby it might be born deformed. She replied that she believed the chromosome structure of a person's body rejuvenates itself within seven years and, since she didn't plan to have a child within seven years, the fact [about deformity] was of no interest to her.

As he told his audience of businessmen, there's something to be horrified about.

Using marijuana regularly are 600 students in the high school, many in junior high school, and some in the elementary grades.

About 100 teen-agers are addicted to heroin or a like hard drug, and twenty or thirty are fooling around with it, in mixtures so dilute as to extend for a couple of months the process of unbreakable habituation.

Of more than sixty attempts at suicide in Ridgewood in the past year, half involved drugs. There are pot parties going on every weekend in many homes in this village.

I predict that there will be a substantial acceleration in the rate of use of narcotic drugs in the metropolitan New York area, including Ridgewood, within the next six months.

I predict that within the next few months some Ridgewood teen-ager will be brought into Valley Hospital dead on arrival from excessive use of narcotic drugs.

Now, Franklin Reinauer is not a square. He is an urbane, cultivated, sensitive gentleman. So he will be tolerant of this doubt of mine whether he's talking to the right audience about the right

31

subject when he warns Kiwanians that with one third of the young people in Bergen County on drugs, one third of us elders will be supplanted in due time by drug users and when he adds:

"As businessmen it behooves you to help eliminate this scourge of our society, for you must protect your businesses and your society if you wish to be in business a decade from now."

There's nothing square about this or in his indignation that old and good codes of morality and civility have gone out of style. There may be something deficient.

"No longer does it seem to be Man's dream to improve his condition by making a better life and situation for himself, his family, his society," said Mr. Reinauer. "No longer does hard work seem to be the 'in' thing."

He's right. That's the way it is. What's missing is a sense of wondering how and why it came to be this way.

And something's missing, unless I misread all the evidence, from the program the committee will recommend to the commissioners. Good as far as it goes, it will propose:

1. Strengthening the police agencies and calling in the FBI.

2. Establishment of a drug information center dealing in educational material and keeping a hot line open twenty-four hours a day.

3. Education in the schools starting with parents of children in first or second grade and bringing in the children at age nine.

4. Development of rehabilitation clinics and reinforcement of family counseling.

That's it, and what's missing, I suggest, is something as square as this:

5. Initiation of a systematic effort, manned by scientists and adequately financed, to find out why the children of highly educated and motivated parents in one of the most affluent of the suburbs, processed by one of the great school systems, take to drugs.

What they're doing the elders know. That's not the problem. Why they do it is the problem. To solve it help is needed—theirs.

Bless Them and Duck!

This is probably a little premature, O friend & brother, but if we could rendezvous about five minutes from now in the gents' room I'd like to ask what arrangements you're making for Aug. 26.

Aug. 26 will be Women's Strike for Equality Day. If I understand the strategy, they don't do whatever it is they do. Their instructions are to do their own thing by not doing their own thing. I guess I don't understand the strategy.

At any rate, the housekeeper won't keep house, the shopper won't shop, the working girl will call in sick or just notify the boss she's doing her thing and why doesn't he (she) do his (hers), such as go fry an egg. "Don't Iron While the Strike Is Hot" is the slogan.

What I have to know, brother, is how you're planning to deal with the crisis.

Some of the problems won't be problems. Rockland County's firm and unsmiling Betty Friedan, founder of NOW (National Organization for Women), is quoted as saying women in Boston plan to distribute 4,000 cans of contraceptive foam on the Commons that day, Aug. 26, which is being observed as the fiftieth anniversary of the amendment conferring on women the right to vote. The amendment was ratified Aug. 20, 1920. I apologize for the snide male chauvinism. Aug. 26 is the anniversary of Aug. 20, and if anybody hands me a can of contraceptive foam I shall accept it and distribute it impartially among migrant mosquitoes.

But I'm worried about my own responses to Strike for Equality Day. Does one bow and smile? Is one expected to affect shock and grief? Shall one cry for shame or huzza?

I'm serious because a deplorably—that is to say, admirably—

large number of women are, and I'd like to be on their side if I could find which side it is.

At the fish store the other day I stood aside on my way out and held the door open for a woman with the undershot jaw and earnest forward lunge of our gentle friend the barracuda.

"You can just stop that right now," she said, zipping through the door, however.

Not twenty-four hours later I got into an elevator in a classroom building at Rutgers. A woman professor was standing in the hallway chewing out some wretch, lank-haired and trousered but I believe male, and she was inching toward the elevator. I asked her whether it would be all right if I held the elevator for her, and, by the kind of coincidence that ought to be avoided, she said, "You can just stop that right now."

I'm not sure what was offensive. There are immense gray areas. The demands, I think, are:

Respect but not so much respect as to seem a thing bestowed, a condescension.

Dignity but not so much of it as to suggest worship, exaltation, the pedestal.

Attention but not much of it as to convey or imply the notion that the object thereof is a sex object.

Equality, and if I ever find out what equality as among people is I'll let you know.

Equality in wages I dig and advocate. I can think of no excuse in law or ethics for paying women less money than men for doing things they do as well as men or better. The proposition advanced by a Maryland doctor that women do less work because they're subject to incapacitation by the menstrual cycle and menopause is arrant guff. Dr. Edgar F. Berman, a member of the Democratic party's committee on national priorities, was explaining to Rep. Patsy Mink of Hawaii why the party shouldn't award a high priority to women's rights.

Dr. Berman is a scientist. He has access to clinical statistics. He should be challenged to produce hard evidence that women in the throes of hormone imbalance cost the economy more than men absent from duty by reason of hangover, hypochondria, or the virus disease called don't give a damn.

And it seems to me unnecessarily paternalistic to propose in defense of the shocking wage differential—it runs as high as two to one—that the man is the head of a family and has expenses to meet that women escape. Millions of women are heads of family. Millions more are working to help keep the family together, get kids through college, indeed get Father through college. It is grossly impertinent of the whole society to agree that, no matter what she does or how well she does it, a woman is of less value to it than a man simply by reason of being a woman.

That much I get.

What can't be understood is why this injustice, which is actionable, cannot be approached within the system—by legislation, by action at law, by due process. What can't be understood is why the system has to be struck in such a way that hurt will be done.

Very well, that's a stupid male chauvinist speaking, and I gather that nobody except a woman can understand a woman's rage any more than anybody who isn't black can comprehend why anger is the only appropriate response of the black to his condition.

What I'm asking, brother, is how you propose to deal with the events of Aug. 26. My conditioning up to now suggests that, no matter what we do, we shall be told we can just stop that. And if we do nothing, we can stop that too. Can we arrange just not to show up for the game?

Neighborly Settlement

In the deep glen across the way from the house where we live sprawls the long, low, yellow brick disposal plant of the esteemed

35

Northwest Bergen Sewer Authority. It is a good neighbor—minds its business, stays severely on its side of the property line, never violates the speed laws. Yet when I got up to walk the two-o'clock cramp the other night I found myself wishing for a reckless moment that it would pick its immense bulk off the floor of what used to be a lovely woods and would go the hell away. Just go away.

In the summertime when the trees are in full leaf it is invisible by day from our hillside, and at night its lights glimmering in the treetops are no more than a bluish moonshine. Even in winter, the naked black trees etching netted patterns against its blank walls and flat roofs, it is about as inoffensive as any public building can get.

But its continuous-process machinery groans and grunts and mumbles, 24 hours a day, month in and month out. It is scarcely noise. It is a presence. But even to proper megalopolitans accustomed to noise that is not noise—the grumble of the distant highway, the almost insensible thunder of the cities beyond the horizons, the 60-cycle hum of clocks and lights and refrigerators and oil heater motors—the singsong drone of the disposal plant machinery can seem intrusive.

So at 2 A.M. I heartily wished it were elsewhere.

At 2:01 I went to the window, apologized to it, and assured it that as far as we're concerned it is welcome to stay as long as it likes.

Another trade-off had been consummated.

Some scholar at Columbia University—trust me to have mislaid his name—proposed not long ago the theory that there is a constant and irreducible minimum of evil in the world. It is a dazzling insight. Evidence in support of it is leaping into your mind.

New York City needs electric power. If it doesn't get power by added tens of millions of kilowatts it is doomed to lose people, business, industry, its lively arts, everything that makes it New York. But power must be generated. And the same New York

36

that can't get along without power can't get along with generating stations.

Evil in one form or the other is unavoidable. A trade-off will have to be made.

Generating stations and high-voltage power lines festooned nakedly on great steel towers stalking across the countryside, air pollution from steam plants burning fossil fuel or heat pollution of rivers from nuclear plants, they're evil. We can choose not to endure them. That won't do away with evil. It will merely transmute evil into another shape: bone-freezing cold in winter, unescapable heat in summer, unemployment, dreariness, the crime that skulks in shadows, the fall of a great city.

A trade-off will be consummated. When people can't or won't make up their mind, almighty evil has its own way of handing down the decisions.

Agricultural sprays are evil. DDT hasn't a friend in the world, and as far as the world is concerned all the chemicals used on plants are DDT. Along in mid-August farmers in Illinois, Indiana, and Iowa began to notice grayish tan spots along the leaves of cornstalks. There wasn't a thing they could do about it. A peculiar strain of the so-called southern corn leaf blight (helminthosporium maydis) has swept through the heart of the nation's corn belt.

Until the harvest is finished in late October or November nobody will know how bad the damage is. But traders in Chicago guess the yield will be down 20 to 50 per cent. That means higher prices on everything from meat and eggs to bread, breakfast cereal, and whisky. It means a sharp setback in the struggle against inflation.

Agricultural chemicals are an unmitigated evil, then, but the blight and inflation and the ruin of farmers are absolute evils too. Well, which?

We can have reeking chimneys or hard times, we can have television with all its violence and brainwashing and piffle or do without a magnificent machinery of education and communication, we can have the automobile and its capacity for pollution and manslaughter and the degradation of inner cities and distant mountains or go back to isolated hamlets and lives circumscribed by the ambit of the horse.

We shan't accept the alternatives proposed. Antibiotics and medical technology have reduced infant mortality, lengthened life, and produced a population explosion that annoys and frightens us, but there's no going back. The fulfillment of the Negro's dignity and this grudging but growing respect for women's integrity have wiped out such pleasures as the minstrel show and the scatological joke, but the trade-offs have been made.

For years I had mourned that runoff from septic tanks in northwestern Bergen County was killing the streams. The trout were gone. Not since the 1940s had we netted fat green crawfish in the brook below the house. And for years I had been writing prim reproaches of people who demanded roads and hospitals, schools and colleges and—and disposal plants—but, when government came with these goodies to bestow, shrieked, "Not here!"

Big Yellow, the disposal plant, grumbles and minds its business. Going back to bed, I reflected I might gracefully try to do as well. We've made our trade-off.

. . . and to Come Rejoicing Back

Edgartown, Mass.—It is time now to take down the whale-shaped weathervane and return the little boat to its plastic cocoon in the garage and batten the windows behind sheets of plywood against the gales and scouring sands of another winter. It is time for the return from Eden to the world of noise and violence and smog and the sound of weeping. So it is time for a reexamination of Eden.

Why doesn't it work? Why hasn't it ever worked?

The Lord only knows. This is a statement of fact.

The Eden he deeded in fee simple to Adam and Eve must have been much like the way it was at sunrise this morning here on the point where Katama Bay takes its turn to the right and narrows, between the main island of Martha's Vineyard and the outermost point of South Beach, into the Mattakesset herring creek.

And Adam would have roused his wife early, as gently as a man would waken such a child of his as she was, and led her across the dew-starred grass to the edge of the beach, and they would have stood stunned by the stark perfection of the world into which they had been brought.

The bay was an immense glass in which were reflected the little moors and the woods of stunted oak and pine on Chappaquiddick. Away to the east the ocean stirred and glistened beyond the barrier beach, but since a great storm last winter closed its last access to the bay the people in Eden remember it is there only by reason of its thud and rumble. On the bay drifts a raft of great Canadian geese, barking and chuckling among themselves, and on a shallow bar stand six blue herons contemplating their reflection in the water.

Eden must have been not much different from this.

I do not think that theologians have granted sufficient consideration to the possibility that Adam and Eve got into their trouble with the police knowingly and deliberately because they were just plain bored.

The tendency has been to attribute their fall to the serpent, but I invite your attention to the fact that the pusher came on the scene late, exploited a market—an appetite—that was fully developed before he got there, and that he made his sale in despite of the most powerful parental authority in the known universe.

The kids were bored stiff. They had nothing to do but stand around admiring the landscape and remarking to each other how well the vegetarian lions and lambs were getting along, and it seemed to them that one carefully controlled experiment with a mind-expanding drug like an apple could do no harm.

They wanted out, and when the serpent sauntered over to them on the playground and said, "Ever fly, man?" they were ready.

I do not think that parents and statesmen now are considering seriously enough the possibility that young people are bored by this technological paradise—bored to and beyond desperation.

It would be callous as well as unrealistic to attribute to sheer ennui all of the youthful aberrations from our norms that disturb us elders. Many young people if not most are persuaded that their parents' values are phony and corrupting. They cannot reconcile themselves to the persistence of hereditary poverty side by side with affluence and conspicuous waste. As the Bergen County Prosecutor's Office survey of drug use and current opinion among students demonstrated, they do not trust the political system or politicians. They are demanding changes in society, economics, and education.

Some of them are motivated in their colleges now by the same spirit of sheer vandalism as impelled them a few years ago to break all the windows in the oschool or rip down the headstones in the cemetery.

"The youngsters who rise up in protest have not formulated a program for action," says Justice Douglas. "Few of them want to destroy the system. The aim of most of them is to regain the freedom of choice that their ancestors lost, to be free, to be masters of their destiny." He couldn't let it go at that, of course. "We must realize that today's Establishment is the new George III," he had to say. "Whether it will continue to adhere to his tactics we do not know. If it does, the redress, honored in tradition, is also revolution." That's what got him into trouble. Nobody is satisfied with letting well enough alone.

The kids on Martha's Vineyard call it The Rock, and yearn for the September when they can escape from Eden into college and the world. In the meantime, like young people in Englewood and New York City, in London and Paramus and Peking, some of them—too many of them—take to drugs. What else?

We should be satisfied in Eden. We aren't. It takes a lot of learning to be a Thoreau or a Schweitzer or a Joseph Wood Krutch, and enjoyment of existence is a thing we do not teach. Be content, we instruct young Adam; be happy; and all he knows is that he is uneasy and unhappy. The market preexists the serpent.

Ten tiny quail are following their mother and father under the window where I'm working. They are being instructed in the art of sheer survival. These are the last of the juicy bugs, they're being told; next month you'll grub for seeds in the snow. They seem content. It is time to be taking in the boat and the weathervane. Even in Eden it is well to be moving on.

The State as Pusher

Having been born with the human species' normal portion of rapacity, I shall not be at all surprised, although I'll be ashamed, to find myself purchasing fifty-cent tickets in my sovereign state's crumby number racket once they go on sale this month.

The odds are ridiculous. They are a million to one against winning the first prize in the weekly lottery drawing ($50,000), 11,111 to one against winning a second prize ($4,000), and so on down to 1,111 to one against winning a lousy $40.

As every crapshooter has learned expensively, odds do not improve no matter how often you play, and the house vigorish in this game is a guarantee that the collective sucker can't win. The government of New Jersey will take in $500,000 a week. It will pay out $158,000.

It seems to me a change for the worse in the moral climate of the state will have taken place when the tickets go on sale in stores and supermarkets and restaurants week after next, then shortly in saloons and liquor stores and racetracks. This is going to be a tax on the budgets of the people who can least afford to be taxed, and moreover . . .

> Number playing, like all gambling, is immoral; it is a bad risk mathematically; it perpetuates the delusion that it is possible to get something for nothing; it encourages other illegality; to legalize number playing because people play the numbers is as absurd as legalizing murder because people kill one another.

This is the case against the government-sponsored lottery as it was summed up last week by William Raspberry, a black reporter on the staff of *The Washington Post.*

It is a powerful case.

Mr. Raspberry is campaigning for legalization and government operation of the number game in the District of Columbia. For, not against!

Hear him out. William Raspberry's argument in favor of the state's taking charge of the racket is impressive because it begins with a fair statement of the objections raised by critics like me:

> When you've scarcely enough money to buy the groceries and pay the rent, they argue, it is a bad thing to gamble even a few dimes of that money away in an enterprise in which the odds are 1,000 to one against you. It is equally immoral, they say, for anyone else to encourage poor people to take that kind of risk.

But what is at work here, he says, is middle-class morality. Save your dimes today, and they'll be dollars tomorrow; hard work and frugality lay up a good foundation against the time to come; and cf. Poor Richard; and, says Raspberry bitterly, appealing as these platitudes may be, for poor people they simply are not true.

He undertakes to prove this.

> The hardworking and underpaid busboy or janitor is not likely to work his way up to chef or resident manager, nor can he save enough dimes to lift himself out of poverty. He knows, whether or not middle-class folk know it, that nothing good is likely to happen for him no matter how conscientiously he embraces the Puritan ethic.

42

To be sure, in New Jersey the odds will be 1,000 to one and mercilessly rigged against the chump.

> But if he is denied the hallowed American dream of success through hard work, he can have one dream: that he will hit the number. . . . And that possibility, however remote, may be the only thing between this poor fellow and utter despair.

William Raspberry is a notorious idealist, and he advances some sound idealistic reasons for taking the number racket away from the mob:

We are wasting too much money and manpower sicking the police on the numbers, to no effect whatever.

The racket flourishes because substantial numbers of rational people see nothing evil in playing the game.

The racket takes money out of the inner city. The government can put its ill-gotten gains back into the city.

Legalization will deprive organized crime of one major source of income.

The fact remains, middle-class morality or not, that in too many cases the 50-cent New Jersey lottery ticket—and in due time the $2.50 ticket entitling bearer to a million to one shot at the millionaire lottery—will be a tax on poverty.

And I suspect it might be something so odd as cynical to propose that, as long as we aren't going to do anything about the realities of poverty, we might as well arrange for the poor to enjoy their hallucinations.

Perhaps, though, that which seems cynical in Washington is nothing of the kind in New Jersey. We don't have so high a percentage of poor people, although the number is rising and that's one of the reasons why the state needs the money. Most of the persons who buy their 50-cent dream at the checkout counter will be able to afford it, and everyone, rich or poor, is entitled to his illusions. Maybe, considering the price of wigs and other forms of self-deception, an illusion is cheap at 50 cents.

Considering the fairness with which frailty distributes itself among us, I shall not be surprised to catch myself investing four bits in this baleful nonsense before the month is out. I trust I shall have presence of mind enough to be ashamed of myself.

The Cricket in the Crock

The world in December is lousy with things over which a man might mourn more constructively, I keep growling at myself, and furthermore it is farfetched if not impossible to grieve coherently over the death of a creature whose name one does not even know.

Yet I have not been able to put its ordeal out of my mind. Perhaps this will serve.

I went to the cellar Saturday morning to bring up the big old earthenware crock in which we brew the Four Thieves vinegar. We give it, along with other home-wrought confections, to people at Christmas. Into a couple of gallons of wine vinegar go mint, garlic, rosemary, tarragon, peppercorn, allspice berries, mustard seed, thyme—we don't use rue anymore, because a lot of people are allergic to it—and it's supposed to sit covered in a warmish place for a couple of weeks, swapping flavors to and fro, before being bottled.

So I tottered up the steps with the crock and set it in the kitchen sink to be washed and scalded, and there in the bottom of it, there in the year's accumulation of dust, lay this thing, dead.

It was an insect. I don't know insects well enough to identify it by name. It wasn't a grasshopper—too squat and low-slung to be that—and it wasn't a cricket, because a cricket is deep brown or black and opaque, and the exoskeleton before me was pale yellow and translucent. But I shall have to call it something. Arbitrarily, it was a cricket.

It had been long dead. When I tried to pick up what was left of it, the legs and segments shattered; it must have died months and months ago, and the intricate chemical broth which was all the life it ever lived had dried away and the molecules that had arranged themselves to spell l-i-f-e had distributed themselves in the overheated air of the cellar. The way they flushed what was left of the ball turret gunner out of his plastic cocoon in Randall Jarrell's poem, I flushed the cricket out of the crock and scoured the crock and sterilized it and went ahead with the Four Thieves vinegar.

The poor damned little thing is on my mind.

To be appreciated is the danger of anthropomorphizing—of attributing to animals or inanimate objects like stones and ships and cities the intellectual or sensual qualities of humans. Birds in their little nests agree, babbles Isaac Watts, or: "How doth the little busy bee/Improve each shining hour," and one knows the man to be a maudlin jerk. There is danger.

But it is a risk that will have to be taken. Don't ask me why.

The more I see of them, the less I can believe that animals are mere copies of each other, incapable of such feeling and evaluation of feeling as make the youness of you and the peculiar meness which is I. I am unable to follow the almost painfully sensitive Loren Eiseley when in his wonderful speculations on the secret of life in *The Immense Journey* he falls to wondering about the drained seedcases that lie about us in the fall:

Beautiful, angular, and bare the machinery of life lies exposed to my view. There will be the thin, blue skeleton of a hare tumbled in a little heap, and crouching over it I will marvel, as I marvel now, at the wonderful correlation of parts, the perfect adaptation to purpose, the individually vanished and yet persisting pattern which is now hopping on some other hill.

Life, the life of the species, goes on, he seems to be saying, and the doom of the individual ant or hare or cricket is irrelevant.

But it isn't irrelevant to the creature. Over the meadow outside our house on the island a hawk works its way to and fro, to

45

and fro, like a man plowing a field or mowing a lawn, and suddenly it drops into the grasses, and the shriek of the rabbit in its talons is a shriek of terror. Gulls riding the thermal currents, terns slanting down the wind, geese sunning themselves on a glassy bay are engaged, I am now sure, in the enjoyment of life. They know what it is to be glad to be alive. Not gladly do they die.

Sometime last summer the cricket got into the crock and couldn't get out. I suppose the angle at which things of that species hop or flutter is a flat angle. Given air space enough, it could make the altitude of the rim of the crock, but it was not equipped for steep or vertical takeoff.

The cricket in the dark would not know that it must very shortly die, and there seems to be no such thing in Nature as self-pity. Gently, hour after hour and perhaps day after day—I have no idea how long it takes an insect to starve to death—it threw itself against the sleek black wall of its cell, and after a while it found that it could not gather itself to try again.

It had no words for its situation. It had no way of supposing that, though it might perish, its species would persist to fiddle other summers away. It did not panic or reflect bitterly on the folly that had brought it to this pass, and I suppose that if its juices had any dim comprehension of the enormous change it was about to undergo, they scarcely gave a damn. All I know is that I am terribly sorry it had to be that way.

Listening to Silence

It is quiet in the schools and on the campuses this fall. Some of my elderly contemporaries think the quiet is ominous. I agree. But it is not ominous for the reasons my contemporaries repeat to each other.

They suspect that student activism has gone underground and that in due time, perhaps next spring, youth will be back on the barricades with new demands more outrageous than ever and with new techniques of harassment up to and including organized violence.

Only an incurably romantic idealist could endorse a conspiracy theory as large but tidy as this. It requires a long series of improbabilities: that there is in fact a cohesive and coherent student organization, that its existence can be kept secret, that 20 million or 25 million young people can agree on a list of the things they want, that the vast majority of them who want no part of anybody's violence wouldn't have hollered cop the first day of the fall semester.

I don't doubt there'll be violence someday maybe soon. It might even be highly effective violence. A few vandals can bring the New York subway system to a stuttering stop, and it can be presumed this has been noticed in revolutionary circles young as well as old. A few gallons of the right kind of chemical could poison a whole water system. A few bombs in a telephone switching plant and broadcasting shanties could raise hell with communications.

But there's a difference between acts of individual violence, up to and including assassination, and the emergence of a functioning revolutionary movement, and we'd do well to keep the difference in mind when we talk about ominous calms.

What's to be feared is that this is the calm not before the storm but after it. What's to be feared is that the young people who turned away from violence and resolved to work within the system have simply given up on it.

It cannot be supposed that they are substantially more content with the environment they turned out so dramatically to rescue from the predators last April. Changes have been made, yes: people are switching to unleaded gasoline, recycling waste products is as popular now as integrating hot dog stands and public swimming pools was only yesterday, and in most Eastern colleges and some schools students are sitting on faculty committees, sitting with boards in their meditations on codes of discipline.

But to suppose they have been appeased by such pro forma concessions would be to demean them.

They still consider a large part of the college experience a bore, the freshman year a ridiculous and expensive repetition of things they are taught in high school, the school's curriculum educational only to the extent it imparts the skills of test-passing, its diploma meaningless, its discipline merely tyrannical, its tenure usages devised only for the protection of academicians' jobs.

They have not been appeased. They've been turned off.

Yorick Blumenfeld is the unlikely name of the European correspondent of *Editorial Research Reports*. Mr. Blumenfeld has been lecturing in colleges across the country this fall. From Toledo, Ohio, he filed a dispatch the other day saying flatly the end of the cult of youth is just around the corner. He has some evidence:

The tragic death of the rock superstars Jimi Hendrix and Janis Joplin may have symbolized the end of that era. They not only were hooked on drugs; they had come to the end of the road—musically they had no more to say.

Young people feel rejected and hence dejected. They had vowed last spring to work for a new Congress. They didn't work. They didn't even work for lowering the vote in the ten states that rejected age-lowering propositions on the ballot Nov. 3.

They are frightened—and not only by the Nixon-Agnew rhetoric and the officially approved violence of the hard hats but by the feel of the economic atmosphere.

"There is fear among the ex-flower children," Blumenfeld wired home as a matter of reportable fact. "The seniors are concerned now about where the next dollar will come from."

He senses confusion and dismay on the campuses. He senses a sudden uncertainty among young people as to where they're

48

going. He finds them sick of rhetoric and fruitless protest and endless jabber about easy solutions.

And this, I propose, is what's ominous about the calm. The oscillation of a fickle civilization from contempt for the Silent Generation in the fifties to youth worship in the sixties back to hostility against anything that even looks young in the seventies is nothing to be alarmed about. Nor is its rediscovery of the virtues in experience, wisdom, and the hardening artery.

But if young people have shrugged and given up, if they have abandoned hope that the system can be changed, that's cause for alarm. It's pretty clear that their elders have no clear idea what to do about the mess we're in. If the young have subsided because they've run out of ideas too, the quiet is more ominous than a siren in the night.

JUST AMONG US SAVAGES

Just Among Us Savages

Deep in a rain forest on the southernmost of the Philippines last month a team of government social workers discovered a little tribe of savages living on a drifting island of time. The Tasadays are a Stone Age people. Backward?

"The Tasadays could be among the few—if not the only—people in the world who do not know of or use tobacco," said Dr. Robert B. Fox, the Texas-born director of the Philippine agency called Presidential Assistance for National Minorities. That backward they are, he said.

I seem to find this boyish gasp of astonishment subtly irritating.

Moreover, the Tasadays go naked except for a few who wear orchid leaves the way Adam and Eve wore fig leaves and maybe for the same reasons—to keep evil spirits away from the genitalia. They don't use salt or sugar. They seem to Dr. Fox to be intelligent, but they'd go 0 for 0 in any well constructed I.Q. test:

"They have no linguistic terms for rice and other cultivated plants, which they don't plant, much less eat," said Dr. Fox.

On the other hand, I'm not sure whether this arrogance is exasperating or delicious.

The use of a people's vocabulary to test or measure its backwardness might be counterproductive. There are Eskimo tribes, I'm told, that have twenty-five or thirty different words for the various phenomena that we dump into the crude catchall noun "snow." There are snows driven horizontally on the wind, soft perpendicular snows, sleety snows, snows that melt on contact with the ground surface—more kinds of snow than you or I can imagine, hence more than we can have a name for.

I don't know how the Tasadays or the Eskimos elaborate the

varieties of love, but there's something unmistakably Stone Age in our use of both noun and verb. In our language, a Tasaday anthropologist would report to the appalled directors of his museum, "love" covers everything from a partiality for strawberry ice cream to admiration of a football or guitar player to carnal knowledge to compassion to adoration to a preference of curriculum subject matter to reverence for all things great and small to the all-embracing benevolence of the Almighty to . . .

We are impoverished in ways the Tasadays aren't. We can teach them a word for tobacco and teach the poor devils to use it, after which they will devise for themselves appropriate linguistic terms for blessings they are unable now even to conceive, such as emphysema, lung cancer, laryngectomy, and cigarette-stained teeth. We can teach them words for rice and other cultivated plants they've never seen, the same way we teach children in the Paterson ghetto words for fun, fun, fun in the suburbs with Dick and Jane and show them pictures of swimming pools they aren't allowed to use.

They can be educated.

I'm not worried about them. We'll have them hauled into the Twentieth Century before they can invent a word for phosphate detergents. Let's worry about us and our capacity to be astonished that not everybody in the world conforms with our concept of civilization.

They believe in spirits. We got over that years ago, and by virtue of the cool enlightenment of science we shall teach them to believe in cosmetics, iron tonic for tired blood, higher education, the two-party system, vitamins, tonsillectomies, lanolin, chlorophyll in the toothpaste, bus timetables, tranquilizers, jogging, court calendars, exercise bicycles in the cellar, patented fish lures, Dr. Spock, hot pants, presidential infallibility, nuclear deterrence, saccharin, and the rest of the blessings that have enabled us to obey the Lord's command that we have dominion over the Earth.

We can teach them all these things. But how shall we undertake to persuade ourselves that a civilization or a society is any way of organizing people that works? Whether or not it has a dictionary listing words for which there are no corresponding realities, such as our "unicorn" and "mermaid," are people backward merely and precisely because they are different?

The question is not rhetorical. An answer is wanted. The people of this country are divided. We belong each of us to one little Stone Age tribe or another, and we are constantly stumbling over each other and sending arrogant little messages back to our home agencies. If we aren't black we're brown or red or, in certain circles worse, white. We eat spaghetti or soul food, collards, okra, hominy grits, or codfish cakes.

We wear our hair long. To many an anthropologist it seems amusing when we wear it crew-cut or wear somebody else's hair. Our tastes in music divide us more deeply than does a ten-year age differential, but, no matter which side of the cleavage we're on, we are superior to the rabble on the other side.

Backward, the man said. The Tasadays, being quiet and gentle and cooking their wild plants and jungle animal meats over an open fire, are a step or so ahead of the avant garde of American diet nuts and peace crusaders. Maybe they're uncivilized. After World War III we shall really have to look them up and see.

Funny Thing About Ethics

Says Canon 24 of the American Bar Association code of judicial ethics:

A judge should not accept inconsistent duties; nor incur obligations, pecuniary or otherwise, which will in any way interfere or appear to interfere with his devotion to the expeditious and proper administration of his official functions.

Says Section 4 of the Principles of Medical Ethics promulgated by the American Medical Association:

> The medical profession should safeguard the public and itself against physicians deficient in moral character or professional competence. . . . [Physicians] should expose, without hesitation, illegal or unethical conduct of fellow members of the profession.

Every trade has its little pleasantries, usually gilt-framed and hung on the wall alongside the license to practice. Real estate, banking, accountancy, journalism, the removal of ugly superfluous hair—I guess every one of the great old guilds except perhaps burglary has a code, drafted by a committee of humorists, guaranteeing to the customer that whatever befalls him now will be not at all irregular.

But it does get a little steep when members of Congress recommend that the justices of the United States Supreme Court and the other federal judges be brought under the strictures of the congressional code of ethics.

They have noticed that Justice Fortas took a $20,000 payment from Louis Wolfson's family foundation and sent it back when Wolfson got into a jam for stock manipulation. To some sensitive critics that interfered or appeared to interfere with &c.

Abe really should ask a good doctor to have a look at his smeller.

But impose the congressional ethics on judges? If there is one more outbreak of hilarity the bailiff will clear the courtroom.

Indeed both houses have codes. The Senate code restricts ouside employment and fund raising by employes, who are not to be confused with Senators. It requires reports on contributions received from testimonial events and on honorariums of $300 up. It requires each Senator file a detailed report on his income.

It is not entirely true that these reports are sealed in leaden casks and committed to the Atlantic in the next dark of the Moon.

Under Rule 44 the truth, filed with the Comptroller-General, is confidential. Only by vote of the Senate Select Committee on Standards and Conduct can even the committee itself peek. You can't.

The House code is at least as entertaining. Under HR-1099 (1968) the Representatives and the ranking employes of the House must list in public the sources of their major income from sources outside their full-time $42,000 job. Major income means business interests in excess of $5,000 and income of $1,000 or more from a single source.

The Congressman identifies who's paying him off. But the actual dollars and cents of the loot are returned in a sealed envelope. Again, a majority vote of the committee on conduct is prerequisite to opening the envelopes—to the committee only, not to you, you snoop.

Sen. Dirksen, who is now bellowing most loudly for legislation requiring judges to tell the world the whole truth about their income, bellowed most loudly last year against the meager disclosure measure just described. It would make him a second-class citizen, Dirksen complained. So he proceeded to vote for it.

It passed, 67-1. When Sen. Case of New Jersey and Sen. Clark of Pennsylvania proposed an amendment requiring detailed public disclosure of income in dollars and source as well, the Senate rejected it, 40-44. Dirksen voted nay.

I guess all I'm saying is that there are no absolute standards of ethical behavior. Some Cabinet officers are expected to divest themselves of stock. It's all right if others sock it in trust. Presidential appointees at Grade 16 or $22,835 a year file annual income reports. Other appointees don't. The rev. Justices of the Supreme Court disqualify themselves from voting on a case in which they—or even a member of their family—may have a personal interest. Members of Congress don't, and members of Congress have been made wealthy by measures for which they have not only voted but lobbied.

So the Congress is the stronghold of cynical privilege, and its ethical codes are an uncouth joke.

Having said this, there should be space enough left to say that in every calling is an immense majority of professionals who take their ethics seriously indeed. You know them—grave lawyers, stern doctors who are sternest in their demands on themselves, newspapermen who would rather blow an exclusive story than prejudice the rights of innocents, actually believing that the Fourth Estate is a great and noble institution.

It is sad and curious that when it comes to forming the public opinion about a profession the minority always rules.

A Reckless Singing Before Breakfast

The cardinal is a beast as simple-minded as it is handsome. It thinks well of itself. The quality is rare in the world we have contrived. One tends to forgive the cardinal its ostentatious winsomeness.

Reeking of coffee and vitamin pills, cloaked in my clouds of guilt and apprehension, I totter out of the house at dawn to start the journey to work.

Somewhere in the treetops that are sweeping the last stars westward, somewhere high in the nervous rustling, the cardinal sees me and says the year's at the spring, the day's at the morn, aren't we lucky to be alive? "Birdie, birdie, birdie," says the cardinal, actually. The biologists say its purpose is to serve notice on other cardinals that it owns this territory and they'll muscle in at peril of their tail feathers. All my cardinal says is, "Birdie, birdie, birdie," hanging there like a small old Chinese lantern glowing red against the paling sky.

It is not a bright bird.

Alcoholism, said the young priest at a meeting an afternoon or so ago, has become a socially acceptable form of suicide. Indeed, he said, it is a socially acceptable form of manslaughter. Show him a man who has been an alcoholic for as much as a year, and he will show you a family that is deathly sick.

The scavengers' trucks are out early in the politer towns. As the sullen collectors dump their bags of household rubbish into the bins of the trucks the bottles clank and crash.

"Birdie, birdie, birdie," says the cardinal. It insists that it's great to get up in the morning.

Out on Long Island the kids are killing the time that hangs so heavy between childhood and death by doping themselves with a relatively new tranquilizer whose name I want to forget. It's a beaut. Any one can kick marijuana, most can kick barbiturates if they try, and a few can choose in agony to break themselves of heroin. But this one is the boss slavemaster.

The addict can't go off by himself and confront his soul and sweat out his abstinence from the pills. If he does it alone he goes into systemic collapse. Deaths have been certified. Withdrawal must be done in the hospital under constant watch and rigorous controls.

The boy or girl who chooses to throw away his crutch and stand alone is doomed by his own conscience, his own bravery. By rejecting suicide he incurs it. How's that for Greek tragedy? How's that for existential absurdity?

The year's at the spring, the day's at the morn, God's in his heaven, all's right with the world, says the cardinal. It has not been notified that in several major cities in the East at least 75 per cent of all births are illegitimate and that 50,000 persons were killed last year in automobile accidents 90 per cent of which are judged to have been preventable.

I know too many things that cardinals don't. Venereal disease, which was hammered down to an incidence of something like 3 per 100,000 of population immediately after the resort to penicillin therapy, is back up to something like 59, and syphilis and gonorrhea are beginning to turn up in the town's best families. Everything-hating beatniks and snobbish homosexuals are taking over the old family resort towns. To qualify for membership in a big-town gang a boy must show blood on his blade. In the ghettos the old-settler Negroes and Puerto Ricans are allied in hostility to the newcomers. Knowing what thy're doing, hating what they're succeeding at, young executives are driving themselves to death on purpose.

The cardinal is doomed, but it is too perfect a fool to know this. Some dawn ages and ages hence, long after its bones have whitened and crumbled into the soil, it or at any rate an exact replica of it will shimmer in the dawn over a troubled man below or at any rate a replica of him, and it will say look at me, look at me, and the year's at the spring and summer will come. It is stupid and does not sing well, but the cardinal is a sweet friend, and a dawn would be dark without it.

The Pirates and the Absent-Minded Rebel

In the wilted weeds at the foot of the stairs to the Susquehanna station platform lay four bicycles, two of them crudely re-painted. On the platform were not four boys but seven. They looked startled when the man came from the steps up through the door into the little shed.

They were watching him. "Relax," the man said. He sat down and got his book out of his pocket and was trying to pick up the twisted thread of the author's argument where he'd dropped it yesterday, but the boys were watching him, and he looked up uneasily.

They weren't much to have noticed in the first place: five skinny bodies and two chubby ones, clothed in dungaree-and-soiled-T-shirt uniform, with blank half-completed faces. The man supposed for a moment he read hostility in sóme of the eyes, but he wasn't sure which ones, and he has come to suspect any-way that often the eye is not so much the window of the soul as a symptom of thyroid pathology. Contented with this aphorism,

60

he went back to his book, and then another man emerged from the stairs into the tacky, smut-scrawled shed which is the station.

That resolved the crisis. Something was done among the boys —the man didn't look up from his book to see; he was deep in its discussion of the behavior of neolithic man—and then four of them went back down the stairs. "Thanks," said one of the three remaining on the platform. "Gee, thanks," said another.

"What the hell are you thanking them for?" said the third. "Because they gave you back your own dollar?"

What we're reporting now is not the sordidness of existence in the crowded city or the misbehavior of the young; it is, to our own consternation, the ultimately unforgivable sin of us and our generation—our failure or refusal to rebel against the world these children have constructed around us.

We sat there, still absorbed in neolithic man, only half-listening, but before the train pulled in we had overheard enough of their squabbling to know what had happened:

The three had come over to Hackensack from Maywood, maybe to go swimming or to the movies. The four on bicycles had stopped them at the foot of the station stairs and demanded money of them. Two of the three had argued—this all came out in the dialogue—and one had shrunk back, on the point of crying. They had given up a dollar.

When the grownups arrived the dollar was restored.

That's the end of this street scene, except that the other man overheard as much as we did. Being a true child of our generation, he managed to get the whole thing utterly balled up.

"You shouldn't steal," he told the three innocents magnificently. "It's a bad habit. Don't you go to Sunday school?"

"Oh, Lord," one of the boys said.

Another said:

"It's getting so you can't go anywhere any more but you get shaken down or beaten up."

And what was your correspondent doing all this time? Having been dragged, sullenly resisting, out of 10,000 B.C. into the twentieth century, he was taking mental notes. It did not occur to him until some seventy-two hours later that in like circumstances Abraham Lincoln might have bestirred himself to do something as constructive as summon a policeman, that Joan of Arc or Oliver Cromwell would have contributed to the integrity and continuity of society to some such modest extent as overhauling the four little buccaneers and clattering their skulls together until they could tell one form of evil from one form of good.

We didn't learn much about boys from the supercilious notes we filed away that day. We did learn something about grownups —and that generalization is valid.

To go back to the third person, the man with a book in his pocket is sensitive to the subtle pressures in his society, and he tries to resist them. He esteems himself as a nonconformist, and rebels when he can against false gods and phony values, in the way he learned from Gandhi and Thoreau. He is on his guard against Cadillacs and commercials, theology and the country-club crowd and the ease that saps valor.

But he consents to see injustice done. He consents to children's dictating the terms of human existence in a way no sweat-shop magnate or coastal pirate ever did. He does not rebel against the pollution of the race by its spawn. A little child shall lead us straight to hell, but that's the way it is. The man takes notes and writes a column. He didn't learn much about children, but he understands modern art better.

When Can You Call a Man Moral?

Joseph Wood Krutch picked up a college textbook on psychology, and it fell open at the beginning of the chapter titled "Morality." It was the shortest chapter in the book.

"We call a man moral," it began, "when his actions are in accord with the laws and customs of his society."

The author of the text let this definition stand without qualification, without limitation, without even a furtive footnote indicating an awareness that under certain conditions we can call a man moral only if his actions are not in accord with a bad law or a nasty custom. And Dr. Krutch, who is old (67) and wise (*The Modern Temper, The Measure of Man, Human Nature and the Human Condition*), was still volcanically smoldering when the University of Arizona summoned him from his home in the desert last month to address the graduating class.

If you accept this psychological concept of morality as no more than mores, [Krutch said,] then you are logically compelled to assume, for instance, that in Nazi Germany a man who persecuted the Jews was a moral man and one who refused to do so was immoral, since persecution was certainly both the law and the custom in the society of which he was a part.

When humanists talk like this, taking in vain the names of sciences like psychology and (as Dr. Krutch earlier did) sociology, it is usual and popular to say they are anti-intellectual and thus destroy them.

It seems to your reporter the real question raised by Dr. Krutch and such colleagues of his as Robert Oppenheimer is whether such sciences are not themselves anti-intellectual. Remember Oppenheimer's chilling question?

Nuclear weapons and all the machinery of war surrounding us now haunt our imagination with an apocalyptic vision which could well become a terrible reality: the disappearance of man as a species from the surface of the earth. It is quite possible. But what is more probable, more immediate, and in my opinion equally terrifying is the prospect that man will survive while losing his precious heritage, his civilization and his very humanity.

The argument these troubled men seem to be advancing is that the science which dictates what man shall be, the laws and customs that make his decisions for him, are anti-intellectual pre-

63

cisely, no more and no less than a denial of the power of the intellect to make choices.

There is a gigantic paradox—on this hand, the gigantic growth throughout the world of what is called social justice, the concern over human rights and civil rights, the perhaps by this time irresistible drive toward one world; but on the other hand, the withering away of what will have to be called private morality.

Let's not run through the catalogue in detail; in shorthand let's say bribery, payola, protection, ice, quiz shows, Ph.D. thesis ghost writers, the broadcaster's yacht, the Congressional junkets, oil taxes, tax write-offs, the well considered use of loopholes—that which everybody's doing, that which really harms nobody, that which is just about legal, fully customary, hence moral.

What's the matter with that?

You may think that personal integrity and self-respect are not what you want more than anything else [said Dr. Krutch]. You may say that putting them first would make it too difficult to get along in the world; that you would rather have money, power, fame, or even (you may smugly say) the chance which money and power and fame will give you to do good in the world. But if you do say any of those things you will be making an unwise choice; you will be surrendering that which cannot be taken away from you to gain something which can be taken away and which, as a matter of fact, very often is. . . . Only he who possesses himself and is content with himself is actually secure.

It was one of the great initiation-ceremony speeches of a vintage year.

The time may come when you lose hope for the world [the old man said]. But it need never come when you lose hope for yourself.

If what the textbook said is sociology he hates it. But don't call that anti-intellectual.

The Knack of Thinking on the Dead Run

I was not at all surprised when I tottered into the Larch Avenue, Teaneck, quarters of the Ethical Culture Society a Saturday morning or so ago to find serenely presiding over a discussion of ethics Richard T. Baker, assistant dean of the graduate school of journalism at Columbia University. I am not surprised when I find Douglas G. Gemeroy, Ph.D., professor of physiology at Rutgers the State University, any evening exhorting a rumpus-roomful of American Cancer Society crusade volunteers. When Walt W. Rostow, whose business is teaching at Harvard, pops up at Purdue to lecture on United States strategy because he is chairman of the Policy Planning Council of the Department of State, I say, "Of course." Of course you expect to find professors in Washington and New Delhi, teachers engaging district attorneys in debate on teen-age drinking, deans installing anti-aircraft batteries and designing submarines, college presidents writing legislation, running governmental errands to mangy and dubious countries, designing Senate investigations.

Of course, you'll say.

Jacques Barzun, the distinguished dean of faculties and provost of Columbia University, has his doubts.

He expressed them at an alumni convocation called "Columbia in Washington" at the capital late in March.

The liberty is taken of suggesting that the word "school" may without harm be substituted for "university" in his summing up:

A university has a unique service to perform—to remove ignorance. And it must not allow anybody or anything to distract the institution or its members from that traditional task. A university, no more than an army, should tolerate the division of its forces. If it does the fragments will soon be scattered and destroyed, and no one—not even the temporary beneficiaries—

65

will be grateful for the failure of will that brought about the defeat. For the victorious enemy will be, once again, that powerful antagonist ignorance.

Evidently this misappropriation of the teacher is coming to a head.

The master of the new Churchill College at Cambridge, England, had inaugurated his tenure by announcing that the purpose of the college is to increase the output of highly trained scientists and technicians for industry. He's a physicist.

From neighboring Peterhouse responded the novelist and scholar Kingley Amis: "A university does not exist to serve society, and must never try to do so."

Dr. Barzun said they're both wrong—the scientist in his proposition that the university or college or school shall serve society directly, on demand, and the artist in his proposition that the proper use of the institution is uselessness.

The purpose of education and the educational institution, Dr. Barzun said, is to remove ignorance.

That's broad enough to cover both teaching and research, he said—by teaching to remove the ignorance of the young, by research to remove the ignorance of the old. And that's enough job for the most dedicated and energetic man.

He is tired of hearing teachers importuned to drop what they're doing and go do something else:

> The institution as a whole is requested to help world peace or social welfare or local culture by providing the means, the place, and the talent for some worthy cause—an exchange program, a clinic, a survey, a world conference on fingernail biting. . . . And the philosophy behind these incessant demands is not wrong: it amounts to saying that the power to do creates a burden of obligation. But I feel more and more strongly that the application of the philosophy needs constant review. . . .

Why should the teacher consider himself responsible to do more than is imposed by his professional obligation?

> The physician removes pain and disease; we do not ask him to deliver the mail in his spare time; we do not task the lawyer to cure toothache on the

66

side. Why should the scholar and teacher be asked to fix the finances of Ruritania, invent new weapons for the Army and Navy, and entertain the P.-T.A. with free lectures on modern art?

The only answer he can conceive is that the scholar is the only man in town who can do these things with sufficient good nature to do them at no extra charge—besides which, he loves to fiddle in the laboratory, and he loves to hear himself talk.

But he has begun to wonder whether he is doing himself or his society a favor. I thought you'd better be warned.

Prayer in the Garden

In the long run, the story of the year may be the story not of masses of people in vast convulsive movement but the story of lonely separate persons standing very still.

Mississippi is a part of the story. One goes alone, bearing witness, into the dark against the guns and the gasoline throwers.

Washington too is a part of the story. Until the civil rights bill was passed by the Senate, for twenty-four hours each day at the Lincoln Memorial in teams of three—Protestant, Catholic, and Jewish—the theological students stood vigil in silent prayer.

The loneliness hasn't made headlines. Indeed, how do you count out a headline about the way in which young people are making an asset of their loneliness—testing their values and proving them by going alone up a dark street in a Mississippi village to do so humdrum a thing as ask a Negro to register for the vote, testing themselves by standing all night to pray for justice and maybe wonder what it is? It is not a streamer. But it's a story.

The names of the organizations involved in making loneliness effective are crowded names: the Students Nonviolent Co-ordinating Committee, or, for short, Snick (Mississippi); the Theological Students Vigil for Civil Rights, Student Organized Inter-faith Interracial, and that's the letterhead (Washington). They make themselves sound as stuffy as 35-year-olds.

But each goes as a volunteer, uncoerced and alone, to face the guns or the jeering. Something goes on that we'd better try to understand.

Thousands of seminarians took part in the remarkably under-reported Washington vigil. Joining in organizing the demonstra-tion were the Jewish Theological Seminary in New York and Roman Catholic seminarians who set up a vigil center in Wash-ington, but headquarters in the North was Union Theological Seminary in New York, where the idea originated. Seminaries in the West sent two or three students each if they could afford passage. Otherwise they convened vigils on their own campus. Catholic nuns did not participate, although non-Catholic women theological students did; though earnest to join, the nuns kept a traditional kind of vigil within the convent.

Catholic seminarians organized the Washington vigil center, and it was sheltered in the basement of Holy Comforter Roman Catholic Church in southeast Washington, under the chairman-ship of students named Hooley, Leatherwood, and Levine.

Between Holy Comforter and Union Theological Seminary was set up a regular automobile shuttle service, and as the stu-dents checked in at the center they'd be assigned to go to the Lincoln Memorial and stand watch in interdenominational threes for 3 hours at a time. Between tricks they'd call on their Senators, rest, eat at tables replenished by councils of women of all three churches, then stay up all night arguing the origins and meaning of morality, ethics, law, history, government. They recorded their experiences in notebooks. "Senator Russell was most cordial, but . . . said he expected us to be for the bill because most women and preachers are." "Be very familiar with the bill; dress warmly at night."

Not every one gave to their use of loneliness the reading I attribute to it. A diary describes a perturbed middle-aged woman

68

who stalked twice past the silent vigil. "My grandpappy done told me the people have a right to make fools of themselves," she rasped, "and you sure are availing yourselves of the opportunity. You're brainwashed. Aren't you? You're Communists. Aren't you?" By April 27 the vigil had a competitor on a street corner not far away: the lonely and alienated souls of the American Nazi Party, heiling and handing out rattlebrained pamphlets.

Don't ask what it means. But if you propose to understand the world as it'll be tomorrow it might be useful to know how some of its people came to the decisions they'll have made. They came to a garden, and said, sit ye here, while I go and pray yonder.

Marriage à la Mod

Through the intricate tank traps of the Long Island Expressway, through the high-rise brick wilderness of Ultima Queens, my wife and I slogged out the other night to confer the honour of our presence on a mod, I think, wedding.

It may have been hip. Swinging? Yip? Groovy? I do not profess the idiom. The bride wore white, all the way down to where my wife wears a swim suit. Mod is what I say it was.

And mod I knew it would be the minute we opened the invitation. The bridegroom's parents requested the honour of. The wedding and the reception would be at their house. The aberration from the middle-class norms was only a degree or two to the Left, but the nonchalance as to the conventions was explicit. "Mod," I remember murmuring; "mark my words, woman: mod."

We hadn't a thing to wear. The only authentic mod clothes I have to my name—dungarees, a yellow Swedish storm cape, a couple of mildewed canvas sou'westers—smell somewhat of clams and squid and deceased bluefish. My wife's few admissibly mini garments hang today in a tool shed behind the house at the island with her clam rake and goggles and spear.

I wore my gray flannels. She wore the little white go-anywhere dress I gave her three Christmases ago.

We were a scream.

The bash—that is to say, the ceremony—was a little late getting under way, like, man, forty-five minutes late. We didn't know anybody involved except the bride, whom we'd met at the island and had liked a lot because she had the peculiarly likable knack of liking whatever there was to do.

That's why, and I kept reminding myself her friends would be folks like us.

And maybe with their clothes off they would be, but as they drifted in wearing turtleneck sweaters and saris, clanking necklaces (on the men) and see-through pants (on the women), Edwardian ruffles and bell-bottom trousers and unisex coiffures— as the merrymakers gathered and the sound of rock suffused the little house I found myself wishing I had her knack of making the best of whatever weather there was.

We kept introducing ourselves to people who seemed to have a kindly curiosity about how such obviously queer fish happened to be there, and at last somebody said the bride's party was ready and we'd please go out to the terrace and be seated. A big yellow circus tent had been raised over the concrete terrace out back. The walls of the tent were a plastic sheet that swayed and rustled in the wind. At the far end of the terrace stood a white trellis decked with smilax. At the near end, against the wall of the house, was a bar with the hardware—bourbon, vodka, scotch —attended by a solemn square in the only evening dress I saw all night. The champagne punch was in silver bowls on a table over there by the door. People were taking a double hooker of whisky and going to their places, carrying the glass.

After a while the minigowned bridesmaids oiled in, carrying bouquets that trembled conventionally and wearing their hair over their eyes, and my wife and I both sighed and I recognized the relief in her eyes. We had both been meditating over our hooch on the probabilities whether the wedding party would waltz in naked.

The processional march was Glenn Campbell, on tape, singing "Gentle on My Mind."

Let him who would snort pagan go read the plot of *Lohengrin* and *A Midsummer Night's Dream,* whence cometh the march music of the conventional nuptials.

The splicing went off with no more than the irreducible constant of ritual clinkers. The minister had to remind bride and bridegroom both of their own name when it came time to repeat the vows. He translated a lot of the majestic English of the charge to the combatants into 1969 East Side American, which one incorrigible square will insist is not an improvement on the poetry and mystery of the original.

But in the end a girl and a boy had looked into each other's eyes and had sworn to love, honor, and cherish this fellow human being, this beloved stranger, in sickness and in health, in joy and in sorrow, come what may—as come it will—until death do them part.

The rising wind rustled the acrylic curtains of that odd oxygen tent, and the reflections in its folds made great gaunt glowing specters that formed themselves against the darkness outside and loomed and vanished. "Until death do us part." The clink of ice in somebody's glass shattered silence. It might have been less conspicuous if one could have blown one's nose on a red bandanna. Dancing was to follow, but we came along home. Things seemed to be shaping up just about right.

Picasso in the Car Pool

We don't seem to be getting the class of creative thinking that we're entitled to expect around here.

(Creative thought: Have you ever noticed that whenever a sentence ends in the phrase "around here" it states a complaint, invariably in a quarrelsome whine?)

And in a three-day symposium at the Rockefeller Institute in New York a jury of distinguished scientists has been trying to decide what or who is responsible for the creative-thinking shortage comma around here.

They incriminated the utilitarian view of science—the theory that the only research worth supporting is the kind yielding data and ideas immediately and profitably applicable in industry.

They incriminated the task-force research method which may be Edison's greatest invention and which can spell things as various as "atomic bomb" and "Salk"—it makes a mere administrator of its best research man.

You observe that their search was itself a pretty good specimen of the task-force method. And for contrast, by the most interesting possible coincidence, on hand was a specimen of the individual creative thinker.

This inspired solitary, who abruptly saw the problem whole and perceived its solution, is Dr. Isidor I. Rabi the Columbia University physicist. And what's the reason we aren't getting any creative thinking done around here?

Answer:

The suburbs.

Dr. Rabi said too many people on university campuses who ought to be thinking about the ultimate secrets of the universe are instead thinking about car pools, cesspools, back-yard swimming pools, and all the other earthy minutiae of their suburban living. In his opinion a man cannot be both a good suburbanite and a creative scientific researcher—or for that matter a creative writer or a creative artist:

I can't imagine Picasso arriving at work with his car pool, painting furiously for a few hours, and quitting about 4:30 to return home with the car pool to work on the garden or the cesspool.

Dr. Rabi lives in an apartment at 450 Riverside Drive, within leisurely walking distance of his office on Morningside Heights, and it is impossible to foreclose the suspicion that this wholly and brilliantly distinguished thinker let himself carry on in public an argument he had just been having with Mark Van Doren or Dwight Miner in the Faculty Club elevator.

We are not conscious of a proprietary interest in the suburban life as an ingredient of the creative process. If Beethoven and Wordsworth, not to mention the late Homer, could have worked better out of an office in town, society was not well served by their galumphing about in the open. But before we can come to any conclusion about it we may have to know something about how the creative process works and even what it is.

Picasso in a car pool is obviously a contradiction in terms. But the mathematician Poincaré left a detailed memoir on the way his solution of some extremely difficult Fuchsian variables occurred to him. His foot was on the bottom step of the bus. Dr. Rabi's cesspool, the very symbol of contamination, sounds terrible. A scientist wondered about an unpleasant green mold contaminating a slop of culture medium, and that opened the creaking door in the mind that led the way to penicillin. Brewster Ghiselin has made a book of creative thinkers' accounting of their own creative process. If the accounts agree at any point, they agree that, once you've worked on a problem hard enough to get its elements firmly in mind, you never can tell when the lightning will strike—or where or how or especially why.

Silently and secretly, in a way almost frightening in its independence of will and consciousness, the mind drudges away; the circuits open and close, in a car pool or a skyscraper; and you go to the desk and write your equations or symphony. It's not awfully efficient. But it seems to be the way this goes.

It does seem to us, not by reason of any personal experience but by asking people to whom the creative accident does from time to time occur, that one good way of suppressing the creative act is to press too hard. The physicist who plays the cello, breeds rhododendrons, or distills his own bourbon knows what he's doing, whether he's doing it on Riverside Drive, in a little development town up the Northern Valley, or Clinton, N.Y., or Brunswick, Me.

A Small Planet To Visit

As soon as the astronauts are ready, we've a planet for them to discover.

It's the fifth biggest in the large system of satellites that revolve around the central star, its mean distance from the star being on the order of 93 million miles. On it there is a firmament in the midst of the waters, dividing the waters from the waters, and there are a day and a night.

Its surface brings forth grass and the herb yielding seed, the fruit tree yielding fruit after his kind, whose seed is in itself.

It has climate. It is surrounded by an envelope of atmosphere, and the axis on which it rotates is inclined to the plane of its orbit at an angle of 23.5 degrees.

And so there are winds. There are waves on its many seas, and their tides beat and crash except where the sea lies frozen, and because the gases in the atmosphere refract the light of the central star it seems to rise very swiftly into a vault of gold and green and amethyst and scarlet, and when it goes down it sets the sky aflame. There is a season of the year when leaves are burned, making a strange sad incense.

The planet is inhabited.

It is about three or maybe six billion years old; and so it has done with the convulsions of youth and adolescence that are still torturing so many thousands of other planets in the universe—its continents and oceans are in balance, and its volcanoes and earthquakes are rare and mild.

The inhabitants have articulate speech. However, they have evolved many languages. It is their custom to hate and, when possible, kill others who do not speak their language.

Some of their race memories are very old and beautiful. Their male young fish and climb trees and wrestle, because in their blood they are hunters and warriors, and the female young play with dolls, being mothers.

It is, of course, fortunate that the surface of the planet is exceedingly irregular, having great deeps in which most of the water is firmly contained. If the surface were smooth the planet would be completely covered by water, since the oceans have a mean depth of 2¼ miles while the mean elevation of the land is but a half-mile.

If the rate of procreation were controlled by safe means long since devised, there would be food enough for all of the inhabitants. As matters stand pending the arrival of superior intelligence, a majority of the inhabitants never know what it is not to starve, and many millions die of starvation. This is for the loftiest ethical reasons.

In the crust of the planet are mineral resources of great variety. To the vegetable food which grows abundantly on most of the land surface and to the all but unlimited food fish occurring naturally in the sea the inhabitants have ingeniously added a third source by domesticating certain animals and slaughtering them. While the race is only about 70,000 years old and has a conscious existence of but 6,000 years, already it has created materials and even elements not found in nature, and has developed its arts and sciences to a state of great sophistication and beauty.

It is relatively safe against the common accidents of interstellar space—collision, for instance, or the senility and catastrophic collapse of its central star. The system itself is far enough removed from the center of the galaxy to hold it immune against invasion from other systems.

There are a winter and a spring, a summer and a fall, and only during summer is food plentiful in growth; thus is necessitated an elaborate system of distribution and storage. There are intricate cities, many of them handsome. The varieties of inhabitants have evolved each of them great philosophers and priests, who have laid down ideals that are all but identical with each other.

They are aware of all they have in common: their ancestry, their environment, their relatively brief life, the constituents of safety and happiness, their deep-rooted need for each other, their heritage of pain and wonder and sorrow and hope.

They might make some god a wonderful family.

They are about to exterminate each other, for no reason thus far defined.

They deserve to be discovered at our earliest opportunity.

An Off Day for Liberals

Nobody knows so well as a writer knows when he's in a slump. Nobody needs to tell him everything's going to be all right in a day or so—he learns in time that if he'll trust in Jehovah and the autonomic nervous system his typewriter will resume behaving itself in a day or so. Sure, sure; shoulder the world, my lad, and drink your ale; yet there are moments, and this is one of them, when one writer whom I know, after having lived inside his skin for a while, would just as soon plead guilty to three charges which last week would have infuriated him:

He is a tired liberal.

He is an agent and spokesman for the establishment.

If he knew what's good for him he'd get out of the way and let the new generation take over the world he has helped to defile.

I certainly am a tired liberal.

I am tired of a labor movement that has grown out of a clean and starry-eyed childhood into a fat and reactionary senility which has no use for the workingman if he be black or brown or red.

I am tired of being called a participling honkie by Negroes with whose parents I tried not very brilliantly to get enacted the laws which had to spell it out that human rights are for everybody.

I am tired of art which has turned the hard-won right of free expression into a dull and dirty joke.

I am tired of sophomores, trailing clouds of afterbirth, who use the painfully widened right of free speech and freedom of assembly to deny free speech and freedom of assembly to persons of whom their fuehrers do not approve.

I am tired of young men and young women who charge their parents $4,000 a year so that as students they can write letters home denouncing their parents as middle-class phonies.

I am tired of the hypocrisy of little leeches who live off the sacrifice of their families and who assure each other that anybody aged more than 30 is a hypocrite.

I am tired of the fiction that it takes great physical courage to throw a rock in the dark at a campus policeman or a college president on condition that absolute amnesty be granted for the atrocious assault.

I am tired of working for reforms in government—the Bergen County charter is in point—which would have strengthened the power to serve their people of the very mayors who opposed it. I am tired of fighting educators for changes in education. I am tired of defending tenure for teachers who have corrupted it into a job-security guarantee and who wouldn't know what to do with the academic freedom which is the only justification for tenure.

I am tired of black students' demanding in their schools and colleges the separate but equal apartheid that 100 years of experiment has proved to be a fraud and a failure.

I am so tired of the demands made by self-righteous numskulls who don't know what they're demanding that with Dr. Benjamin Fine I'll ask questions which may be dangerous:

Are the militants who have made black studies a nonnegotiable demand afraid they can't compete in the prescribed course of study?

If black studies are installed to defer rioting, will they be academically sound? Or will they merely qualify black students to teach black studies to black students, and why would this circle be less vicious than the other ones I've been bitching about all these years?

If we go into black studies, do we go all the way in?

I am the doddering apologist for an establishment that has tended to reward talent and work and accomplishment rather than drug-bleared daubs and shrieks, and as of today I'd be delighted to get out of the way and let the pure in heart take over and run this mess its way.

But except for a parcel of drones and squares and preppies in the hard sequences I cannot find that the go-go girls and their hairy consorts have evolved any way of their own of running anything, from the hot water up.

I don't think the administration of law would be improved by repealing the statutes or shooting policemen; I cannot believe that, with all the love in the world, a kid who can't add should be running a bank or a railroad system; a nation's food supply cannot be safely entrusted to persons whose only experience with the subject is opening a can of ravioli.

A lot of us are tired of long days and sleepless nights and a sense that we may be responsible for a generation of vipers.

Maybe tomorrow will be better.

The Death of a Teacher

When a great man dies and the world puts on its funeral vestments and kneels to do him reverence, there may remain one last service that no man is too humble to attempt performing for him.

We might try to understand what it was that made him great.

Pope John XXIII will be remembered by this one of his untold millions of non-Catholic students and disciples as a man who insisted on understanding and who began by insisting that he be understood.

He was a patient man, and his peasant origin accounts perhaps for the genial optimism with which he seemed to deal with nature's, including human nature's, sluggishness. In one of his eight encyclicals, the one beginning *Mater et Magistra* (*Mother and Teacher*), he outlined a theory as to the organization of society which offended the world's haves, the ultraconservative Right. His concern for little people who earn their bread in the perplexity and loneliness and hazard of modern civilization seemed no more radical or astonishing than the concern expressed earlier in the century by Leo XIII and Pius XI. But in the United States he was accused of trifling with economics and politics; a sneer was popular for a while: "Mater, Si; Magistra, No!"

He had been thoroughly and systematically misunderstood. He set out to make matters clearer.

The Second Vatican Ecumenical Council was a gigantic effort to make understanding possible.

Consider the range of the effort. Here at one level, the level at which the 2,500 cardinals and bishops and leaders of the Roman Catholic Church met in Rome from last October 11 to December 8, Protestants and officers of the Greek and Russian Orthodox Churches sat as invited guests and observers. They were able to come away uttering the word "unity." Some of them seemed to be discovering that Christian churches have a lot in common.

And here at another level Roman Catholic specialists debated reform in the direction of better understanding—such reform as priests' saying parts of the mass and administering the sacraments not in Latin but in the vernacular tongue of the people there in any church.

Not a day after his election in November 1958 had elapsed before the Pope of peace went on the air by radio to appeal for an end to war. As if he might be apprehensive lest the world mistake that for a pious cliché, he undertook to make it understood he did not mean creating peace with one's friends—he meant removing the causes of friction with people taking no pains to make themselves lovable. He began to seek out some manner of working arrangement with governments behind the Iron Curtain in behalf of Catholics in what is called the silent church. Moscow was at first startled. Then it seemed to be encouraging him.

He must have known he could not live to build the many kinds of unity the world will need. But he was determined that there would be no misunderstanding of his purpose. *Mater et Magistra* having left a few rugged Christians in doubt, the Pope composed his masterpiece, the "Pacem in Terris" of April 11, and made one meaning clear at the outset. Instead of addressing it as a letter to Catholics only, he addressed it: "To All Men of Good Will." He appealed for peace, disarmament, the absolute renunciation of nuclear weapons, and the organization of the civilized state in such a way that little people can fairly share in the abundance they help create. He spelled out the world's need for an international or supranational organization powerful enough to keep the peace and promote the general welfare. Without denouncing Communism by name, he said that in its present form it is the enemy of human freedom; yet, he said with his infinite patience and hope, its form can change.

He lived each day as if it might be his last, with an intensity whose glow suffused us all. When he died all of us, including millions who have no church or deity and very little faith in anything, suffered with him in his agony and knew when it was over that a friend had gone. That much was clear.

Companions in Misery

Except that they would have made an unmanageable multitude in our little dead-end street, I wished that I could have had with me Sunday morning the moralists who complain the decay of individual responsibility is what's wrong with the country.

The scene was, of course, ridiculous.

Not the scenery: the scenery after the ice storm was sublime— the trees glittering in a sheath of ice, the houses packaged for Christmas in a film of silver, the sheeted lawns, each street in that upland reach of the country a river frozen over its mysterious black depths.

Stunning, and now and then in the silence that signified traffic had slid to a dead stop on the distant highways, a great branch on some overburdened old tree would give way with a crack like an artillery piece's and would come floundering down to sprawl dead still twitching and crackling.

But the scene was ridiculous. In house after house as I teetered along on the ice men and women were standing at the window staring out, their faces drawn with worry, and at a dozen houses within a couple of blocks men bundled as if to confront an Arctic blizzard were chipping ice off the driveway, scattering sand or salt, even getting the car out of the garage to make little test runs out to the main thoroughfares and back.

I knew what they were doing: the same thing I was doing; they were determining whether they'd get out of the house and on the way to work next morning or had better start then and there and perhaps hole up for Sunday night in a motel en route. And I knew what they were thinking: that the way a chap responds to the unpredictable crisis is the measure of his quality. I was just thinking the same thing myself. It was, of course, ridiculous.

In the context of history and human experience, that weekend sleet storm was about as significant as a summer evening breeze on the surface of a lake. It came; it went, perhaps actually interrupting electrical service for a few minutes here and there; it was utterly superficial. I had been reminded how superficial our weather is when I had a letter from a farm in upstate New York last week observing that the town road crews had just gone past doing their last chore before the winter plowing starts.

"The guys in the truck were hammering into the ground at the edge of the road big six-foot stakes, one every hundred yards or so," the letter said. "Each stake has a little red flag tacked to its upper tip. They said that's so they'll be able to know where the road is when they have to plow it open, over and over again, during the winter."

When the boy who wrote that looks out his window next month and sees the little red flags fluttering just above the surface he'll know it snowed during the night.

That, as against a half-inch layer of ice that'll rot and shatter and melt whenever the temperature inches above 32 degrees Fahrenheit—that is winter.

And thousands of us, hundreds of thousands whom the mobile society has carried eddying here from the upper corners of the country, know better than to equate an overnight freeze or a foot of snow with physical adversity. Don't let any of us get started on that, but at the farm the drifts in the lee of the old house would reach to the sill of the bedroom windows, 12 or 15 feet above the surface of the ground, and there were nights under the shifting purple curtains of the Northern Lights when the thermometer on the barn showed 40 below and a boy's hand would freeze to any piece of steel it touched, but don't let any of us get started on that.

Here at the windows of a sheltered street in Megalopolis they stood, these children of Maine and the Great Plains states and Appalachia, staring at the husks of fallen ice on their lawns and worrying.

Men don't change. Contexts do. Take a tough middle-aged corporation executive out of Glen Rock or Palisades back to the countryside he came from, and he'd listen to the hiss of the storm and the creak of branches, light a fire and a pipe, and let'er blow.

The deadlines are different. If the cows aren't milked by 6 A.M., they'll last till 7; if the machinery awaiting repairs in the shed isn't fixed today it won't go away, and it won't be needed, any of it except the snowplow attachment on the tractor, for months and months; the deadlines are in terms of hours at the closest tolerance and seasons at the loosest. Let 'er blow!

We walk at a different pace. We hear a different drummer. If Chick Robinson can't get out in time to make the 6:30 A.M. airport limousine at the Howard Johnson on Route 17, he'll not catch the 8 o'clock plane out of Newark, and if he misses that, why there'll be a conference hall full of men much like himself waiting in Chicago or Miami Beach or Dallas this afternoon to hear him lay down the new company policy on widgets and he won't be there.

As baseball and football are games of split seconds and fractions of an inch, the game urban Man plays is a game of minutes. It is a game of crises. He has responsibilities to meet, one of them being his responsibility to himself, and it should not be surprising that he worries about them. What might be surprising is the faithfulness with which he meets them.

Let's Try One Nation

Sometimes I fly down east to Martha's Vineyard to see whether the bluefish are in. Sometimes I drive a car, as I did last weekend, and they're in. What I see through the window of a plane and through the windshield of an automobile looks as if it were two separate countries.

One United States, the one you see from 8,000 or 10,000 feet aloft, is an immense forestland, glittering with gemlike lakes and the silver esses of rivers, washed by the endless sea, dappled with little towns shining white among their trees, here and there erupting in the awesome craters of great cities.

It is still Thoreau country.

From the air!

At ground level, especially if you squirm off the landscaped parkways and turnpikes and go the secondary roads, the United States is a desert, a wasteland, an endlessly unreeling belt of clutter and purposeful mediocrity.

Some of the horror is pretentious: the neon-lighted pizza stands alongside a sweet and brimming pond, the jazz modern regional schools located the maximum possible number of miles from the people they're built to educate, the immense assembly-line industrial plants, with their hideous acres of blacktop parking lots, converting a mountainside into an angry indictment of the right of free choice. And some of the clutter is merely pathetic: halfway to nowhere, get your palm read or buy a genuine factory-guaranteed antique or do stop in and get yourself overcharged 100 per cent for a blueberry pie in a hovel that a housefly would hesitate to enter without an armed escort.

The two Americas are not only simultaneous; they coexist within a few feet of each other, and neither seems to be aware of

84

the other. On a back road in Massachusetts or Rhode Island stop the car in the parking lot of a barbecue hell (grinders & submarines), and walk a dozen paces away from the road, then look around you.

You are in the forest. This summer, the rain having been abundant, the forest is thriving—growing so luxuriantly that it is creeping back across the margins from which it had been beaten back.

It occurs to you that the forest is waiting, that everywhere among the trees eyes, little glinting eyes, are watching you.

If one day we wipe the human race off the face of the globe, the forest will sweep over our traces like a great green surf, and within 5 years, except for our bottles and coins and the rusting hulls of the cities, there'll be no sign we ever existed.

Indeed, the signs that we exist now are thin. They are the cities, which are not so very numerous considering the expanse of the country, the surrounding suburbs, and the strip slums connecting them. Such things should not depress the quality of all life. But they do. One comes home from an automobile trip convinced that this is a nation of slobs, dimwits, and con men, and it may be that the factor which has made the degradation inevitable is the automobile.

Wherever the automobile can go, people can go, carrying money in their pockets, and this means that wherever a road is built some jackass will set up shop on its shoulder and build a better mousetrap.

It is all the far frontier, even if its name is Route 17, Paramus, or Route 59 through Rockland County. We are all of us pioneers, just about to strike gold or oil, and we have no State or national agency with brains and muscle enough to point out that this is not 1849 and the country cannot afford to let us believe that anything private initiative elects to do is the American way and hence the best way of doing it.

We need a new kind of national zoning which would prevent inner-city business and industry from moving out into the country to avoid the taxes and letting the city go to rot. We need controls on where and how suburbs can be built, and the controls will have to be stronger than town government, hungry for new tax revenues, is willing to impose. We need laws enabling the government whose duty is to safeguard the common happiness to sweep the junk off the roadsides, make the roads be roads and not flimflam parlors, and preserve the city as city, not a warehouse for human rejects, and the country as country, not labyrinth of squalid clip joints.

There are two Americas. They should be made one nation, indivisible, under God, who sees them from a high place, higher even than a Northeast plane.

Beggars of Life

By day the beggar on the street confronts you with a clear-cut question. Mind you, the solution is no pushover; some of the equations are extremely difficult; but you understand the nature of the test—you know what it is in you that's being tested.

The beggars in the night ask you questions for which there are not even words.

There is hunger in their eyes but there is danger too, and you remember the beggar boys in Tennessee Williams's *The Garden District* who tore the sleek stranger to bits. But what shall you give nighttime's beggars who cannot say what they want?

Well, we had come downtown that evening to a pipe shop that stocks the peculiar brand of tobacco we affect, and Main Street was looking busy and bright and affluent. It seemed to be a little more cluttered than it is of a shopping Friday morning, but you don't stop on the sidewalk to adjust your glasses and put your chin on your fist and wonder what you mean by "cluttered"— you go in and get the tobacco.

A man was walking along the edge of the sidewalk, the curb edge, weaving a little, not because he was drunk but to avoid the spaced parking meters. He was a little old guy, dressed not exactly well-to-do, but he was wearing a gray homburg, which indicated an effort to look sharp and think well of himself. This time, when he veered out into the main stream on the sidewalk, a tall boy in a leather jacket, coming up behind him, veered too, so that his shoulder belted hard into the old guy's shoulder.

The boy slowed. When the old guy veered again to pass the next meter the boy shouldered him again. He wasn't fooling. He was looking for trouble. The old guy just kept puttering along, and the boy had to pull ahead past him, looking back as he went up the street, looking for trouble.

That's how it was, and then things seemed different, as if you'd stepped through a flaw in time and didn't know when this was going on. On the corner stood six men. They were staring diagonally across the street at the far corner. There stood four kids. The men were colored. The boys were white. They were looking for something.

A jalopy idled past. A girl at the back window leaned forward and yelled something, and then was yelling something else that wasn't laughter. It was meant to hurt. A little colored kid stood on the corner and looked up the alley where the saloons are. He was waiting too. On the step of one of the recessed doors leading up to the flats over the stores hunched three boys, maybe twelve years old, passing a cigarette back and forth. Our little boy was tooling along with us, and he happened to be wearing his khaki camp shorts and the scarlet sweatshirt we got him at the Rutgers bookshop last spring. On it in black is stamped the University seal or the Q or some other symbol. The boys on the doorstep didn't like it.

One said, alto, he wished he had pants like that.

One said he thought he'd like a sweatshirt like that.

The other said he'd like to meet that boy when he didn't have his old man with him.

Old Bill waltzed along imperturbably. He's been through this sort of thing at camp and school.

"What did those guys want?" he said halfway home, fifteen minutes later.

We'd both been thinking. What do they want—what is it that we all want, not just down there in the teeming bazaar that is any main street at night but everywhere we go angrily and dangerously asking for something to happen to us? It's not meant to be a rhetorical question. There has to be an answer for it.

Maybe all they want, before they go home to bed and their six or seven hours of death, is affirmation, some certification that they exist and have an identity of their private inviolable own. In the clockwork routine of the lives we lead, in the gathering crowd that presses in around us, perhaps there are times when in an abrupt panic we know we are faceless, we are nobody, emerged from nowhere and going nowhere, and we need to matter and to find who we are.

Maybe our search, sweaty and squalid and vulgar as we tend to make it, is the search for dignity. Maybe even in the depths of the asphalt jungle what's being sought at the point of a gun or a knife is even the punishment that crazily testifies a boy is to somebody important. We have not yet minted the coin that will buy off these beggars or the conscience they awaken in the night.

THE WISDOM OF THE GULLS

The Wisdom of the Gulls

Along with the jewel-toned jellies and jams one fetches home,
along with the frayed ropes to be spliced and whipped, the fishing tackle to be rinsed and cocooned in plastic bags against
another summer, the driftwood to be shaped into birds and
candlesticks—along with such rough-textured certainties, one
brings back to the city the parable of the gulls.

Now, no matter how abstruse its veiled meaning may be, a
parable should be told in the simplest and clearest terms possible.

So let's begin with clear and simple matters of fact.

On the bay in front of the house the gulls congregate by
dozens when the tide is low, to pick clams and scallops and small
crabs from the shallows over the bars and fly them ashore, drop
them to crack on rocks or hard-topped driveways or the roof of
your car, and eat them.

Most of them are herring gulls, the gull vulgaris, and over them
reigns a gull we chose years ago to name Elmer. This property
belongs to Elmer, and the other gulls know it. Elmer sits on a
small bench overlooking the beach, and whenever another gull
presumes to land within 100 feet of Elmer's property line Elmer
steps down from the bench and stalks over to where the invader
is standing and growls. If the stranger affects to ignore Elmer,
the tyrant raises its wings over its head, as if posing for a portrait
of the eagle on the back of a dollar bill, and the other gull backs
away. There is no contact, no violence.

We are talking now (a) about herring gulls (b) as a population thinly distributed (c) under natural conditions, and we are
talking about the pecking order.

We humans that share the premises with Elmer blundered into

an experiment. We cooked too ample a pot of pork and beans, and after eating beans morning, noon, and night for three days we surrendered the rest of the pot to Elmer. Superficially a herring gull appears to be a selfish fowl, but somehow it cannot suppress news of a windfall, and no sooner had Elmer peered into the pot and perceived it was half full than he stood atiptoe like a cockerel and crowed beans, lads, beans, and all the gulls on the bay came sailing in, adjusting their bibs and saying where, where?

Elmer took charge. It was Elmer's bean pot, and the other birds acknowledged this. Among them were bigger and younger gulls, but when they approached the pot and Elmer raised its wings they would turn away and duly raise their wings and frighten off other gulls, which in turn would go find some poor little brown slob of a yearling gull to bully.

The great black-backed gull is the aristocrat and knows it, and —God knows how—so do the lesser gulls know it. It is not much bigger than a full-grown herring gull, but in some way the other birds are aware that it is craftier and swifter, more danger- ous, and when it settled on the lawn and advanced on the bean pot, stately as an ambassador in dinner dress, they fell away, Elmer first of all. The black-back took its place at the bean pot, glanced around to see that the candles were lighted and the crystal and silver were in order, and began dinner. An unlettered yearling strolled up and asked how's pickings, and the black-back drew itself erect and examined the poor child as if through a glittering monocle, and the yearling panicked and fled.

The town dump is a great man-made hole in the ground maybe 100 yards in diameter. Into this noisome crater people throw their garbage, junk, brush, automobile tire carcasses, wrecked or played-out cars, collapsed furniture, mildewed bedding. Fires are always smoldering in its depths. Year by year the crater advances across its inland hill and last year's scene of horror is covered with a few feet of sand, and here live the city gulls, crowded shoulder to shoulder, hundreds on hundreds of them. Here in Hell they are born and live and die, fighting over the garbage and forgetting the look of the sea. There is no pecking order. Do not ask me why. Do not ask me why, when people are crowded into an artificial environment in any concentration per square mile higher than some mystic optimum, law and order deteriorate.

The gulls at the dump go into the fires to fight over garbage, and devil take the hindmost. Their wing tips are scorched, and the beaks of most are blackened and of some are burned away to stumps.

I am not arguing for the establishment of a peace by pecking order in human relations—we have our pecking orders, and need no more. What may be suggested is that when any population reaches a certain density the rules which make savagery intolerable are suspended or perhaps are not adequately transmitted.

There may be a literature on the subject. What I can report is that as my wife went about the burning-ghat picking asters the gulls turned toward her and formed a ring, silent and converging, and that as she went back to her car in something that was not quite terror she saw, beside her own shadow on the sand, the shadow of a slow-hovering gull which had not learned it was not a bird of prey. That is the parable of the gulls. I shall have to take it out from time to time next winter and see what I can make of it.

Beach Plums and Pirates

Over the long weekend the bride and I oozed up to Martha's Vineyard to see how or whether the house had weathered the winter—the wind blew eighty miles an hour from Christmas to Easter, or so swore the man who watches our foundation for us— and to reconnoitre the beach plums. Now, I'm not sure whether two people's journey backward into spring is going to warrant stopping the presses, and you may not give a damn that the shrews have eaten the two coconut fiber chairs and the master-piece I left beside the typewriter in the shed. I consider it impor-tant that along the Connecticut Turnpike and away on the island the dogwoods and lilacs and wisteria, even the tulips, are in bloom. It's as if a month of my life had been granted me to live again. So what's in that for you?

And you should worry about my two coconut chairs and my stack of typescript. I do: the chairs were reduced to a litter of shredded tanbark on the garage floor. The only rodents we have are shrews, which are supposed to have evolved to the size of beagles out on our point. And I worry about the masterpiece I found ripped to shreds or chewed to little pellets on the shed floor. I think of other works thus disastrously interrupted—Coleridge's "Kubla Khan," Carlyle's *Sartor Resartus*. I curse the laziness that made me leave the manuscript there exposed to shrews and burglars. Now and then I wonder indeed what it was about.

Well, I cannot expect the world to share my concern in such privy matters, but I believe the adventure of the secret beach plums has a certain universal quality. No matter how unassum-ing he may be in other respects, every one considers himself a close and perceptive student of Nature. Scratch a Wall Street banker, and you will find beneath that horny hide a bird watcher or a tier of trout flies or a trainer of show cats. I go fishing in the summertime with an editor whose most solemn boast is not that he can think the way twelve million Americans think but that he thinks like a striped bass. Every woman I know thinks she knows where the beach plums are to be had when they turn from bronze green to bronze purple in the early autumn.

The beach plum grows, she will tell you, in the lee of the second dune. Along the face of the dune, the dune facing the sea frontally, are the sweet peas and the rosa rugosa and the marran grass. Not until you climb the wind-drifted second dune do the pines and oaks and the beach plum appear. Every one knows this. In the fall everyone tiptoes down to the lee of the second dune, and finds somebody got there first.

But now the beach plums are in bloom, and you walked stunned among them trying to remember what Housman meant to say: loveliest of trees, the beach plum now/is hung with snow along the bough,/and stands about the woodland ride/wearing white for Eastertide. As their fruit and the jams and jellies made of it in October reflect the bitterness of their struggle for existence, so the blossoming now—the sweet soft white flowers close-clustered along the branches—seems to say something about the ecstasy, indeed the gaiety, of struggle.

You do in fact find beach plums along the second dune, but what nobody else knows and we shan't tell is that they have drifted away inland through the centuries, so that whereas they grow in heroic solitude along the beach, in the deep woods they flourish in veritable groves.

It is a fickle plant. Islanders say it produces in alternate years. And since 1964 and 1966 were vintage years for beach plums, so should last fall have been. But the crop failed, and toward the end of the season some of the shops were offering $10 a bushel for beach plums and weren't getting enough even to lend a tint of color to the mail-order jellies.

This fall's will be a bumper crop for us who know where to look, or so we assured ourselves as we scrambled through jungles of wild grapes and scrub oak. We didn't band the trees or mark them with a pennon of red cloth—such tracing devices would be useless. Nobody will ever mistake a beach plum for anything else once he encounters it. It is its own sufficient identification.

But we did make a list of places where the treasure is hidden, and we did draw a bit of a map. And we reflected late one dusk as we stumbled out of an oak cover that someday next autumn, when it's raining and the fog is rolling in across the beaches and nobody in his right mind would go fishing unless he had to, we'll pull on our foul weather gear and go beach-plumming—and we'll know, as does nobody else alive, where.

As we pulled away along the sandy path into the woods another car came up and stopped, and two women got out. One of them carried a yellow scratch pad on a clip board. "In here," one said. "Put it down: half mile off Wintucket Road." They said good day, but it seemed to me their smile was bleak and secretive, hard-faced, as if they knew where they were going.

Ferry Tale for Adults

Edgartown, Mass.—In this report, the gist of which will be that there is nothing to report on the island of Martha's Vineyard except the flowering of beach plums and shad bush, the sensitive reader may recognize a quality that pervades his own life.

We are about to be frantically casual. The ultimate disaster has overtaken the wayfarers. Let us be gay.

A word of explanation is in order.

I am telephoning this copy to the office as if it were an urgent bulletin from some battlefront in Asia or the Middle East or an Ivy League college. It is urgent in only one peculiar respect.

For a little more than forty years now I have been writing a column a day to fill this space for better or worse. I have not thus far failed to meet a deadline. It is not the sort of stunt that people stop and talk about on the street, but it is a record, a habit, that I'd be unhappy to break.

In ordinary circumstances I'd have come up here over the Memorial Day weekend, helped open the house for the summer, and taken the ferry boat back to the mainland Sunday night or very early Monday. In ordinary circumstances, I'd have written on Monday in the office a piece for today's Simeon.

But on this island there is no such thing as ordinary circumstance.

The controlling fact of life is the ferry boat. If boats are running on schedule with their normal loads of cars and trucks and passengers, their existence is taken for granted, no more noticeable or appreciable than is good health. But the season this year is peaking early. The boats are jammed. The waiting lines on the mainland are long. There'll be no room on a boat leaving this island for at least twenty-four hours more.

So here I sit at a bench on the beach overlooking Katama Bay, watching the white terns wheel and halt and plunge headlong into the water to take small fish, and I worry about a deadline which is, as deadlines go, distant in time and space.

It is annoying, of course, to be reduced to such helpless dependance on uncontrollable agencies. It does not please us moderns to be denied instant gratification.

Yet I wonder whether we might not be healthier and happier on the whole if we had more ferry boats to battle and defeat us.

We have been deprived of our respect for space and distance. We have thus lost our respect for our own limitations. We try to be in too many places at the same time: we try to do too many things; we try to be too many persons, and this may be the shattering experience of which psychologists so often write.

Early in the century old Jim Devine, who was the mayor of Hohokus Township (now Mahwah) and a famous blacksmith, would give himself two full days to make his journey by oxcart from his home, just across the state line from Suffern, to Hackensack for the opening of the court sessions.

He could make it as far as Paterson by nightfall the first day, dine well and breakfast early and be in the county seat by noon for lunch and a long talk about the dire state of the republic.

Lean old Jim Devine was a wise man, and I choose to suppose that something of his wisdom developed in his long days of solitary journeying, when there was nothing a man could do but see and listen and think. But he had another dimension. It was impactness. It was a hard personal integrity. He was one man and he did not need or want to be more.

I wonder what sort of distracted committee modern transportation would have made of a man like Jim Devine.

He was shrewd, experienced, respected, persuasive, honest, and skilled in the black magic of bureaucracy. So, if he were one of his successors in this generation, he would be a man besieged to share himself among two dozen good and urgent causes in the world around him. Being conscientious and being needed, he would serve on boards, committees, commissions, task forces, planning councils, policy panels, investigating teams. Thanks to the parkway and the turnpike and airplanes and automobiles he would be in Trenton at 10 A.M., in Washington at noon, in New York for dinner, back in Mahwah in time for a township committee meeting tonight, up tomorrow morning to be in Los Angeles for lunch. Having lived too many lives, he would die early.

Perhaps it has been made too easy for one to subdivide oneself into a posse of men all strangers to each other.

Perhaps one should be compelled to sit still from time to time considering how terns and oxen give their undivided attention to the subject.

Perhaps it is well that sometimes there is no room on the boat.

Youth Discovers a World Too Full

Edgartown, Mass.—The bums' bench is back in its accustomed place under the great old elm in front of the Dukes County courthouse, and the meaning of this is that summer is ended and the danger of a confrontation is past.

But another summer will very likely come, bringing with it boatloads of the migratory young and a certainty of confrontation. That might be dangerous (shots were fired last month); it might be violent, as the trouble was this summer on Nantucket; it just might be worse. There are people here on the island of Martha's Vineyard who have been heard to say they have shotguns and know how to use them.

So the Dukes County Selectmen's Association, which is an

98

unofficial sort of council of the island's six municipal governments, met the other night and excitedly recommended that each town adopt six new by-laws or ordinances enabling uniform tough treatment of vagabonds and undesirables, end quote, or, for short, hippies.

Forbidden would be:

Camping or sleeping in the open on any property, public or private, without the permission of the owner.

The use of obscene or profane language in any public place.

Sauntering or loitering in the street in such a way as to obstruct travelers.

Drinking on any street or parking lot.

Any drinking by any person aged less than twenty-one.

No person shall enter upon the premises of another with the intention of peeping into the windows. . . .

The draft by-laws do not contemplate prevention of the incident of the bums' bench. Perhaps there is no constitutional way of forbidding the young to congregate on a bench of public accommodation. Through the years since the county commissioners installed the bench under the elm it has been occupied by the elderly from, say, 9 A.M., when the shops on Main St. are opened and the pilgrims arrive to be inspected and sneered at, until dinnertime. The old gentlemen who sat daily in judgment except in event of rain were never conspicuously natty. But they were an institution, and institutions are respected. If you were on the bench to while away a wife's shopping hour and one of The Boys tottered up you'd rise and give him your place.

The kids this summer had not learned about this custom, or had no use for such decadent proprieties. Long-haired, barefooted, clad in sweat shirt and dungarees, they would take over the bench at 7 or 8 A.M., and when The Boys reported for loitering the young not only declined to go away but told The Boys to go get lost, pappy.

The county commissioners couldn't contrive a legally tenable way of removing the kids. So they removed the bench. There was some talk among the young people about drawing up some non-negotiable demands—either put back the bench or we'll blow the courthouse—but it never came to anything. Now the kids are gone and the bench is back.

The things the draft by-laws proscribe are the things that troubled Vineyard people this summer. Young people, notified by the underground press that on the island the livin' is easy, swarmed over from their cities and campuses bringing with them precisely the adversities they were trying to flee: noise, crowdedness, the smell of gasoline, the sense of being not wanted. They did indeed loaf and saunter. They drank sometimes too much, and they had drugs. After the bench was gone they'd roost along the Main St. curb and sneer at the bourgeoisie, and the use of the four-letter words was calculated and ostentatious.

I just don't think, you see, that the selectmen's uniform by-laws get to the taproots of the Vineyard's problem. Given police manpower enough to enforce them, they might enable wholesale arrest and imprisonment (for lack of money to pay a fine) of people camping in woods otherwise unusued or sleeping on beaches otherwise deserted. They might inhibit the use of obscenity on Main St. and the calculated rudeness of pre-empting the whole sidewalk, although here's a dime to your doughnut that the appellate courts would make hash of any law that didn't define more narrowly than these what's profane, what's obscene, and what's sauntering.

They don't get to the root of the Vineyard's problem, because that problem is everybody's problem everywhere.

There are too many of us in this corner of the world, and this corner of the world is running out of the things we all want and need and should have a right to enjoy in equal measure. It is not fair that because some of us have been lucky or came early we should repel and indeed hate people seeking, because they are human, the look of sea and sand, the sound of wind in the gnarled pines, the medicament of solitude. This is my beach, a man told some kids, and in *The New York Times* Anthony Lewis reported their answer, and it makes you wince: "But, you see, we don't have a beach." And on they came.

On they are coming, millions on millions, and the beaches dwindle and the tides sicken, and we had better begin wondering whether the problem can be solved when we are the problem. I don't think it can be done by pulling up the town bench or passing by-laws.

The Fearful Old Sea Dog

Because I am the kind of trembling little twirp that expects to be arrested for interstate transportation of drugs because he keeps a deck of aspirin tablets in the glove compartment, I do wish the House would stop goading the Coast Guard.

You don't see the connection.

At the island we have a boat. It is named Boat II. It floats. Often, when it has a 3-knot wind behind it and the tide is fair at 2 knots, we can bang her up to 5 knots. That's full throttle.

So I am a pilot. I don't know anything about piloting a boat. I don't have a license—and the fact millions of others don't have a license does not relieve me of my guilty secret. All I know about navigation is that if you head due west you'll hit the North American continent.

Every time I take Boat II off her stake and go thundering up the harbor for the mail I expect the Coast Guard to lob a cannonball athwart my beams or avast my scuppers—just getting the hang of the idiom, you know—and send a boarding party to haul me off to prison. Don't ask me what the charge would be. I don't know what laws I'm violating.

Last summer I was terrified. This summer the House Government Operations Committee will want the Coast Guard to get tough with me.

The fact that the Coast Guard has not up to now come within 25 miles of Boat II isn't reassuring. The House committee wants the Coast Guard to take more aggressive leadership.

While the number of motorboats increased 7.9 per cent from 1962 to 1966, the number of boating accidents increased 41.3 per cent, of personal injuries 59.2 per cent, of fatalities 24.9 per cent. Property damage was up 82.1 per cent. Damage totaled only $7.3 million in 1966. Isn't that an interesting use of the word "only"?

Meanwhile, the committee said, almost half the pleasure boats boarded by the Coast Guard turned out to be in violation of the statutes or the regulations, but in fewer than 20 per cent of the resultant proceedings was any penalty imposed on the violators. And the average fine was only—I think "only" is defensible usage in this case—$10.

Such a record of diligent nonenforcement should be reassuring. It isn't. The Coast Guard is a proud service. It will not suffer such needling gladly. Mark my words. It can't compel amateur sailors to take a test and get a license—only Congress can do that, and Congress has so far refused to concede that a drunken six-year-old at the wheel of a 600-horsepower cruiser is a menace to the general welfare. The Coast Guard can't pass laws. But it can enforce the laws that are on the books.

It's scary enough now. When I wade out to take Boat II up to town for a can of tobacco, 1 doz. eggs, and crumbs to dust and oil to fry the fish we won't catch that afternoon, the bride asks me whether I have the lifebelts aboard. Yes. The horn, in case of fog? Boathooks? Bilge pump? Compass? Charts? It's about three miles, and you can't miss the town dock without charging spang into the Christian Science reading room. Running lights in order, fore and aft, green and red along the sides? We don't have any running lights. Off I go, quivering, absolutely sure that this time a great white cutter will rear up beside me and a man with a bullhorn will order me to pull over to the side.

I keep trying to tell myself that the Coast Guard even when incited to fury by congressional criticism wouldn't be interested in clods like me—it would get after the states to pass laws meeting the 1959 federal safety standards; it would press manufacturers for research on safety devices; it might, reversing itself, insist that anybody in charge of a powered boat pass an examination something like the automobile licensing tests written and in motion; it might argue, against Treasury counsel's dictum, that the licensing process would be the most effective safety education possible.

Besides, it would be suicide for a Coast Guard cutter to chase me into our reach of the bay. Anything drawing more than 4½ inches of water would go aground in the mud, and the maddened clams would swarm out and eat the crew alive.

I tell myself all this. But if you've ever caught yourself in the car six blocks from home with your driver license in your other pair of pants, you know how cold is such comfort. I wish the Congressmen had let well enough alone. It was bad enough.

Translation of a Sigh

You must have noticed a little exhalation of relief that went breathing through the countryside last weekend. That wasn't spring—not yet; we've one more snowstorm to cross before we make it to spring again. It was the newspaper business, sighing nationwide its delight and gratitude that Mr. and Mrs. James Reston had bought *The Vineyard Gazette*.

When newspapermen sigh these days, too often they stand stricken at the grave of some beloved old monarch. Say *World Journal Tribune*, and weep.

The news from Edgartown, Martha's Vineyard, Mass., was that the *Gazette* would live. In the hands that have won two Pulitzer Prizes a little country weekly would be safe.

But it had come to be a close thing. Henry Beetle Hough,

editor of the *Gazette,* is as spry and competent as any of the birds whose comings and goings he chronicles along with shipwrecks and hurricanes and the price of eels and sand dabs. But his own Pulitzer Prize was awarded in 1918, and he knew—as newspapermen everywhere knew—that even on an enchanted island time must have a stop.

He does not take himself very seriously—his humor, whether it be grim or merry, is based as all good humor is, in a hard bedrock of humility—but he takes seriously a newspaper's responsibility to reverence the fact, pursue the truth, and hold the mirror up to its community.

So although his composing room foreman, whose only name as far as I know is just Bill, had sworn he wouldn't go through another island summer of frantic emergencies and his senior aides are very senior indeed, Henry Beetle Hough had to draw a line. He was willing to sell. He wouldn't sell out.

Newspapermen assumed a queer sort of holy obligation to preserve the *Gazette,* with its limpid editorials, its grunt-by-grunt minutes of the town meetings, and its stern insistence that an island's values were to be preserved. It is an Edgartonian unashamedly patriotic. It is conscious of Tacitus' admonition that patriotism consists of honorable competition with our ancestors.

To the island in the summertime come whole glistening schools of millionaires. So do small ragged detachments of newspapermen, some of them fallen into the regrettable habit of writing books.

And every so often a newspaperman would steer a millionaire from the Yacht Club up to the cluttered little office on South Water Street, and the millionaire would say that he'd like to buy the *Gazette,* the price being right and the tax write-off generous. The temptation must have been sore. The work is hard, and since Mr. Hough's beloved Betty died three years ago the old sense of fun has leached out of it.

He knows how to ask questions. Episode after episode, he'd satisfy himself that the visiting millionaire wanted the *Gazette* the way he'd want a Rembrandt drawing or an award from some foreign potentate—something to hang on his living-room wall, a little gewgaw, y' know.

The newspapermen weren't much better, take them for all in all. Too typically, one said he'd rather like to be a country editor—sounded like a pipe-smoking, flannel-shirt job, maybe 10 A.M. till time for a swim at 2. Henry Beetle Hough showed them the door.

Like so many others in so many places I got involved to the extent of trying to find a buyer, trying to interest universities in establishing the *Gazette* as an off-campus journalism school (it has trained some great writing men), and trying not to worry. It looked hopeless. The dean has a way of looking through you when you propose the need for training the young in writing —in the organization of the material, of ideas, no matter what the medium.

The other day a girl gave me a book, in which she had written a note professing gratitude for something and wishing me well in my new venture. I gather it had been deduced that since a fellow was interested in saving the *Gazette* he must be promoting a snap flannel-shirt job for himself.

I love Henry and the *Gazette*, among other things, but there are other loves. I have promises to keep and miles to go before I sleep, miles to go before I sleep, and the miles are hereabouts. So much, then, for a small suspense story—enough to explain a sigh of relief to know that Scotty Reston and his family are standing by and ensuring an orderly transition rather than another damned funeral.

There's a Seagull in This Cookbook!

Edgartown, Mass.—Waking early yesterday, he heard a quiet music at the bedroom door that opens to the deck of the little house. Rain, that had to be. He sat on the edge of the bed listening to the shower of sound and trying to decide what was rainy about it. Well, it was music without rhythm; it consisted of millions of minute, flickering, oddly colored points of sound; it occurred in irregular gusts and trickles; each note, no matter how pianissimo, was being struck separately. He knew rain when he heard it.

He got up, took his armful of clothing from the closet beside the bed, and tiptoed out of the darkened room into the kitchen.

The Sun, its dazzle multiplied by its reflection in Katama Bay, was blazing in a cloudless east. He put on his sunglasses and turned away from the hurt of the glare to start the coffee.

It takes time to get accustomed. The music at the door had been a little Japanese wind chime, eight or ten bamboo tubes hung on strings from a crosspiece so as to jostle each other in the merest whisper of a breeze.

That was yesterday. Today he woke to music at the door, and reflected that it would be another brilliant morning. He'd get the boat out of the garage and into the water, and one might do worse than pack a picnic basket with bread and meats and cheeses, not forgetting a small bottle of clean white wine, and run across the bay to a secret place on Chappaquiddick where the marsh heather would be glinting purple. He went into the kitchen, squinting in anticipation of that shocking glare.

It was raining. The wind chimes hung mute in the windless air. The music he had heard, the millions of tiny notes struck separately, each having a quality of hollowness—the music was the rain that it should have been yesterday but wasn't and shouldn't have been today but was.

It takes time to get accustomed. At home he cooks breakfast on a gas range. Here the range is electric. At home he turns on two burners, one flame high to boil the water for tea, one low, but not too low, to warm the big shallow cast aluminum pan for the omelet. It takes perhaps three minutes to haul out the makings.

106

In many a summer of dealing with electric ranges he has not learned how to tell how hot a heating element is by looking at it the way he looks at a gas flame. If the metal spiral glows red he knows it is too hot. But as a measuring device this is crude. It can be too hot and usually is long before incandescence occurs.

When he drops the dollop of butter into the pan he observes that it skitters about and melts fast and that the puddle of fat is browning—indeed, blackening—at its edges. Yet he tells himself frantically that browned butter imparts a dark nutlike flavor to foods, and his alimentary canal assures him it could use more omelet and less Hamlet. He sighs and pours the materia into the pan.

It explodes. Its edges pop and bubble. He slides his fork under the hardening keel of the omelet and lifts it, and the raw egg runs underneath and sizzles. He takes the pan off the heating element, tilts it to and fro so that the uncooked liquid can form a smooth new edge around the periphery of the ruin.

He folds it out on the plate, and, pouring tea, sits down to contemplate the disaster. He pecks at it. It is tough and rubbery. Perhaps a filling of strawberry jam would redeem it? The answer is no. The answer is that no treatment yet invented can render an automobile tire tube toothsome. The only decent use of this by-product of American technology is to be taken down to the beach and offered to the gulls.

The gulls are fewer in number this year, and they are behaving in a way not explained or even mentioned in a shelfload of books about birds. These are herring gulls, the common gull of the shore and now of the inland city. Last year they swung in clouds over the bay. Except at low tide, when they convene on the exposed shoals and bars to grub among the weed for garbage, they are as scarce this fall as flickers.

Perhaps the reason is no farther to seek than the tip of the stake on which we moor the boat. There, grim and silent, presides a great black-backed gull, called sometimes the saddleback, the coffin-bearer, the minister, or the turkey gull. The black-back is bigger than the gray herring gull. It is a solitary. It is aggressive. It does not kill herring gulls. This is unnecessary. It can put a hundred of them to flight by dropping among them and raising its wings.

It eats herring gull eggs. Put another bird on your list of endangered species.

And so the omelet is submitted to the gulls on the lawn, and the cookbook that awaits the writing will be *Gourmet Garbage, or, 1,001 Messes Easily Prepared in the Home Kitchen.* There will, of course, be the recipe for Electric Range Omelet, and the great field and stream writer Bill Backus has a way of marinating breast of crow in red wines and subtle spices and broiling it on a plank, after which you throw the crow to the gulls and eat the plank.

But the underlying theory of the book will be that a lot of us moderns cook for the sake of cooking. There's something Freudian in all that chopping and slicing and pounding and getting up to one's elbows in goo. To the dedicated cook, especially the male cook, it doesn't matter how the stuff tastes or whether anybody eats it. It is not necessary that art be useful. If people are hungry they can go out and scuffle up a bug.

The Trouble with Stars in the East

The *Barbara and Gail,* a squat little scowlike scalloper out of Fairhaven, Mass., lost her rudder and stove herself in and sank on a shoal in the snowstorm off Nantucket the other day. Five men were drowned. Five survived. You'd suppose experienced sailors would steer clear of the Great Rip, steer clear of any of the rips east of the Vineyard, where the sea stands on edge, roaring, and sucks in any boat and chews it and spits out its bones. But even at this time of year people take their chances in the rips and not always understandably for money the way scallopers do.

There were these pilgrims in their stinkpot barreling in from the east, and they mistook the Pogue light for the lighthouse at the entrance to the Edgartown harbor.

If you know the country, either you're laughing or you've turned pale. If you don't, why then you must piece it together in your mind. Here on the treacherous shoaling Atlantic east of Martha's Vineyard is a big chrome-and-mahogany motorboat. On it are three off-islanders, a lawyer and a doctor and a merchant prince. They're cruising up from New York to spend the holidays on the island, as more and more people do these days, and they've managed to grope their way out of the Sound into open water. Night has fallen.

They've consulted their charts and their instruments. It is time to be heading from the open water toward Edgartown, home.

So they turn the boat from roughly north to roughly west, and start looking out for buoys and lights. There are two lights to watch for when you're coming in from that angle. One is the lighthouse on the steep cliff at the end of Cape Pogue. The other is the much smaller lighthouse at the entrance to the peaceful harbor that turns in its magic S below the mansions of the whaling captains. Coming in, you take the Pogue light away on your left side, and, about five miles farther in, you cut the engine of the boat and let the harbor light slide by on your right.

They'd been out through a long, relatively hard day, and it is conceivable that they had been passing a flask to and fro, but in any event suddenly one of them said he saw the Edgartown light dead ahead. The steersman slacked the boat off a little to the left, to clear the harbor light and its pier, and of course you know what happened next. The boat thundered up and flung itself on the rocky strand at the foot of the Cape Pogue light, and everybody fell flat on the deck singing "Nearer My God to Thee" and wondering what sort of play *The Times* would give the obituary.

The boat didn't sink. The beach between the rocks is shallow-sloped and sandy. The men got out and waded ashore, and walked down the beach until they came to a place where they could climb to the top of the cliff.

There's a little shack back in the scrub-oak woods. They asked for help there, but the man who let them in said it was he who needed the help; he said he was very much afraid that he hadn't gotten his wife over to the hospital on the main part of the island in time and she seemed to be having a baby.

The doctor shrugged ruefully and washed up and went to the bedroom and did whatever it was that had to be done. When the story was told to us last summer the emphasis was on the wonderful illiteracy of the three pilgrims who hung themselves on a 6- or 8-mile beach thinking it was the entrance to the harbor. But the men themselves that night talked a long while about the luck that had brought them just that way at just that time, to take part in the miracle which is the birth of any child. The human race is very old and perhaps incorrigible, they said over coffee, but something seems to want it to keep trying; there is some reason to believe that it can be saved and is worth saving, and a baby may be about as clear a statement of that reason as we shall ever have.

They went back and brought up to the shack some stuff from the boat—milk and eggs and some cold cuts and bread and butter, enough to hold the family till somebody could get out there with a jeep or an ambulance and get the mother and baby to the hospital, and in the morning they floated the boat off and came in to town. The three wise guys didn't tell anybody about how they'd gotten their stars mixed up, but the story got out somehow, and by the end of Christmas week every one had heard about it. Despite some disagreement on details, the consensus was that they had been fools to chance the rips at night.

About Time for a Turn of the Season

In the summertime the mountains look convex, rounded, as full-fleshed as a Rubens nude. It is now at the end of winter that you see their bones.

From the Ramapo valley a great hill soars away to the west, and you'd seen it a hundred times, but this time you were startled to observe that at its very crest is a sort of saddle and in the saddle hangs, trying to make up its mind whether this is the right geological epoch for adventure, the idea of a glacier.

A great stone battlement of upended strata rears itself up a little farther north along the Thruway, and that too, you'd have said, you know as you know the veins on the back of your hand.

Halfway up its face is suspended a little pond—dull gray ice except at its edges, where the water, which is very deep and very cold, glows dark blue.

In another month the hillsides in the Ramapos and Catskills and Adirondacks will have flattened away into their old long curves and planes. Last week-end, all the way up the long valley to Saratoga Springs for an inscrutable ritual known at the college as Happy Pappy, a man found the hills are not that way at all—not at all so geometrical and dull as they seem when the trees and brush have greened out. Down their sides, as secretly and delicately as would ancient deer, tiptoe little ponds. The footsteps glint blue and white against the earth colors.

Farther up the valley the streams that run crosswise to the road are choked and grumbling. Pull off the road, and duck under an old bridge. On the upstream side the ice jam has formed. Laced through the immense slabs of ice are the baleful structure's girders—trees fallen and drifted, in some rivers logs

111

trimmed and meant, one takes it, for delivery to market at mills miles away but swept loose in the flooding.

The water mumbles and hisses through the jam, and tumbles into the stream, many feet below, at the other side of the bridge. When those walls of ice go out there'll be trouble.

Up there it's winter still. A few miles farther south a creek comes shouting out of a mountain gap in full flood. A few miles farther yet a little river pulses in its accustomed rhythm, and the added way a man can tell spring is in the air is that its surface is marbled with long streaks of muddy water, yellow to dark brown—up there somewhere a farmer's field has pulled out with the winter.

But down in the valleys where the old farms nestle is where you can be sure at last that the long death is ended and things are going to be all right again.

In the distant hills the colors are all stark—white and black and murky dun. But along the edges of the farms and along the valley roads the woods are beginning to seem red or purple where life has started to stir in the sheathing of the buds, and there are places where a yellow haze seems to hang in the valley and around the houses. Look harder, and it is gone, but look away, and it is there again—the ghost of last spring's forsythia or spring after next's. Afterward you remember that the trees around the barn were willows and might be expected to be impatient.

One takes it the winter has been hard back in the hills as it has been in town. On a long trip a man stops for coffee now and then. In a dingy little beanery this side of Glens Falls the deer-jackers were comparing notes. The deer have been starved out of the mountains. A man can shoot down a load of venison for the New York trade without hardly getting down from the cab of his truck. It's a wonderful race we belong to.

Nothing much happened that week-end. There's nothing to report. One night up there we had a bit of an ice storm, and you could hear the thunder on the roof, and in the morning all the deserted hot-dog shoppes and tourist come-ons glittered as if a province of Heaven had come to Earth for an hour. And some cars and a truck slithered off the road. People got hurt. In a field a little herd of skinny deer stood glistening and waiting.

But down here on Route 17 a few hours later the sun was out and warm, and the road was dry, and the people getting killed in cars had other reasons for going off the road. The hills above Suffern glowed red, and in southward-facing yards little crocuses nodded and twinkled. There's snow to come. But that long winter is over.

The Itch To Get Back at Nature

It was a rum thing to be sitting there on the edge of the bed at 3:25 A.M. reflecting that we built this house here at the edge of the woods so that we could be close to Nature.

Across the street the land slopes away, catches itself and clutches briefly to the brink, then topples steeply down a glen wooded in oaks and beeches and stunted laurels to the edge of Valentine's Brook.

Away in the distance the brook surged over the dam, talking to itself.

That hasn't changed much. It won't. As long as there's a law of gravity water will find its way somehow safe to sea. But not much else is quite the same.

On the far side of the brook when we came there the woods were old and deep. We were told that an old railroad town called Waldwick lay somewhere to the north, and we had the assurance of reliable maps that if a man went far enough he'd encounter civilization in such forms as Middletown, N.Y., or maybe Buffalo or Toronto, but as far as the eye could see there was nothing between Ridgewood and the eternal icefields of the Arctic except the woods. It was like living on the first page of a Norse legend.

Not on purpose does a man get up at 3:25 A.M. to while away an hour with such grim anecdotage. Not on purpose.

The woods beyond the brook are gone now. Where then their groined corridors marched away into darkling mystery is now being completed the treatment works of the Northwest Bergen County Sewer Authority. It is an immense plant, hundreds of feet long, towering story on story above the brook, composed of the yellow brick that proclaims the public institution, from prison to housing project.

Let the record show that this is an observation, not a complaint. That part of the county needs massive sewerage, the plant had to be put somewhere, and the competent engineers and conscientious public servants who decided to build it here did their job.

One of these days the trout and perch will be glinting again in what had become an open sewer, and the kids will wade safely in the long pools for frogs and turtles and crayfish, and we're planting forsythia and kolkwitzia as a screen between us and the disposal plant.

To think, I said to myself at 3:45 A.M., that we came here to get back to Nature.

Nature had come back to us. For the first time in my life I wished I owned a shotgun.

When they started building the plant a year or so ago the deer that used to tiptoe down the valley—how sweet and solemn they looked, like young nuns!—just went away, slipped through the wooded hallways between towns into the blue hills on the horizon. And the birds with options abandoned us: the big piliated woodpecker, the tanagers, the finches and kingfishers and hummingbirds.

The solid middle-class citizen didn't go away. They just moved up the hill to our place.

So every morning now a boy's choir of crows sings matins at sunrise just outside the bedroom window. The basses croak in five-fourths time. The tenors and baritones caw four beats to the bar. The mourning doves say who three times, then pause and swallow, all except one mourning dove from Boston that says whom. The bluejays shriek, the cardinals say birdie, birdie, birdie. Drink your tea, cackles some poultry higher in the tree.

It is sometimes hard to make oneself remember that this is their morning song. As far as they know, they are blithe spirit made flesh, one with the nightingale, and the fact that they sound like a high-class cocktail party is not their fault.

I can stand the junk birds, because I get up at the same time they do, but the nocturnal beasties are making themselves intolerable. Raccoons are darlings to look at, but there is no beast more foul-tempered or, when it can't lift the lid off the garbage can in the garage, more foul-mouthed.

They curse the garbage cans. They curse, page by page, the magazines and newspapers we stack on the lids. They curse the cats and opossums. When the trains pass, honking the ill-tuned horns that will never wake a boy and inspire him with impossible dreams, they curse the locomotives for waking the whole house and making it difficult for a decent second-story man in a black mask to make a livelihood.

It is like living in a brawling slum.

Don't believe what the nature fakers tell you about the raccoon's fastidiousness. These fat tramps don't take the grub down to the brook and wash it before eating it. They kick over the garbage can, pick out the bones and juicier leftovers, and proceed to glom it sitting in a circle on the hood of my car. They leave their little hand prints on the windshield and the rear window. They grumble to each other, so loudly the proprietors can hear them, that the quality of the victuals has gone away downhill. Gorged and glutted, they take a last few dainties up on the roof and quarrel over them in breathless throaty barks—at 3:25 A.M.

In the winter they'll creep into the attic.

We wanted to get back to Nature.

In those days it was to, not at.

Pulse Feeling in the Country

The storm that blew in toward the end of the week was a sincere, hardworking northeaster. Typically a northeaster finishes torturing itself to death along toward the end of its third day in office and leaves the skies scoured, the air washed crystal clear, and all the beasts on Earth, including us, feeling relieved and fresh. I suppose it has to do with barometric pressure.

The three-day rule is not enforceable, and northeasters have violated it with impunity from time to time, but I am trusting in advance that today dawned crisp and transparent, because I'd like to recommend a cure for the glums.

Back the car out of the garage. After breakfast—there's no hurry about any of this, no deadline—haul out the picnic basket or maybe just a paperboard grocery carton and pack a lunch for as many persons as there are in the family plus half again as much. No need for jellied salads or an intricate casserole: let's restrict it to sandwiches big and well buttered, a jug of coffee, a container of milk, a pint of Pouilly-Fuisse for the elders and a couple quarts of soda for the children, apples, a slab of cheese.

Questions may be raised. As for Sunday school or church, you can leave town afterward. As for the football game this afternoon, you can be back in time to catch more of it than you really need.

You're going to go out and see for yourself the world as it is in fact, not as it is represented to be in the frantic yammer of politicians and the incoherent alarums of the front page.

It's a pretty good world. Come on.

If the day is fine the traffic will be heavy. Go with it, as you would go upstream with the commerce on a great river, but once you come within sight of hills do not hesitate to leave it. There

116

is much to be seen from a car moving on a superhighway—the southern reaches of the Garden State Parkway are often reassuring, and the Palisades Interstate Parkway is an unalloyed delight that was built with the sense of sight in mind—but roads like Routes 17 and 46 and 4, like the Turnpike, are a pestilence and make no bones about it.

They are not coldbloodedly constructed to serve an earthy purpose, any more than were the railroads, but, as was the case with the railroads, grubby uses have grown up and coalesced alongside them. Let's not recite the ritual curses on strip slums and billboards and the slatternly power lines and poles, the naked horror of asphalt acres, the smell of frying clams and burning pizza.

Leave the highway where you will, veering always toward the hills, and do not fail when you come to a fork in the road to take the way less traveled by. Take the narrower and less promising of the alternatives, the way the eel or the salmon turns at the fork into the colder and more boisterous of the converging streams. It's the way to find the road home.

One afternoon not long before the northeaster I found myself doing it, though not by any such choice. I had a piece of paper to deliver to a minister at a farmhouse in Upper Saddle River, and, having duly memorized the road map, I got irretrievably lost.

It is a beautiful country. Out back of the highways, away from the cities and the developed towns that have flowed together into cities that don't yet want to know they are a single organism, the settlements are still lonely, very far apart, and the farms and woodlands that ramble between them are glowing red and purple, luminous gold where the maples have herded near water, pale yellow, deep green. People are still raising pumpkins for no purpose other than to raise pumpkins—there can't in all the world be market enough for so many pumpkins—and they lie polished with a hot orange radiance. Watch for deer. I think I saw a fox.

You're the explorer, and you'll pursue your own instincts, but let me recommend the Ramapo mountains, Palisades Interstate Park, the foothills of the Catskills to the west of the New York Thruway; anywhere you range will be sound wine, but you might wish to sample the great vintages.

Even before lunch stop now and then. Get out and walk a while. Look at the trees, now stripped by the storm of all their sooty browns and grays, as if you were seeing them for a first time, with a realist's understanding that any time might be a last time. How many of them can you call by name? And when you come to a great old stone fence alongside a well tended field you might consider that the field is there because very long ago some one felled deep-rooted trees one by one, hauled their immense roots out of the earth, and carried each stone to the edge of the farm and set it in its place firm and true. Stop and touch. Feel a stone. Try to lift it. There were giants in the earth.

The lawns are sleek, still green, and the houses testify the people they shelter are proud of them. It's not housing. It's home, and you know what it means. At a turn of the road stands an old barn. There is no house nearby. We built barns to last. From a house we could move on and up.

It is a lovely country, deeply lovable. Go see for yourself. The winter will be long.

You'll be back in time for the game, if it matters. Maybe you'll find it doesn't.

Men at Work, Dreaming

In the saloon off the ferry plaza at Woods Hole one of the boys ordered beer for all. "Two Bally, two Knick, and two Bud," he said self-consciously, as if they were swear words and he wasn't used to them, and the bartender slid the bottles to him and said,

"Whyn't you guys get down there to the end of the bar to do your quarreling?" "Hoodlum kids, drinking in the afternoon," a man said. He was having a double bourbon on the rocks, acting out platitudes. The boys went to the end of the bar and finished their beer, and that's the last we saw of the six of them as six.

On the ferry, though, leaning against the rail of the upper deck was one of them—the hook-nosed Latin one with the tattooing on his wrists—and he was waving to the other five on the broad bayberry-gray wharf below. They were shambling along grinning up, nondescript teen-agers or maybe in their early twenties, wearing grotesque cheap summer clothes—Ivy League caps a little too loud, shirts in red or yellow or Seventh Avenue Hawaiian, cotton slacks, rubber-soled canvas shoes that needed washing. You see them in front of downtown drugstores. You see them in police line-ups.

"Make money," the boy on deck called.

"Make lots of money," replied the tall Negro.

"You know what for," the Latin boy said.

"We know," the Negro said. The five below clambered onto a squat boat at the end of the dock, and one went forward and, bending, lifted a hank of net. It clanked.

It was necessary to ask what purpose money was being made for, and we did, and the boy beside us at the rail said the six are chipping in to buy a hot rod. Either that, he added, or to get a boat of their own. Depends on how much they have in the bank from their year's work.

What work?

"They're scallopers," he said. "I'm a swordfisherman. They work pretty much all the time. I get called only when the sword-fish are in. They're in now. I'm going down to Menemsha Bight. Couple of nights ago a captain came in with 150 swordfish. They're in."

Would he take along a healthy amateur as unpaid help?

"This is my profession," he said. "Would you take along an

119

unpaid amateur as help in your profession? I hope I said that so it didn't sound rude, but . . ."

Ordinarily, he said, the fish will veer away when it feels the harpoon in its back, and will take out the line and its painted keg and run until it kills itself; then one sends a boat to bring in the keg and line and to signal there's a fish to be hoisted aboard. But sometimes a swordfish will go to the bottom and then turn to come on and kill whatever is killing it. Then you must get away from there very tidily indeed, or . . .

On his first trip as a swordfisherman, the boy said, the captain sent him below to get some rags, but didn't describe the location of the rags. The boy stuck out his head, and said, "You mean port, near those plugs?" During the war, he said, when a ship was holed by enemy fire below the water line a plug would be set in the hole from outside, and the water pressure would hold it firm. "What plugs?" said the skipper, and he came below, and they found that the plugs were bone—old swordfish spears that had been broken off from inside. But the point was, the boy said, that at some time in the past three swordfish had charged the boat and driven their beak through an inch of oaken plank.

One afternoon off Nantucket a fish had been harpooned, and a man went in a dinghy to follow it and bring it alongside his boat. The signal to come and get such a retriever is to bring in the oars and hold them up. The man followed the fish a while, and then sat motionless in the boat, rather starchily, evidently having finished his part of the job yet not hoisting his signal.

They went over to where his dinghy bobbed in the evening sea, and found his fish had come up under him and thrust its sword through the floor of the boat and his own stout plank seat, then longitudinally through him from buttock to shoulder, and both were dead.

"On the market this morning," he said, "swordfish were getting 32, maybe 32½ cents a pound. Say we get 100, and for fun make them average 200 pounds. I could make me $1,000 this trip."

We asked him about his friends on the scalloper, and he said they were the real seamen—out there in any weather, away out on the edge of the continental shelf sometimes, working 16 hours a day dragging their chain-mail nets and shucking scallops faster than you crack peanuts, wearing their silly Ivy League caps and dreaming of hot rods. We heard later they came in from this trip with 11,000 pounds of scallops, which that hurricane day were quoted on the Boston market at 48–48.6 cents a pound.

Mr. Sinatra Aids at a Passage Ritual

To Frank Sinatra and the glamorous company he led ashore on my island I know now that I owe a debt I shall not be able to repay. They have made a Vineyarder of me.

All these years, sullenly I've wondered why the natives on Martha's Vineyard had to detest us summer people—the Pilgrims, they call us, or the dogfish. Why couldn't they just take our money, let us pay their taxes, accept our orders for the next antiques off the assembly line, treat us for our burns, submersion, and delirium tremens, and let it go at that?

The Vineyarder grimly insists on maintaining the difference between himself and the mainland man. It is a haughty difference.

And I suspect that much more is involved than the hatred that goes with dependence. Now that the whale is functionally extinct, now that the New England fishing fleet has been rendered technologically obsolete by the immense floating canneries the Soviet Union has massed on the offshore banks, the Vineyard is a 1-commodity economy. The commodity is tourism. Between the conspicuous affluence the summer people bring with them for two or three months a year and the dreary profitless norm which is the rest of the year there's a gap. Where there's an economic gap there's tension, be it in Iran or Colombia or Massachusetts, and the sleek haves are resented; or so some wise men in Edgartown have explained matters to me. Yet much of New England is thus dependent. Out on the island there's a difference.

The yacht was moored in the outer harbor, and the party came ashore. Mr. Sinatra and Mia and the actresses and their husbands had dinner at the Harborside, walked for a while in the gardens that blossom so bravely at the edge of the sea, and went back to their boat. It is hard to imagine behavior more decorous.

I resented it. And with a pang of recognition I welcomed myself into the secret company of those who will not tolerate their island's being taken for granted.

It would be easy to mistake the reasons for resentment. In the August issue of the travel magazine *Venture* S. J. Perelman makes the mistake. He is talking about Beverly Hills people:

> You meet them wherever you roam, in Helsinki or Hong Kong, Patchogue or Perugia, Moscow or Martha's Vineyard—those aromatic, imperious, gravel-voiced characters with unlit Coronas embedded in mahogany faces, clad in Italian silk suits tailored by Sy Devore. Their fashionably haggard wives flaunt Buccellati's latest brooch or Gucci's shiniest handbag and sprinkle their speech with melting allusions to Billy (Wilder), Irving (Lazar), Harry (Kurnitz), Irwin (Shaw), and all the other gods of Leonard Lyons's daily pantheon. They drive Mark X Jaguars as a matter of status but secretly prefer Cadillacs, maintain a dacha at Palm Springs but yearn for one at Klosters, and frenziedly collect the more abstract expressionists. . . . Whether in Nyack or Nairobi, Bessarabia or Bonwit Teller, 21 or Timbuctu, they are as unique, unmistakable, and easily identified as the water moccasin, and just as lovable.

And so much for how to spot a dogfish; but now what's to resent?

The Sinatra party has been to the island, and now Frank and Merle and Rosalind and all the rest know Martha's Vineyard and will smile and nod when the name is mentioned. They have savvy enough not to utter the curse "quaint." They will pay their memory of the emerald-jeweled harbor the tribute of a sigh. They have not impoverished the gardens by plucking in them an immortal recollection.

But they have no right to love it, to dare say they know it, who have never lived with it when the harbor is deserted and the only presence in Main Street is the winter wind. The party that comes ashore to dine and be charmed by narrow streets and architecture of uncanny purity in taste—what does he know of that on which our values are based: the smell of the storm, the shriek of the hurricane over the ancient graves, the beat and halt and shattering crash of the sea around us?

One must try to keep the contempt out of one's voice and manner, but there are things we islanders know that these smiling, chattering strangers cannot be told. Let them go. Let the dogfish go.

An Ancient Horror of Grave Rubbers

Edgartown, Mass.—Something there is that does not love a gravestone rubber.

Meteorology does not account for the mist that happens when the summer-people women tiptoe into any one of the little up-island burying grounds to press their sheets of bond paper against the face of a lichen-scabbed gravestone and make a rubbing.

Call it art. Call it rediscovery, suggested by the commercial success of the rubbings from the toppled temples of southeast Asia—rediscovery of the humble craftsman, unappreciated in his time, whose technique and grace and wit died with him. Call it Freudian; the crayon is black and greasy.

Something there is that does not love irreverence.

It must be sunny, so that the rubbing can be done in an even register, and the day must be windless, so that the paper once affixed to the face of the stone will not flutter or shift or tear. Such a day in the autumn holds its breath, so that the figure a fly dances against the sky, the wash of wind across a field of dying grasses, or the stumbling of a tiny wave on the pebbles at the far edge of a pond are not sounds but evanescent configurations of silence.

The girls, sweatered and kerchiefed and carrying their big tablets of paper and boxes of crayons, go hushed, and when they work they whisper.

Gravestone prose and poetry tend to be monotonous. The stonecutters were craftsmen, not lyric poets, and it would be astonishing if they had found something droll or touching to say about every corpse that threw its trade their way. By and large, but not always, the inscriptions confine themselves to matters of fact. This stone, goes one for-instance, is erected to the memory of Capt Jno Pease unfortunately lost at sea January 1759. Another for-instance:

"Here lyes ye body of Thomas Trapp Aged 83 years died October the 15th 1719 All You That Come My Grave to See/ Such As I Am So Must You Be/Flee Sin Therefore Live Godly Still/Then Welcome Death Come When It Will."

I had not meant to let such matters of fact intrude, but a peculiarly handsome slab of moss-covered typography stands in memory of a girl actually named Mary Smith, who died, as so many people did in the good old days before antibiotics, at Age 8. The stonecutter was smitten with inspiration:

> If blooming Beauty, Innocence,
> Fine wit, or Grace, were a Defence
> Against the Dart of Cruel Death,
> This Child had not refign'd her Breath

The poetry may be indifferent, but sometimes the carving is exquisite—trees of life, death's heads that range from barebone horror to mocking, defiant caricature; and always there's that magnificent type face.

Not every one understands about gravestone rubbings. When Ruth Cowell got back to Westwood she was telling a neighbor about the wonderful summer's rubbings she had brought home with her. "Wait," she said, "I have some in the car; let me get a few to show you." Her neighbor's husband got up slowly. "I guess I'd better help," he said unsteadily. "Aren't they heavy?" Robbings, he thought she'd said.

The women attest that what follows is truth. No matter how fine the day begins, they say, not long after they have started their gravestone rubbings a little wind springs up, and in the valley which is implied by every cemetery's being a hillside cemetery the mists begin to gather. By four o'clock in the afternoon a gray presence comes drifting up from the soil, gray and dank and bone-deep in its capacity to chill all talk and laughter. The paper whips against its pressure-tape stays, and tends to rip or be ripped, and the women gather their tools and tablets and tiptoe out. By the time they arrive home the sun is shining.

In the old town cemetery on Pease's Point Way, they have been told, is a stone inscribed: "Here doth lie our daughter Charlotte, born a virgin, died a harlot." They have searched and searched, but the days are brief and in the old graveyard the mists are sudden and angry. They have not found the stone. It may be that if Charlotte is there indeed she prefers not to have her daytime sleep disturbed.

In a Nest of Ill Fame

It is wonderfully quiet now in the upstairs room at home in which I close myself to catch up with my loafing, so quiet that the only sound perceptible is the rattle and scrape of the house builders. Irreverently and to my intense annoyance they are laboring through the sabbath day. They should, of course, be exterminated.

They are blue jays. Two couples of them are at work constructing nests—one on the copper flashing across the top of the front door frame, the other, on the opposite side of the house, in the crotch between the downspout from the eave trough and the porch pillar to which the spout is attached. The nests are doomed.

Let no representative of a species that builds its homes on flood plains and the sides of volcanoes speak disparagingly of the blue jay's intellectual capacities. No animal that can survive and flourish in this environment is an idiot. But it is permissible to observe objectively and irritably that the blue jay (cyanocitta cristata) is a slow learner—or at any rate these four are.

Year after year at the nesting season, in their impious lust suppressing their memory of the winter's bitter quarreling and profanity, they pair off and address one another in muted wood-wind hypocrisies, and proceed to build nests in the two specific locations within a mile of here where common sense dictates and experience proves a nest is an absolutely uninsurable property.

Nest, did I say? These habitations on which the jays are at work would depreciate the esthetic values of a garbage dump. They are not nests in the way robins' are—small cozy cradles woven of grasses and straw and strings, anchored securely in the Y where branch meets trunk or in an elbow along a bough. And to the exquisite architecture of the oriole's nest, swinging at the tip of a branch, or the art of the hummingbird's or wood pewee's, camouflaged in lichens and bits of bark, the blue jay's nest is as a jumble of raw lumber to the house you live in.

I have watched them at work. Late one afternoon last week the male jay staggered up out of the shrubbery carrying something in its beak. It was a strip of green paper towel, a big strip, and the paper was blowing up and back into its eyes. The wind was stiff, and the jay couldn't see where it was going. It tried, like a driver whose hood has sprung loose and popped up in front of him, to peer out first this side, then that, of the obstruction, but however it ducked and craned the paper was still there in its beak.

At last it took off by dead reckoning for the crotch in the downspout, and landed all askew in the rubble of sticks and twigs that its wife du jour was rearranging. Surprise, surprise, he

126

said; look what I just picked up for a song in the quaintest little old antique shop; and she examined it coldly, pronounced it junk, and threw it down the wind.

She should talk about taste! I appreciate that we should hesitate to pronounce normative judgments on the ways and works of other cultures, but the female jay homemaker makes a spectacularly seedy home. In the blue jay's concept of a safe and and pleasant place to bring up children shows that relationship to the crow family which its magnificent coloration and its classic crested profile suppresses.

The sticks and twigs are not woven or even crudely interlocked as they are in the nests of herons or hawks. As far as I know I've never seen a jay nest in the woods, but at our house the raw materials are just hauled to the site and dumped helterskelter, the twigs lying parallel to each other. The wreckage would suffice, I suppose, to prevent eggs' rolling out, the way the herring gulls' shallow foxholes in the sand keep a clutch of eggs and fledglings approximately together for the brooding and then the feeding.

But they are terribly untidy, are the jays' little slums; we are somewhat embarrassed by the unkempt character they impart to the premises; the birds are raucous, aggressive, cannibalistic, and on top of it all intolerably sarcastic, with their boorish imitation of other birds and their ostentatious quotations of hawks and owls.

There is a temptation to take a broomstick and whisk their silly nests into oblivion. The species would survive. Let them go lay their eggs in some abandoned squirrel nest. There are a dozen within a minute's lumbering flight.

A defensible case would be made for destroying the nests as a service to the world, indeed to the young jays which would otherwise be brought into life in a hostile and precarious environment.

I can't.

The blue jay is a tyrant, a bully, a slob, a bore, and it would be easy enough to say it is in my opinion an unnecessary evil. But it is a very beautiful animal, and without it and the wintering cardinals the dark night of the year from which we're just emerging would be unbearable.

But besides all this is an element of which we have been made suddenly and miserably conscious: the danger of becoming indifferent to life, the danger of unfeelingness, the terrible danger of apathy with respect to the uttermost fundamentals. Once death is no big deal, as somebody at Fort Benning said it was, then what is?

I'd like to keep my options open with respect to cockroaches and mosquitoes, but as far as the blue jays' nests are concerned and as a matter of policy let's just keep our goddam cotton-picking hands off other creatures' lives.

The Shock of April

April is the cruelest month in much the same way as a mirror is the cruelest of commentators. For a little while they compel us to contemplate what we have made of ourselves. Whether the ordeal lasts a month or a matter of minutes, it is depressing, and the depression has very little to do with T. S. Eliot's lilacs and desires and dreams.

Out on the road these first sunny days of spring 1971, you keep trying to resist confessing to yourself that the old place has gone downhill.

It has.

You remind yourself that now, when the face of the world seems so shocking, it is at a peculiar and defenseless disadvantage. Only yesterday the forgiving snow lay between the eye and the warts and grime and pock marks. Within a week or so the forsythia and azalea macrophylla and after them the bulb plants and the flowering trees and shrubs will perform their accustomed cosmetic wonders. Looking back from June we shall be astonished, as we are when looking back from noon at the cruelty of

128

the bathroom mirror at 6 A.M., that we were so much shaken.

Let's resolve this time to resist forgetfulness.

We should not want to forget that along country roads and streets which could be and so recently were pretty great stacks of green or yellow plastic bags are heaped now day after day. There's a reason, of course, and it makes sound economic sense. The suburbs' system of garbage collection by private contractors having broken down, quite a few of the towns have handed over collection and disposal to their public works departments. These don't have manpower enough to send men with a bag over their shoulder into the backyard of your house, into the garage or cellar indeed, as the private contractor did—and, someone told me, there are insurance problems.

So the householders drag their garbage cans out to the curb or package it in glistening sacks and set it along the front line of their lot where the daffodils used to be.

To an extent we've broken the contractors' comfortable monopoly and brought under control one component of the cost of living in a civilized society.

But let's not assure ourselves that the quality of life has not been affected by the substitution of rows of garbage bags for strips of grass or beds of flowers.

This is likely to annoy some decent and sensitive people, but there's a connection between the deterioration in the quality of life and the kind of government we choose to tolerate—not only to tolerate but to defend as if it were a religious principle. Here in Bergen County we have, thanks to some energetic young municipal lawyers who discovered in the 1890s that the incorporation of new boroughs was rewarding business for municipal lawyers—here we have 70 separate towns, all but a half dozen or so of them being small towns. The system has virtues, which great cities are struggling to duplicate by decentralizing government and setting up district school boards and police headquarters and citizen service agencies. But it has defects, and they show.

They show in the form of deep potholes in the roads and

streets. They show in the flaked patches of paint on asphalt that indicate where lane dividing lines once kept traffic safely divided and do so no more.

They show in the middens of junked cars that accumulate so uncontrollably along back roads. They show in the stream pollution to which so unaccountably often the municipality is the principal contributor. They show in all the ugly inadequacies that have developed because little government doesn't have money or muscle enough to do its job.

The defects in keeping government very small, very passive, and very, very local show on a weekend afternoon in April when the kids swarm into every town that has a main street lively enough to support a pizza parlor and a five and ten cent store. There they stand hour after hour, blacks and whites separate but equal, waiting for sundown, supper, and adjournment to the park or such substitutes for it as the church lawn or the library steps.

One accepts the kids. One had better. What's unacceptable is a variety of government that considers the young people's presence on high-tax shopping streets nothing but a police problem.

As the towns sprawled across the countryside, as the corridors of farm or woodland or bare unused acreage between them dwindled and vanished, why didn't someone—someone in government—ask his colleagues what was to become of the child's privilege to go out and wander and talk about nothing special and do nothing special, just be?

On the sidewalk there's dog dung, in the river at the edge of town float boxes and oil barrels and patches of soiled paper, on the street in front of the hospital lies squashed, oozing blood, the body of a cat or an opossum or a skunk, and there's not much that anyone can do about it. As the Governor said, holding his hand level above the top of his head, people have had it up to here with taxes. They're even asking what they get for the money.

April is the cruelest month. Let May, with its paints and eye shadow and its falsies, come soon. We've a lot to forget.

130

IN DEFENSE OF FREEDOM

In Defense of Freedom

Homeroom 102
Tenafly Middle School
Tenafly, N.J.
Dec. 18, 1969

Dear Mr. Caldwell:

My name is Eleanor Angeletti.

I am a sixth grader at the Tenafly Middle school. My teacher is teaching us about the mass media. What I would like to know is this: Do you think there should be complete freedom of speech on TV and in newspapers?

I would be very pleased if you would answer my letter.

Eleanor Angeletti

Dear Miss Angeletti:

Yes.

William A. Caldwell

P.S. I hope your teacher will agree that my answer, which was abrupt, necessarily has to be abrupt. I did not want to seem rude, but if the "yes" is anything except absolute, if it is hedged with qualifications and reservations and oh-buts and gee-whizzes, it stops meaning yes and it starts meaning sometimes, maybe, or under prudent safeguards and proper conditions.

Everybody knows what complete freedom is. Nobody can say for sure what incomplete freedom is.

So if we decide to settle for less than complete freedom, we need to establish guidelines within which we can exercise incomplete freedom without running the risk of going to jail or being blacklisted.

You know how the blacklist works. Germany under Hitler had

133

it along with beautifully controlled freedom. Soviet Russia has it now. Your class might want to study it sometime this year.

If we're to have guidelines somebody will have to write them, so that when people like you or me sit down to write a take of copy for print or a script for radio or television they can look in the official guide for media and see whether it is legal and hence safe to say what they want to say—what they think needs saying.

I don't know whom we can trust to write those guidelines.

Freedom of speech and of the press has been abused. Offhand, I can't think of any freedom granted to us by the Constitution that has not been abused.

I shall not defend the abusers. Except for one shameful subspecies of abuse, however, we have agreed on ways in which to deal with people who pervert or degrade their access to the public eye and ear and mind.

When they lie maliciously and their intent to do harm can be proved they can be taken to court and compelled to repair the injury. For libel or slander the abuser is liable to an action for damages. He is indeed liable to a jail sentence. For publishing obscenity as obscenity he can be fined and sent to prison. For inflicting sensational or frivolous twaddle on people the publisher or the station is liable to be deemed unnecessary. He can be sentenced to go out of business, and this is a form of control that should be invoked by people like us more often.

There is that subspecies of abuse which is immune from any control. It is represented by the newspaper that knows things are going awfully wrong in town, that the government has gone rotten, that humble people are getting a raw deal, and doesn't report it. It is represented by the station that programs soap and rock when it knows damned well the part of town on the other side of the tracks is about to burn.

I'm glad there's no guidebook that forbids me to say damn.

As long as Spiro Agnew is lurching around threatening license revocation for television stations that neglect to give our leader a big hand I don't think we can trust the White House to write the guidebook. I can't trust a Congress whose sense of smell has so badly deteriorated that it can't detect the presence of a rotten member in the next seat. I can't trust the courts. If they had their way they would obliterate the right of a defendant to pre-trial publicity—and perhaps your class will find time to consider whether public notice of the circumstances surrounding an arrest are not the common man's last best defense against police brutality.

I believe, I have to believe, that a free people's access to the truth and their use of it to form the opinions on which they base their judgments in the ballot box are the only guarantee of freedom.

"Were it left to me to decide whether we should have a government without newspapers, or newspapers without a government, I should not hesitate a moment to prefer the latter."

Thomas Jefferson said it. Look it up: it's in his *Writings,* Volume VI, Page 55.

Not abruptly, the answer to your question is yes. Thank you for asking.

Bringing to Bay the Last Obscenity

It took thirty years for the courts to decide they could not delegate literary criticism to Puritans. It has taken them ten years to decide that evaluating the relative purity of a book is no proper job for courts.

Give them ten more years. They're headed toward relaxing with a sigh of relief and holding once for all that the test for obscenity should be the test they apply to any other crime or tort—what it does, not what somebody says about it.

In its latest tussle with an issue which in this form simply doesn't come into the public domain the Supreme Court annihilated State court convictions of a bookstore clerk who sold a work of doubtful merit to a policeman and of a dealer who peddled girlie mags, if I have the shop talk right.

The Justices handed in four opinions but didn't sign them. In effect, the opinions held that the defendants didn't corrupt youth, invade anybody's privacy, or hawk the junk with a discernible leer. If you had to write a definition of obscenity based on these mutterings or face the firing squad in the morning your name would be mud.

So wise and highly prepared men whose very profession involves the logical use of definitions are backing farther and farther away from the act of reducing to writing any statement whatever about norms of morality and taste.

This is bad?

By the Venus de Milo, by Titian and Rembrandt and the hairier books of the Old Testament, what's bad about it?

We have come a long way since 1927, when a bookseller in Boston was tried and convicted in the State courts on a charge of selling Theodore Dreiser's bedrock classic *An American Tragedy*. The State held that certain passages of the novel were obscene in that they might—not did: might—corrupt the morals of the young. The defense tried to argue that the author's intent should be considered. *An American Tragedy* is not a flattering report on small-town society, but it is an intensely moral work. The defense reasoning did influence the courts in later years. But no federal question was deemed to be involved. The Supreme Court never had a crack at the case.

The Boston decision, absurd as it was, stood until in 1957 the Supreme Court got its hands on a case in which it could hold flatly that a book cannot be held obscene by reason of what it might do to a young reader. To sustain this test, it held, would result in reducing all literature and all readers to the level of fun with Dick and Jane.

It didn't stop there. Later that year it commissioned Justice Brennan to write the threefold test that still stands: whether the book as a whole appeals to a prurient—dirty—interest in the reader; whether it has this effect on a normal grown-up reader, rather than the child or the village idiot; whether it offends the standards of an entire modern community.

Does this mean anything goes? The Court has been troubled, and has tried to answer the question. By and large, the Court has come over to the Black-Douglas theory that a book may be held obscene if it can be proved to cause overt acts but not if it does no more than cause thinking to go on. The social value of a work can count for or against it. The exploitation of the weak-minded is punishable: if the advertising says the book is gummy, the publisher is criminally responsible.

Pandering for profit is out. Dirt for dirt's sake is out. And invasion of anybody's privacy for purposes of making a fast buck, that's out.

But the Court appears to be moving toward the conclusion that what happens inside the human skull is none of its business. The test taking shape is: What does this stuff make people do, and can the State prove they did it because of something they read in print or saw in the form of picture or sculpture or film?

It's a clear and feasible test. Someday it should be applied to the papers and utterances of statesmen, the greatest living masters of the difficult art of pornography. The style is often wretched. But they get results, such as war, the uttermost limit of obscenity.

Surrounded by Soul-Savers

Thanks to the American Civil Liberties Union, we shall most of us spend the next month or so impersonating the United States tourist fallen among foreign waiters—trying to make ourselves understood by saying it again very slowly, very loudly, and very angrily.

It'll be quite a few centuries until the discovery is made that the other guy misunderstands not because he's wicked or dumb but because he speaks another language.

The A.C.L.U. has attacked the National Organization for Decent Literature on the ground that it censors what the American people may read and that its blacklists, boycotts, and certificates of compliance—not at all uncommon in this community, of course—seriously violate the principle of freedom.

The N.O.D.L. was organized as a group within the church by the Roman Catholic bishops of the United States in 1938. As set forth by the episcopal committee, the purpose:

> To organize and set in motion the moral forces of the entire country . . . against the lascivious type of literature which threatens moral, social, and national life.

It has emphasized its intention to protect youth and also, in addition to its negative efforts, positively to encourage the publication and distribution of good literature and develop worthwhile reading habits. "To evaluate the literature of our day in terms of its suitability for youth," the Union said, "the N.O.D.L., at last report, uses a committee of mothers of the Roman Catholic faith in the Chicago area." The A.C.L.U.'s fundamental objection is that the judgment of a particular group is being imposed on the freedom of choice of the whole community.

There are several ways of phrasing the case on both sides of this argument. One such way is the way of a distinguished Roman Catholic, Father John Courtney Murray, S.J.:

> In a pluralistic society no minority group has the right to impose its own religious or moral views on other groups through the methods of force, coercion, or violence. . . . Society has an interest in the artist's freedom of expression which is not necessarily shared by the family. If adult standards of literature would be dangerous for children, a child's standard of literature is rather appalling to an adult.

But it must be suggested as respectfully and genially as possible that this is one more area in which understanding and adjustment—tolerance if you please—are impossible.

People on the civil-liberties side hold to their first principle:

> A novel which may be thought by a committee of Catholic mothers to be unsuitable for a Roman Catholic adolescent is thus made unavailable to a non-Catholic. It is plainly necessary to challenge the N.O.D.L. as keeper, by self-election, of the conscience of the whole country.

So their first principle is that thou shalt not arrogate to thyself the power to prescribe what thy fellow man chooses to read —chooses, in the long run, to know.

And people on the N.O.D.L. side adhere to their own principle:

Filth is filth, corruption is corruption, and in a complex and interdependent society we all of us have a responsibility to prevent the spread of corruption.

We keep trying to drive out of our mind the image of the man they're talking about—or the child. There he stands in the tobacco shop or drugstore, 35 cents in hand, trying to decide whether to shoot the wad on Irwin Edman's *Philosopher's Holiday* because it has a naked Greek goddess on the cover. Nobody's access to books in hard covers has been challenged, remember, at least in this field of proscription—the field of big-money comics, magazines, and paper-back books. As between the reader's right to shoot the 35 and the publisher's right to squeeze it out of him by offering him ecstasy that Edman won't deliver we're inclined to concede that the N.O.D.L. is at least a benign friend of the consumer. But the A.C.L.U. is—in our opinion—right; censorship is an instrument hostile to freedom, susceptible of being hideously abused, and basically subversive of man's trying to get ahead with his perfectibility. To us this makes sense. It is temperate and reasonable to make a distinction, as the A.C.L.U. does, between the right of an organization through its management to express its opinion and the organization's behaving in such a way as to deny a freedom to persons who don't agree with it. But we have no confidence whatever that people who conceive themselves as crusading for purity will consent they subvert freedom when they boycott the likes of Ernest Hemingway and William Faulkner, and we keep trying to live with the fact that no man is so implacable as the one who proposes to save our soul.

It's Always a Shock To Wake Up

The subject tonight is anticipatory self-restraint.

It shouldn't be hard to talk about, but it is. It shouldn't be hard to define, but the only way to define it is to describe how it works.

Your reporter wandered down the Parkway to Upsala College and the annual conference of the New Jersey Scholastic Press Association, to complain to the faculty advisers of school newspapers that the papers don't cover the news in the schools. They present to their student-body subscribers substitutes for news. For instance . . .

The news, the gritty reality of the student body's physical existence, is the school-construction bond issue. As this goes, so will go kids' lives. School newspapers don't talk about the house we live in most of our waking hours. They talk about football teams and the senior play.

The news is that running for the school board is a gaggle of anti-intellectuals whose program is the dismantling of the school system.

The five-column headline in the Upper Mildew Regional High School Weekly Fungus:

"All Out For The Beat-Teaneck Rally Tonight!"

The faculty resigns in a body because the village troglodytes kill the salary schedule, and in the school newspaper the kids giggle over who's dating the hatcheck girl in the boys' gym; the superintendent of schools is fired because he suspended four first-string football players for chronic drunkenness, and as far as the school newspaper is concerned the news is that unless all members of the French Club report for tea at 3:30 o'clock sharp Wednesday the chairman of languages, Miss Urf, will require that they turn in their umlauts.

This is what your reporter was bellyaching about, and he took the liberty of suggesting that so consistent a pattern of behavior cannot be due to accident but must rather be due to systematically teaching young people that there are certain things they had better not think about.

And this, we hold, is anti-intellectual, is the diametric opposite of educational. If at the age of sixteen a child has learned there are certain aspects of his society and culture that he dares not even know about, what could Communism do to make him a robot that capitalism has not already done—in his willing and cheerful conformity, how is he less dead and useless than the ants being produced by Red China? To teach incuriosity, to teach a child that he may be intelligent and alert and challenging with respect to everything except that which is relevant to his existence—this, we were saying to the faculty advisers, waving our arms . . .

"You badly overestimate public-school students," later said a swarthy teacher from a South Jersey school. "They want gossip —who's going with whom, who's the boy in the blue Buick that calls for Jane S. Give 'em what they want."

No, we said; students are serious people. They are worthy of our best.

"Our best cheesecake," said a red-haired teacher from down the shore. "Give 'em legs, and they buy the paper. Give 'em John Ciardi on the race for inner space, and they use the money to buy a soda. Don't talk idealistic nonsense to me. I know."

"Our principal reads all our copy," said two girls from North

Jersey. "Academic freedom, intellectual freedom, or not, he edits the copy. He doesn't stand for election news. So we don't try it on him."

We started to say that was what we were trying to talk about —anticipatory self-restraint, the self-censorship that is the most insidious kind of all. The Lord knows how much of it we all suffer from, but we must try to fight it. We must try to face and trace reality as it is.

"In my school," said a fine crag-faced teacher, a woman, from a big-town system, "we have quite a few Negroes. There are incidents. Do you think I'd let my staff print the incidents?"

Incidents like what? Incidents like, maybe, out comes a switchblade knife during a recess discussion of some problem in philosophy, and:

"Our children need security," she said. "They need to know they are loved and understood. Even if the police made a record of the incident, do you think I'd let my staff print it? No, sir; no! Their security comes first."

We thought that was splendid, and not until later, on the way home, did it occur to us to wonder what comes second. Reality? Truth? The fact, of record, that knives were indeed drawn? To turn, in anticipatory self-restraint, away from this—that is security?

Too Chummy a Way To Run the Law

Off in the northwest corner of the County a little before Christmas the johns picked up an odious twirp, charged him with a series of meannesses as long as the Marquis de Sade's bull whip, and announced with a regretful sigh that they wished they could give the reporters his name. The twirp is aged less than eighteen years. He is a juvenile.

The incident isn't spectacular—not so spectacular as things are when the police scoop up a teen-age gang, chuck its five eighteen-year-old members into the common 'gow and onto the front page, and remand its ice-cold brain and boss to the children's home and sweet anonymity because he's only seventeen.

But the twirp will serve to bring up an almost unmentionable lameness in New Jersey law enforcement and journalism.

In other things we do we go by due process. So and so is dictated by the law. The courts have held such and such. We constrain ourselves to obey the law, as we make ourselves do as the courts have directed, because by the body of common consent they represent the wisdom of society.

The names of juvenile delinquents are withheld from the media of communication—oh, hell: newspapers, the radio, television, magazines. Why? Because some influential people think publication of the identiy of young persons in trouble would inflict irreparable damage on the young persons.

They may be right. A substantial majority of policemen and Prosecutors think the guarantee of anonymity is wrong.

But the Supreme Court committee on juvenile delinquency and the conference of juvenile-court judges, whose members are by no means unsophisticated or weak-minded, insist that the uniform rule of anonymity is an essential piece of the rehabilitation job.

That gets to the point. The key word is "rule."

Now:

1. In no law is it set forth that names of delinquents shall not be published.

2. In no decision of the courts or regulation of administrative agency has that right ever been created or even alleged.

3. The so-called rule exists simply by reason of a benign and woolly-minded conspiracy among the courts, the enforcement agencies, and the media—and it may be necessary to specify that all "woolly-minded" means is that thus far the minds involved have been unable to put the rule and its rationale on paper in

such a way as would not affront due process and the Constitution.

Your reporter thinks the practice should be abolished, not so as to enable newspapers' pillorying innocents and dimwits—the newspapermen would remain as woolly-minded as ever—but precisely for the protection of the juveniles.

As matters stand, they are a criminal class by themselves when they get or seem to get into trouble. They aren't really arrested; they aren't really confronted with a charge; in entirely too vague a way, they pass from freedom into the hands of the police, and what happens then is not always calculated to rehabilitate them or do them justice.

"The time a defendant needs counsel most," wrote the court in Ex Parte Sullivan, a 1952 federal case reported in 107 F. Supp. 517, "is immediately after arrest and until trial. Two friendless, inexperienced boys without a criminal record are tricked by . . . police into making incriminating admissions." In *Our Lawless Police* Ernest Hopkins quotes an American Bar Association committee:

> The notorious fact is that the police do not apply their war theory to the classes of criminals. . . . It is visited on the youthful imitation gangsters, . . . mere indigents and vagrants and morons, . . . illiterates.

The illiteracy often consists of the juveniles' not knowing their right, spelled out by Junius Allison in the December *Journal of the American Judicature Society*, to have counsel not only at trial but at each and every step in a criminal proceeding. Another commentator, David Watkins, has whittled it to a point:

> The door is open to the unscrupulous law-enforcement official and others to become petty local tyrants shaking down the ignorant and the timid-soul members of the community by threat. . . .

If anonymity belongs in due process, it should be put there. If it doesn't, it should be done away with. The right to make a name public or not is too large a discretion to give the cop who makes the pinches.

Look Who's Running the Arena Box Office!

They were standing about eight feet apart in front of the shelves of paperbacks. One was a girl, maybe fifteen. One was a hussy, maybe fifty. They were inching very slowly sidewise, keeping the head tilted to the right, the way a hen tilts its head when it's trying to focus the good eye on a bug in the dust. One by one they were reading to themselves the titles, and their lips formed the words, so slowly you could read the lips: *The Making of the Modern Mind, A Preface to Morals, What Man May Be.*

You guessed they were shopping in the wrong department.

So did they.

The hussy emitted a typhoon of a sigh, half whiskey and half blowtorch. The girl drew a little farther away from her. The girl's jacket had folded against a tray of greeting cards on the counter behind her. When she moved the tray was tugged off the counter. It fell with a clatter, spilling its contents across the floor. She left the mess where it lay.

"I guess it isn't here," the hussy said, letting go another suspiration from the distillery.

"You guess what isn't here?" the girl said.

"I been trying to buy *Tropic of Cancer* for my B.F.," the hussy said.

"I'm trying to buy it for myself," the girl said.

"It's illegal in Jersey."

"The hell it's illegal," the girl said. "It's just hard to get."

"It sure is," said the hussy. She was looking hard at the girl. "It sure is hard to get." They both looked at your reporter, who is terrified by this skywriting form of double entendre, and laughed. They laughed in such a way that it sounded as if they were snarling, which is a feat that must require ingenuity and long practice. Then they went back to digging for dung in the philosophy department.

One cannot be utterly sure of anything, and yet we would be very much surprised if those two pigs wanted *Tropic of Cancer* in order to study the motivations of its author, as a clue to the death-wish component in sex, or as a guide to the judicious use of leisure time. They wanted it, in one man's opinion, because it's dirty. If they get it this will be because some one sells it to them as dirt. In one man's opinion there are no ifs, and, or buts about that.

And in one man's opinion we dues-paying members of the Society for the Preservation of the First Amendment will have to gird up our loins one of these days and see whether we can't devise some substitute for the ignominious position we've wriggled ourselves into.

We're defending the freedom of the press, freedom to write, freedom to read, freedom.

Our sword is the Constitution of the United States and the Constitution of New Jersey. Our buckler is Milton's *Areopagitica* and United States District Judge John M. Woolsey's decision in U.S. v. *Ulysses* of Dec. 6, 1933. We're putting in a hell of a fight. And in the little zone of safety that we've made in the name of liberty the smut peddlers have dragged up their huckster cart and are hawking filth to morons.

There's no question about it, or there won't be very much longer.

The next essay in freedom of expression that'll hit the market will be pornography on phonograph records—*Music to Strip By* (with a free G-string as bonus), *A Trip around the World Is Not a Cruise, If I Embarrass You, Tell Your Friends*. The Cowles magazines' December 11 "Insider's Newsletter" says the stuff is about to flood the market. It's the hot item in Miami supermarkets. The Post Office Department is ready to confess that it's licked—it did refuse mailing privileges to a small operator on the West Coast, but a district court slapped an injunction on it, and

146

the Justice Department won't prosecute. What's to prosecute? A sample record, low on overhead production costs but for the last year and a half big on profits, is titled *Erotica,* and on the sound track is nothing but creaking bedsprings, heavy breathing, and a bongo-drum beat in the background. What does the prosecution allege, and how does it (a) set out to prove it without (b) making a jackass of itself?

Up to now we friends of the First Amendment have clinched our case by asking how the state can set up restrictions on bilge without setting up an apparatus that can be used against art, truth, beauty, the proper provinces of freedom. We've asked the question. One of these days we shall have to do better than that. We shall have to take part in the search for the answer.

This Magic Doesn't Seem To Work

Your reporter was upbraided lately by a Fort Lee patriot whose patriotism takes the odd but popular form of supposing Communism will bury us.

We had been muttering that we don't think there are Communists in the Fair Lawn High School student body. This is what offended our man in Fort Lee. He said we are walking hand in hand with the Communists. It was quite a spirited conversation. . . .

Time out.

Will some one explain this cross-eyed, upside-down, inside-out form of loyalty we're constantly exhorted to swear? The schools have been taken over by the Communists. The Communists have seized the churches. The Government itself is infiltrated by the Communists. So are the arts and sciences. Labor is Red. Agriculture has gone all the way into Marxism. As for the armed forces, one question: Who promoted Peress? The bill of particulars is brought by people who characterize themselves as patriotic. To what are they loyal, the real estate? They fear or despise every institution and nine of every ten persons in their environment, and to a man they consider themselves a majority.

Well, the upshot was that your reporter asked the subscriber to settle himself to his desk and at his leisure write a definition of this Communism the subscriber was talking about. We shall later reiterate our appeal to the adult-education schools for courses of study, beginning with the fall term, of Communism as it is postulated in theory and as it works in reality. We cannot possibly defeat the enemy unless we know what it is.

In due time, from our man in Fort Lee:

Dear Mr. Caldwell: Whether or not I know the proper and correct definition of Communism is not too important. Let's take the word "columnist," and I am sure that from 30 people you would get 28½ different definitions, or from any word of more than 4 syl.

There would be divergence of opinion as to the Fair Lawn witch hunt. Your face sure would be red if subsequent events proved that Communists were operating in the high school. But it is not really important that you be right or wrong on this issue.

Here are interpolated sundry compliments to Franklin D. Roosevelt and Churchill. They could be wrong, and often were.

The whole point of this is that great men can come out with some real lulus and get away with it, the public has a short memory. . . .

Now, here is my idea of COMMUNISM.

C. Cowardly bullies who let 4 million nonconforming farmers starve to death in the early days of the revolution.

O. Outside the realm of all that is good, decent, and worth while.

M. Malicious lies spread all over the face of the earth.

M. Making trouble for America, the ally that gave them billions of dollars' worth of foreign aid in World War II.

U. Unfit to mingle with decent society in the U.N., and should be expelled.

N. Nothing is too low for them to descend to in extending their slavery to other nations.

I. I am running out of ideas, Bill.

S. Self-perpetuating dictatorship which machineguns all opposition.

148

M. Marx's creed says the world cannot exist half Communist and half capitalist.

The showdown must come. God help us, Bill, if we lose. There is no place in their scheme of things for either you or me.

There is nothing the matter with this man's heart. Where he's deficient is with respect to his information. Such incantations as his are really worse than useless. The Communists are sending across the earth trained troublemakers to preach a highly complicated gospel, the gospel spelled out in Marx's *Capital*. It is a gospel that appeals to the impoverished, the dispossessed, the alienated, all the angry people in the world. It gives them something to hate: us and our way of life. It supplies them a heaven, and in its theology man becomes the god, creator and master of his environment, and we had better not dare try to sneer it away.

We are dealing with people peddling an article bearing the stenciled label "Salvation," people who mean to save the world by altering its character radically, by violence. We can't vanquish them by reciting the alphabet.

Note Dropped from Weapon-Factory Window

It may be that the time is at hand for the President to appoint a national commission on the freedom of the press.

Its assignment would be to find fact and write recommendations. It wouldn't legislate; it couldn't. Questions of fact:

1. Do we have a free press?
2. How do we make use of such freedom as the communication mediums now enjoy?
3. Is absolute freedom compatible with the preservation of the national security and the realpolitik of the cold war?

149

4. What [here would come the page of recommendations]—what should be the relationship between the Government and the press, which term for these purposes encompasses the newspaper, television, radio, magazines, books, billboards, latrine walls, sky writing, the works?

Britain is proud of its press freedom too. In both countries the tradition traces back to the propositions of old Milton's *Areopagitica*. They do things differently in Britain. When Her Majesty's Government want the papers to let a hot ground ball roll out to the left-field fence and cool off they issue a D notice. It suggests to editors that the Government would be gratified by discreet treatment of certain evidences that, say, troops are being shipped to the Suez area. The press lays off. So:

5. If the impact of the news involves the national safety, doesn't it involve a national responsibility? Should the Government shrink from taking charge?

My own prejudices on the point are too elderly now to change their ways. The free flow of information is necessary to the democratic decision-making process (this is a cruel abridgment of my prejudices), and this principle is not disparaged by the occasional abuses of it by dimwits and knaves.

But the question is brought to life by the protest of a Washington friend that I've taken part in wronging Arthur Sylvester, the Assistant Secretary of Defense for Public Affairs, in attributing to him the statement:

"In the kind of world we live in, the generation of news by the Government becomes one weapon in a strained situation."

My Washington friend happens to be Arthur Sylvester. He simply denies he ever uttered the line that is getting him toasted at Sigma Delta Chi meetings from coast to coast—if toasting is what's done with boiling oil.

"Don't believe all you're told, Bill, any more than you believe all you read," Mr. Sylvester adds. "The fact is that in the last twenty-three months the Pentagon has put out more clear, solid, undiluted news, judged on any basis you wish, than it has in any comparable twenty-three months."

He will say again, as he did November 2, there has been no distortion, no deception, and no manipulation of the news cleared by the Defense Department during the Cuban crisis. Simultaneously he will stand by what he said then:

I am sensitive to the people's right to factual information about their Government. But as a public official I am also aware that in a time of extreme national peril there are other considerations in addition to the news business. . . . We have . . . protected national security and the lives of the military personnel directly involved in the current crisis. This is our primary concern in releasing the news.

It may be a small point. Judge for yourself. The line about generation of news by the Government was originally attributed to Mr. Sylvester by the *Washington Evening Star*. He insists that the phrase he actually used was "news generated by the actions of the Government," and so it was taken down by an Associated Press interviewer. The *Star* itself interpolated this passage in a story reporting Mr. Sylvester's disclaimer:

It is clear that Mr. Sylvester was referring to Government reports of the actions during the blockade and not of the falsification or manipulation of news.

It is a small point. But an official who has been through an experience as traumatic as this with respect to a small point cannot be blamed too sonorously for wondering how the large points are apt to turn out in next day's papers.

There'll never be final answers. There'll never be absolutes in any kind of freedom, otherwise I'd tell you now how many hydrogen bombs we have and where they are and how many men we have doing what kind of fighting in Vietnam. We may never get an answer. But it would do no harm to raise a question.

The Blacklisters that Got Away

A little before midnight June 28 a jury in the Supreme Court of New York came in with its historic verdict on the crime that had been done to John Henry Faulk. Justice was done.

It awarded this amiable and intelligent—and no longer young

—radio-television commentator and disc jockey $3.5 million damages for libel, to be collected from Aware Inc., Vincent W. Hartnett, and the estate of the late Laurence E. Johnson.

They had undertaken to destroy Mr. Faulk by calling him a Communist. To the extent of his consignment to a special kind of hell for six tortured years they had succeeded.

Now, thanks to his own genially stubborn refusal to surrender his integrity to any stickup man and to his attorney Louis Nizer's simple genius for relevancy, Mr. Faulk had caught up. The respondent Johnson, the Syracuse supermarket tyrannosaurus who had enforced Hartnett's and Aware's verdicts on actors' employability by threatening advertisers with boycott, was dead in hiding in his Bronx motel. Hartnett will pay. Paul R. Milton, his colleague in Aware's blacklist for profit, will pay.

Justice had been done. There was dancing in the streets.

Justice?

Not by ten hundred vindications, not by ten thousand conspirators, not by a hundred million verdicts!

The job Aware Inc. and its merry men did was a pretty loathsome job, but Hartnett and Johnson and Milton couldn't and didn't do it alone, and to see any animal however fragrant made to serve as scapegoat just sticks in a man's craw.

Mr. Faulk qualified himself for ruin by daring to run for the presidency of the American Federation of Television and Radio Artists as the candidate of a dogged middle-of-the-road element which was fed up with Aware's bullying and proposed to fight. That was in 1955. Since the early 1950s Aware and its nasty little people had been making a handsome living selling blacklists to agencies and advertisers and selling to actors clearances—removal from the blacklist. Faulk had to be wrecked.

He was.

But it cannot be said he was destroyed by the arrantly phony bulletin Aware cooked up inventing a Communist-front record for Mr. Faulk.

He was destroyed by the actual and potential employers to

152

whom this document was sent—radio and television houses, newspapers, advertising associations and agencies, motion-picture studios, and sponsoring corporations, plus patriotic organizations, columnists, magazines, actors' unions, and law-enforcement officers.

Wherever he went looking for a job the bulletin went too—out across the country. And where the bulletin went the doors creaked shut. Nobody wanted to hear him tell the truth. The truth, the operational fact of the matter, was that in the United States of America it did not matter if a man was innocent or guilty. The only truth the industry knew was that to be accused was to be damned—and that the justice-loving people of the country stood ready to enforce this law with all the power of their orders for beer and soap and process cheese.

Here and there advertising executives, broadcasting management, even whole communities would balk. The flesh-eating Right tried to organize a boycott of Chet Huntley when as a commentator in Los Angeles he said something generous of Unesco. His sponsor, a coffee company, stayed with him, and Los Angeles liberals began to swig that brand of coffee in quantities above and beyond the call of habit. A.B.C. was instructed to fire Elmer Davis. It refused. John Kelley, S.M., in the University of Dayton *Alumnus* has told how in 1961 a meeting of volunteer firemen in Dayton—business, journalism, religion, and education—evolved a plan without a name (that's the name it uses) to make character assassination under the flag of Communist-fighting impossible in one town.

There have been exceptions. But the long sorry history of the Faulk case is the history of great interests, great communication media, and great communities that didn't have wits or guts or energy enough to rebel against a shadow government. If you want the names of the tyrants' collaborators in a shameful—and thoroughly ominous—abdication of responsibility, get John Cogley's *Report on Blacklisting II: Radio and Television* (Fund for the Republic Inc., 1956).

It is the history of a people that sat bemused in its colosseum and watched, in the name of entertainment, human beings thrown to the animals.

Justice will never catch up. You have nothing to worry about.

A Difference of Opinion

We should be grateful, I suppose, for anything that sets us in the other fellow's shoes, lets us feel the way he feels—in a word, teaches us sympathy.

And so newspapermen should, I suppose, be grateful to a couple of politicians named Robert J. Manning and Carl T. Rowan.

As wanton boys with flies, so play newspapermen with politicians. We damn them if they do. We damn them if they don't. The same man—cf. Johnson or Eisenhower or for that matter Herbert Hoover—can find himself denounced in the public prints because he is too liberal, too conservative, lazy, energetic, weak, power-drunk, insensitive to people's needs, a veritable sycophant to the cranks and whims of the rabble.

Now I know how it feels.

Mr. Manning is the Assistant Secretary of State in charge of news manag—that is to say, public information. As a speaker at a joint symposium of the Massachusetts press and bar Mr. Manning denounced the newspapers for their aggressiveness: a mindless devotion to exposure for exposure's sake which serves mainly to expose this country's policies and intentions to its potential enemies.

Mr. Rowan is the director of the United States Information Service. The trouble with the press in the United States, he told an American Civil Liberties Union audience in Washington, is that it is nowhere near aggressive enough.

154

Both are experts. Both are onetime newspapermen. One says we're recklessly pugnacious and invasive. One says we're recklessly timid. The answer is that this is how it feels. The question is whether both of them may not be right.

A case at hand is the war in Vietnam. The reporting on it has been energetic enough, I suppose: it persuaded us that if it were not for the corruption and laziness of the Saigon Government headed by Ngo Dinh Diem the South Vietnamese people would wipe out the Viet Cong guerrillas in twelve seconds flat. It has not been explained why the substitution of the win policy for the no-win policy hasn't produced victory. But the reporting has been vigorous and colorful.

Yet it seems to me the most significant of the war stories is going unexamined and unreported. This would be the story of the professional military's pressure on the Pentagon's civilian management to commit this country to direct involvement in the fighting. The influence of that military-industrial complex against which General Eisenhower warned us has become so pervasive that, far from resenting it, we don't even notice it.

It should not be necessary to labor the point. Let it be said that too much space has been squandered on Mr. Johnson's forays into impoverished Appalachia and too little attention has been paid to our own countryside's development of the preconditions which produce an Appalachia, in particular its indifference to education.

We take notice when gangs of young Negroes in Harlem declare war against society, and couldn't care less when policemen and social workers warn us that young people who have been alienated—doubly or triply alienated by race, by economic status, by social rejection—cannot very well be expected to behave otherwise than as aliens. We walk blithely past festering slums until one of them takes fire and a dozen poor blanks are incinerated. Then it's Page 1.

I suppose something of this sort is what Carl Rowan had in mind when he said:

But where the press has been timid, where editors themselves have been motivated by animal gland rather than by human intellect, we have seen the erosion—sometimes tragic—of human freedom.

Perhaps the area of agreement would be about here:

We tend to be raucous about the wrong things. When we report a Bobby Baker scandal, a teen-age rumble, a traffic massacre, a tenement fire—or any of the overt acts that make it to the front page—we report a failure; we report a failure of the press's itself. But preventive medicine is a new and very difficult science.

Open Wide and Say Cesspool

The scrupulous fighter for the cleanliness of other people's minds will never refer to the magazines he's hounding as being obscene.

The adverb is "never." The punctuation is an exclamation point (!). The command is issued in Bulletin No. 1 of *Common Cause*, house organ of the United Community Decent Literature Committees, 387 Passaic Avenue, Nutley, N.J. 07110.

Never call a magazine obscene, and what is this access of lenity—a qualm of doubt whether we are competent or entitled to make judgments for other people, a twinge of humility, a gentle concession that what seems obscene to us may be another man's Song of Songs Which Is Solomon's or yet a third man's irreducible and necessitous scientific literature?

The problem is more sophisticated than that. Under the heading "Avoid Legal Pitfalls" the bulletin counsels the faithful:

Never refer to magazines or other publications as "obscene"! In almost every State the word "obscene" means "criminally violates the State laws on obscenity." To accuse another of a crime is itself libel. You can be sued for damages because of the careless use of this word. So many other words, e.g. filthy, vile, smutty, cesspool, raw, bawdy, lurid, perverted, revolting, etc., are safe and more expressive.

So much for one pitfall. There are others, usually based on thoughtful consideration of the buck:

1. When you organize a crusade in town, incorporate the committee. "This . . . will remove your members from personal liability for actions by others of the committee."

2. Don't badger or harass dealers, and never organize a boycott of a defiant dealer. "Conviction can be followed by an award of triple damages to the complaining store owner."

3. And join the United Community Decent Literature Committees. And (Pages 2 and 4) send money.

So maggoty with this accursed relativism is my own mind that I'm not sure anymore what is obscene and isn't. But I can admire the purity of people like the ones described in a Page 1 story about the Penns Grove crisis. The decent-literature committee in Penns Grove arranged to confer a decency certificate on stores stripping their shelves of books on the committee's index, the distributor sued for an injunction and $100,000, and a town meeting had been convened. Go on with the story:

So Lewis Wright [chairman of the citizens' group] stood before the assembled onlookers that night of January 28. He was flanked on both sides by wooden display racks to which were affixed some 100 magazines just purchased from local stores for 25 cents to 35 cents apiece. Their opened pages revealed a parade of nudity, homosexuality, and perversion such as possibly never before accumulated for public inspection except on the display racks of countless soda shops and confectionery stores frequented by juveniles.

I cannot be sure what to make of this remarkable passage. Possibly Havelock Ellis would have plumbed its limpid depths. "Without an element of the obscene," he said in "Impressions and Comments," "there can be no true and deep esthetic or moral conception of life."

Send money.

157

Here is why decent citizens must unite (Page 3, Column 3):

It's common knowledge that full-length female nudes with the narrowest covering of solely the organs of reproduction glare defiantly from the pages of many of these magazines. Some nudist monthlies feature complete sections devoted to pictures of both sexes whose genital organs are fully visible, uncovered and unretouched. . . .

And over here on Page 4 is Dr. Nicholas G. Frignito:

Pornography is a scheme of avaricious and depraved psychopathic persons to enrich themselves.

"We spend hundreds of dollars to educate our children," says *Common Cause.* "A few dollars toward the fight against this cesspool epidemic is only Common Sense protection of these investments."

It never said "obscenity." It never even said "economics."

The Blind Panic of the Censor

Against the effort of a small lay committee in Englewood to arrogate to itself the right to license booksellers can be made an argument which has always resonated orchestrally but which I suspect is itself as naive and fusty as is amateur censorship itself.

The stock-model case against stock-model book suppression depends on assumptions which cannot be carried to the point of demonstration.

They are:

1. The people initiating the censorship effort are small-minded, mean, and illiterate.

2. Their purpose is to invade my—your—freedom to read.

There is a better case against censorship—a better and a bitter case. I think it can be taken to a demonstration. It would argue that book censorship, no matter how honest and benevolent, is doomed in its nature to treat not a cause but a symptom. By the time James Baldwin writes a book about a sickness of society, the society is sick, and to destroy the book is like—precisely like —undertaking to control an epidemic of spinal meningitis by burning the doctors' charts. By the time Henry Miller writes a book pandering to depraved appetites—and for the argument's flow let us allege that this is what Henry Miller does—the appetites have been long since corrupted and not by Henry Miller.

Peculiarly in the Englewood of Texas, the Fourth Ward ghetto, the Englewood of Man's indomitable inhumanity to Man, there is something dirty. It isn't books.

The traditional case against lay censorship is the one made by John de J. Pemberton, executive director of the American Civil Liberties Union, when a newsletter of the Maryland Junior Chamber of Commerce reported a national plan to issue a seal of approval to drugstores which would promise not to expose young people to pornography. The national Jaycees disavowed any such plan. Mr. Pemberton congratulated them. He seized the opportunity to emphasize the A.C.L.U.'s distinction between the right of an organization to say what it thinks about any publication and an attempt on its part to function as a censor to the community.

Such coercion, he went on, brawnily whaling away at the dead horse—such coercion would deter patrons from doing business in a store lacking a seal of approval and would force stores into accepting the Jaycees as a review board screening the stores' stock of books and magazines. He needn't have stopped there. Once the censor is ceded the power to bless the inventory, what's to stop him from sanctioning or forbidding the sale of cigars he doesn't like, fruits, frozen broccoli, girdles and wigs and cabbages? The answer is that there are indeed towns in the land of the free where the censor has proscribed the sale of Polish hams and woven baskets from Yugoslavia.

That he means well is precisely the point.

Too many of us tend to confuse symbol with reality. The government itself runs up its "Under God" pennant on the town flagpole, and, having examined the evidences, I gather it is supposed that if people will look up at the pennant they will not see that at ground level the town is shabby, disorderly, for abundant reason ashamed of itself. We stuff a gag in the yammering mouth of James Baldwin, and thus we need not know that the sickening truth about which he writes is the truth about our town.

An instinct for self-preservation asserts itself blindly and unintelligently [writes Gerald Sykes in *The Hidden Remnant*]; the members of the mass "regress," as we now say, and, if examined closely, they give every evidence of panic. They demand faith, secular or religious, in a way that never won it. They demand protection against their enemies. . . .

Such people, says Sykes, are entitled to the understanding which their panic prevents them from giving others. They do not often get it. They are an important and a moving social problem. It will no longer suffice to dismiss with archaic maledictions them and the panic which seizes them when they see what we all have done to art and mankind.

OF TWIGS AND BENDERS

Of Twigs and Benders

If I have read once I've read a hundred times that the real problem is not juvenile delinquency but parental delinquency—indeed, in the course of my career in the guesswork business I do believe I've written it a hundred times.

And I'll bet it's true, at that.

But what does it mean? What is parental irresponsibility? Rather, how should the responsible parent come to understand and discharge his responsibility? I am puzzled by reproachful lectures on what the parent should be, to wit, a good parent. I need to be told what it is that the good parent does.

And so I am grateful to Paul Harvey, writing in the February issue of *Future*, for specific counsel—do this, don't do that. Mr. Harvey points out that of all arrests made in the United States last year 10 per cent entangled persons aged eighteen or less and that the incidence of juvenile crime is increasing.

He means parental delinquency. But he does not stop there.

In many cases [writes Mr. Harvey], parents could have helped their children if they had been aware of the danger signals which, experts in the field agree, indicate that a boy or girl is headed for trouble.

There are ten of these danger signals. Ready?

1. Truancy.
2. Evidence of alcohol or drugs on the breath or needle marks on the arms.
3. Cruelty to animals.
4. A sloppy appearance or a manner of dress that exaggerates sex.
5. Unexplained cuts, bruises, or scratches.
6. Unexplained late hours.
7. The appearance in the house of strange articles that were not purchased.
8. Possession of unnecessary weapons.

163

9. Flagrant disobedience.

10. Association with friends he/she never brings home.

One or two of the items in Mr. Harvey's catalogue puzzle me. It is not clear, for instance, what sort of weapon ordinarily carried by teen-agers is an unnecessary weapon. When Mother and I pack the tads' school lunch pails, for instance, we always clip a .38-caliber Smith & Wesson and a couple of hand grenades into the recessed top of the container, on the theory that if the day is nice the children will play outdoors during the noon butchery. But suppose they plan after school to go downtown or out to the shopping centers for a little relaxing larceny; against the total fury of the adult bargain shopper, what armaments shall the helpful parent deem necessary? We happen to think that a healthy youngster can survive almost any shopping emergency if equipped with a shotgun, a sword, and a light but reliable flame-thrower. The children whine and threaten, but Mother and I see absolutely no need for thermonuclear devices. That is our decision. Do you think we are wrong?

Again, it may be difficult for the nonhep parent to be sure when his teen-ager's manner of dressing is sloppy. It sometimes seems to me that the longer the teen-agers in my life spend up-stairs grooming themselves for some crucial social occasion, the likelier they are to come down looking as if they had just been run over by a freight train.

There are ambiguities, then, but every parent who suspects himself of negligence and to whom is supplied by experts daily evidence of his nonfeasance will be grateful for the little homely tips in Mr. Harvey's brief counsel.

The sudden appearance in the child's possession of articles he did not purchase, for instance, must have confused all of us from time to time. We might like to think of him as being an un-assuming, hard-working, straightforward little crook. But can we be sure? How do we know that unbeknown to us he has not be-come a patrolman, a police commissioner, even a State legislator? Might not that account for the scratches and bruises, the un-

164

explained late hours, the sloppy appearance, the friends he never brings home, as well as the unearned swag?

Never, you gasp. But are you sure? Aha!

I do not believe anything can be added to Mr. Harvey's perceptive hints with respect to alcohol and drugs on the breath or the punctures of the hypodermic needle on the arm. A boy or girl who takes drugs habitually, as the experts agree, is probably headed for trouble. They have not stated the case a bit too strongly. The addict is indeed in grave danger of addiction. Now go do your duty.

A "They" in the Mist

Professors often say with a labored chuckle they are surprised and saddened to find years later that students remember them not by reason of the skill and erudition with which they taught the subject but by reason of some joke or by-the-way or digression with which they padded forth a miscalculated hour.

And turnabout is fair play.

So the visiting windbag who was talking with the English classes at Westbrook Junior High School in Paramus the other morning will remember those students by reason of just two questions—incidental, by-the-way, forget-it questions—out of maybe a hundred.

One of the questions, addressed to a man working on the editorial page, was:

"After you've written your copy do they make any changes in it?"

The other was:

"Don't you think it would be better if the newspapers didn't talk so much about our failures—like our failures at Cape Canaveral?"

The visiting windbag thinks they are disturbing questions. To a man who believes that language should be used to communicate and that clarity in language is dependent on clarity in thought, the appearance of the pronoun "they" without an antecedent noun is a shocking experience. It is deadly important that we use the language precisely—that we put clear hard noun and efficient verb and clear hard noun together in such a way that they convey a meaning. This is a time of day when a phone might ring in the Kremlin or the White House and feed into the mind of the man who picks up the receiver a combination of nouns and verbs that would set the world on fire. The example is extreme. It is meant to suggest that we must learn to use words as fastidiously and conscientiously as a surgeon chooses and uses the things which are his tools.

Who is "they"? "They" is a pronoun. What is the noun it stands for?

And there's a cloaked and soundless "they" in the question about suppressing the facts about this country's failures. Who would decide which facts must be withheld? What agency of existent government could be trusted to run through its screen the ocean of possible choices which is any day's report of the news and to decide which truths are too true to be made known to the people of a democracy whose life depends on the knowledge and wisdom of the common mass of us? If no such agency exists, how do we create it—by act of the Congress that has visited on us such confections as McCarthy, Eastland of Mississippi, J. Parnell Thomas, the House Committee on Un-American Activities?

Such testy questions are by no means beside the point, which, last time we looked, was the use of language.

For it seems to the visiting windbag that there is no way of differentiating between clarity of language and clarity of thought. But it also seems to him that some one more eloquent than he must try to tell young people that the search for clarity in word and idea is about as exciting a game as can be played in this vast gymnasium between anybody's ears. The search for that antecedent to "they" might be brief, of course; it might be "your editor" or "the boss" or "well, like our faculty adviser." But it might lead a student into reflecting on the meaning of the Constitution, on the struggle for the Bill of Rights, on the stodgy miraculous rightness of informed public opinion, on history, law, the tripartite system.

It might lead him to wonder how many other "theys" inhabit his intellectual premises.

It might lead him into the lonely and dangerous search for nouns, some of which are friendly but some of which are horrifying.

It might lead him to the suspicion that whenever any of us, even people of great humbleness and simplicity, undertake to drive an idea into a corner and make it tell us the truth about itself, we are doing something not unlike the stern and necessary work that the very great poets do. It is not quite a coincidence that when men are straining to tell the truth—as one did, for instance, at Gettysburg—they cannot avoid speaking poetry.

One of the boys shrugged.

"It's in fourth grade," he said, "they put the girls to reading poetry and the boys to reading sports stories."

You can guess, alas, which they he meant.

You Can Stop Tolling That Bell

Teachers have entertained each other for years abhorring themselves and in sackcloth and ashes repenting that they answered their wretched calling. Thus it is refreshing to find the current issue of *Teachers College Record* (that's the Teachers College, the one at Columbia University) devoted, cover to cover, to teachers' telling each other, sometimes angrily, that beneath these ragged overalls an honest heart doth beat.

Now let's see whether they can teach the rest of us the kind of pride in which, as Chamfort said, are included all the commandments of God.

Desperately teachers have been needing to be told, as they're now being told by spokesmen for industry and labor and the community, that only teachers themselves can make teaching an honored profession.

But just as desperately, we all of us need to be told the converse of Donne's dictum is the truth: that our diminishment of ourselves diminishes all mankind, and the bell that tolls for thee alludes also to people you don't know.

For instance:

Government is the loftiest of callings, simply because it subsumes every other calling—physics, psychiatry, mathematics, communications, to name a few currently reverend. We are now in the ultimate throes of a campaign whose effect is to persuade us that government and politics are not an art or discipline but the world's oldest profession.

For instance:

We make it a habit to read the Negro press. It summons the Negro to live his dignity. Too often also it talks to him in terms of superstition and numbers to play in the next day's lotteries, charms and aphrodisiacs and illegitimacy.

For instance:

Medicine insists on its selflessness and nobility. But whenever in the last quarter-century have been proposed ways of getting all the benefits of modern medicine out to all the people—not just the people able to afford them—medicine as an interest has talked not human lives and happiness but money.

For instance:

An illustrious publisher in the State reproached us with gentle sternness the other day; too many words in our copy, he said, that he doesn't know, and the dictionary's twenty feet away. We're duly chastened, since any failure to communicate is a failure, and yet . . . And yet it seems to us the people running the communications industries are wrong, disastrously and mischievously wrong, when they set out to reduce the terms of writing (or radio or television or the theater and films) to the terms of the least competent. To dilute a difficult idea only because it is difficult, to substitute grunts and zowies for accuracy in meaning, is not a way of communicating; it is a way of forbidding communication. But, besides that, it seems to one somewhat rattled struggler that to deal with people on any terms lower than one's own best is an act of condescension—not only wretched manners but essentially fascistic.

For instance:

The only excuse for labor organization—the only excuse loftier than the level of the fraternal lodge or the pool room—is to emancipate people from slavery and exploitation. Instead of being grateful for automation, which further reduces man's commitment to slavery, and for the exposure of such exploitation as Hoffa's and Beck's, organized labor is, of all things, sullen.

Who of us couldn't use a little more pride, if not in ourselves then in the work we've chosen to do or had thrust upon us?

The teacher who stands before his class and sardonically compares his wages with the brewery truck drivers' commits an intricate crime. He imparts to children a hideously false system of values. By proposing that the worth of an institution is to be measured by the splendor of its plant and the size of its budget, he teaches them a Farouk is worth a dozen Schweitzers. He traduces many a community, whose people pay dearly indeed for education. Not incidentally, he demeans, to no good purpose, the honest and exacting business of driving a beer truck—which is essentially not different from driving an ambulance or a fire truck.

But the worst of his crime is against himself. Pythagoras was deadly serious when he told his students, "Above all things, reverence yourself!" Without self-respect how can a man have morals and convictions or laws except as inane and annoying rituals?

169

An Alternative to Disgust

Call her, for long, Lynette, and you may find you know her
though not by that name. The other kids at the school say she's
one of the great teachers.

She has decided she can't afford to teach. And she is not talking
about the money teachers are paid.

She is majoring in English. During her senior year she has been
sent down into the districts around the college to practice-teach.
Lynette has some theories about what's English and what's
teaching—she is willing, for instance, to go through the stately
rituals of the *Ivanhoe-Silas Marner-Tale of Two Cities* syllabus,
but she has been insisting that the world of J. D. Salinger and
Hemingway, Camus, T. S. Eliot, Freud is the one the children
live in and must know. She has insisted on assigning the tough
moderns, and the students in the high schools have insisted on
being interested, and the principals have insisted Lynette take
her highfalutin ideas back to her campus and mind her business.

She said, not bitterly, that if teaching consists of imparting to
innocent children an incurable hatred or contempt for English
literature she won't teach.

One does not argue with stern-minded young persons in the
throes of decision. I asked her what she thought she'd do. She
said the life of an insurance adjuster rather appeals to her.

One does not argue. But it may be recalled that last summer
in *The Antioch Review* was published a translation of an essay
by the Spanish philosopher Ortega y Gasset which bore the
innocent title "The Mission of the Librarian" but which dealt
with destiny.

Ortega y Gasset always steps at once in deep water:

170

While calling to mind and considering the various kinds of life possible to him, a man observes one of them attracts him more than others—draws him, claims him, calls to him. This appeal that a certain kind of life has for us, this imperative cry, is called vocation.

In vocation, what is necessary for a man to do is not imposed upon him but proposed to him. . . . But the vocation itself is not in our hands. That is why every human life has a mission. A mission is just this: the consciousness that every man has of his most authentic being, of that which he is called upon to realize. The idea of mission is, therefore, a constitutive ingredient of the human condition; as I said a while ago, without man there is no mission. We may now add that without mission there is no man.

That's step No. 1 in discussing you, Lynette, in the third person. For step No. 2 consider the counsel of Rufus E. Miles, Jr., in the current issue of *Antioch Notes:*

The men and women of every generation who live the fullest and most satisfying lives are without doubt those in whom vocation and mission are joined. That a vocation should also be a mission, not merely a means of acquiring income and status, is an idea which should lie at the core of our educational system. . . . Yet most students leave college without ever realizing that the opportunity to merge vocation and mission is more precious than gold and if seized will make economic security and prestige seem like the fool's gold that they are.

Rufus Miles, a trustee of Antioch College, is a public-service career man, Administrative Assistant Secretary of Health, Education, and Welfare. He is biased. In his opinion young people should be training for public service because in government—in the public service at any level—are the forces that must be used to counteract the centrifugal forces that are tearing society and the world to pieces.

That's his case.

Mine's a little different. It seems to me that Lynette's argument is not with the English curriculum; it is with an educational system, in the end meaning a political system, which has forgotten or never knew why the English language is studied. Lynette is the medical student who writes bitterly and anony-

171

mously in avant-garde magazines about disillusionment. She is the law student who has discovered that the business of law is not justice but victory. She is all of the kids who came in answer to a challenge and found they were not wanted.

We need them, not to teach English but to begin building a society which will remember the names of the challenges and will want to meet them.

They're needed in Washington, Trenton, the Poles, Africa, the town hall, the Moon, London.

You might call it, at that, a form of insurance adjustment.

The Teacher's Time Off

Mason W. Gross's big frame filled the doorway of the little hotel room, and his deep-lined features were arranged in that prompt inclusive smile, but he braced himself with a deep breath before he came on in, and you could see that he was tired. When he said hello you could hear he had a cold. Nothing much, he said—just can't seem to shake it off. He made his rounds of the room, saying gay things to people he knew and the right things to people he was meeting.

He stopped at a window, looking down, and his face was lined and tired.

For an appalled moment you comprehended that the president of Rutgers the State University is fifty years old, human, mortal.

If you're the average Jerseyman you don't believe it. Over his three-odd years of presidency at New Brunswick Dr. Gross has persuaded most of us that he's either an all-pervasive sprite or a secret fraternity. Go where you will, there's Gross laying a cornerstone, dedicating a school, upbraiding a congress of planners, building a dam, exhorting a P.-T.A. Note-comparing Rutgers men insist they can prove Dr. Gross was lecturing on

172

philosophy in Cape May and addressing an alumni fund-raising klatsch in Tenafly simultaneously.

The introductions done, he stepped back and leaned, sagging a little, against the door frame. He was tired.

He had a right to be, one guessed. That week he had gone to Washington, Pittsburgh, Boston, and New York to speak where his speaking was needed. He insists on meeting his philosophy classes in the college on schedule. He's running a vast, explosively growing, crotchety university. His six-feet-three sagged. Any other framework would have been squashed flat. One was impelled to wrap this precious resource of ours in fluffy woolens and take it home and put it to bed.

But grown-ups can't let that kind of concern show—God knows what would become of us if we let our sympathy get out of control.

What had he been in Washington for?

"Oh," he said, "that was the National Conference on Urban Life, and I wanted to say something about this—well, this damned mess they call the megalopolis."

He drew himself up, and his fine face hardened. "It is absurd, Bill, it is irresponsible," he said, "to cross-identify this sprawl with a city. A city is not what it's called. A city is what it does. . . ."

He had begun to move up and down the corridor. He was there in Newark that night to give the kickoff-huddle speech starting the American Cancer Society crusade in New Jersey, and the people on the program had met upstairs to get their timing settled, and in a little while Dr. Gross was striding in the corridor and saying again that if the city is dying this is because it has been allowed to become meaningless to the people in it.

And the fact that he says he earns his most honest dollar as a professional philosopher may have nothing to do with the phenomenon I was looking at, but it seemed to me there was something ancient and forever valid in the enormous gusto with which this big and gentle man responds to the things that matter to him and the unfailing taste with which he decides what matters.

An hour or so later in the dining room he was explaining to 400 cancer-fighting volunteers the way in which modern research has reduced to a hairline the gap between the atomistic philosophy of Democritus and the monadism of Leibnitz and Giordano Bruno. Science has yet to set in place the bridge between the living monad and the nonliving atom, between the dead and the undead and back again, and this is the fugitive truth on whose twisting track research is pounding now. He did say again, as he has said before, that the air is electric, crackling, with promise—that in many disciplines, marching side by side even if they don't know where, there is an almost unbearably exciting sense of imminent breakthrough. . . . But much of what he said was not far short of technical. His audience of laymen sat there entranced. Suddenly the idea of the search for truth as the most important thing in human life was clear—the remorseless search which may be all the truth we'll ever find and which lives at the heart of the effort against cancer.

A great teacher stepped down from the dais, and passed the back of his hand across his forehead. Dr. Gross said he'd better be getting home. Isn't there a way of telling a man to take care of himself so he understands you mean he's to take care of himself?

The Teaching of Teaching
of Teaching of . . .

Margaret Mead the anthropologist belted out one of her better lectures the other day at Paterson State College—gist of what she told the teachers in training is that they must equip themselves to prepare children for survival on a planet where no one will ever have been till they get there—the Earth as it'll be tomorrow.

This is a curious form of criticism.

It was a good gruff Mead lecture, down to its haunting suggestion that this generation of our own is already a stranger on an Earth which it doesn't understand and which has become unknowable to it.

It's odd to find oneself tracing the performances of anthropologists as if they were football teams or pianists—Mead seems to be a little rusty in the timing of her attack; in *Darwin's Century* Eiseley does not sustain the lyric line of *The Immense Journey*. Yet one takes one's excitements where one finds them. And, with due gratitude for what she did say at Paterson, one wishes Dr. Mead had told the students a thing not enough moderns have heard her say before.

It is that the way in which education is transmitted has undergone a revolutionary change that will control the way things are learned from now on and that may already, unnoticed by us strangers, have taken control.

In a stable old or isolated society (so went Dr. Mead in one of the memorable games of the last season) education is vertical. It is transmitted downward, from generation to generation, and a boy learns from his father how to tie the knots or set the traps or plan so as to have the gilts farrow down about the end of March, a girl learns from her mother how to sew and cook and make home brew and track her man until he catches her. In a child's life there is all the time in the world, and in a society that has settled on its skills and destinations there's a limit on the bulk of the culture that has to be transmitted.

But, if I understand her, Dr. Mead proposes that, in the world as it'll be or even is, the learning process must—not may or should; must—go on and on day by day until the day we die. We must teach each other, and we do. There is too much to learn. There isn't time enough in the first fifteen or twenty years of anybody's life to learn anything except the tools—language, mathematics, basic attitudes, the methodology of curiosity.

Try within your own experience her argument that we teach each other.

Every time a new machine comes into the shop, a little seminar takes place. Every time a new product comes into the market, a million women enroll for a course of home study which might involve just reading the directions on the back of the package but might extend into the abstruse arts of the home freezer. The pharmaceutical companies' celebrated detail men, who call on doctors and peddle new drugs but stay to talk of dosages and side effects and incompatibilities, are obvious teachers. For better or disastrous worse the television screen is a teacher when educational T.V. is farthest from its thoughts. A seven-year-old teaches his grandfather the sometimes abstruse skill of tuning a clear picture on the set. I was complaining the other night that a lot of American art isn't art and isn't American, and a man taught me, saying: "What you find in a pyramid is Egyptian art, no questions asked, and what you find in the ruins of an Ionian temple is Greek art; what you find in a New York museum may be good or bad, but it's American art, isn't it?" Yet I've learned important things in the last month too from a bus driver's imperturbability in traffic, from a medical doctor's way of controlling his anger until he was ready to use it, and from a small boy's indomitable refusal to remember that he had been hurt and had a right to bear a grudge.

We do teach each other, and it is astounding how badly we do it most of the time. A professional teacher would be fired out of hand if he treated his pupils the way the run of us treat the rest who are our pupils, to wit, brutally, sneeringly, as if we were annoyed or bitterly reluctant to impart to the people on whom we depend the skills on whose use our happiness and—for instance, in the educational institution called a traffic jam—our very lives depend.

We must be taught to teach. We're going together to that

176

planet where no one has been, and we aren't yet half ready. It's a rum form of criticism, and yet that's what I wish Margaret Mead had told the teachers.

In the New School a Room for Magic?

The schoolhouse of District No. 2, Schuyler County, N.Y., was a small one-room building, painted duly barn-red, warmed by a wood-burning potbellied stove. Over the front and only door was a big brass bell. It didn't have all the necessities—our instructions were: in case of fire, jump out of the nearest window—but we had a biology laboratory down in the little brook that feeds Watkins Glen, and you could scarcely beat our gymnasium and play yard, which were all outdoors.

I don't know that I remember anything I learned at the little red schoolhouse in all the disjointed months, scattered across the years, I went there.

Oh, maybe little things: I was taking the Regents' examination for fourth grade, and threw a wheel on a question that seemed to me utterly inscrutable. One of the upperclassmen, a pimply troglodyte named Butch, had to leave the room. He passed my window on his way to the backhouse, and I asked him what the hell was the starched-collar capital of the world. "Troy," the teacher said. "If there are other questions covering material the class studied before you got here, come up here and I'll fill them in. You deserve to pass, William. Don't ask Butch for information. He doesn't have much to spare."

Troy is the starched-collar capital of the world.

Troy is the starched-collar capital of the world.

Despite my best intentions, I find myself thinking of the little red schoolhouse and its teacher of kindergarten through eighth grade, Mrs. Bolt, whenever I am told about the brave new concepts in education—that is to say, oftener than I should.

A report titled *The Schoolhouse in the City* brings it up this time. I have no quarrel with the report. Issued by the Educational Facilities Laboratories (Ford money, $8 million), the book has this as its thesis:

"The schoolhouse is aged, crumbling, ill-equipped, a symbol of the decay surrounding it. . . . Almost never does it boast the facilities needed to serve the community at large."

This is not a pitch for the construction of modern schools—or, if you insist, palaces and country clubs—in the slums. It is a plan for radical new concepts in the use of urban space for schools.

New York and Chicago have placed elementary schools in public housing projects. New York has a junior college running in a high-rise office building.

Schools are being built over railroad yards, highways, and in at least one case (the United Nations School in New York) salt water.

Schools are more than schools. In New Haven they're senior citizen centers, public libraries, community theaters, community auditoriums.

The thrust is toward use of the school as the cultural and social bone structure of the inner city. It holds people in town. It brings wandering people back to town.

Mrs. Bolt was young. She had red hair and green eyes. She didn't have much to work with by way of books or human tissue. She made a bewildered boy understand that somebody did give a damn how he was making out.

Since they are colored by his own lenient opinion of the confection emerging from the process, nobody's recollection of his school days are admissible as evidence on any subject. So I shall add that by the time my brother and I were brought down from the farm and thrown into the New York school system's hamburger grinder Mrs. Bolt had made us pretty much immune to permanent damage. She thought highly of us, and let us know it, and lately in a classroom whose kids are there because they had given up on themselves, I've seen again that nobody, nobody at all, is wholly invulnerable to the magic of being thought highly of.

That's all. As I read the budgets and blueprints and see the schools of the future loom out of the ground I wonder what happens inside the walls. Troy is the starched-collar capital of the world, but there's more to growing up than that.

What's the Matter with Old Gutter U.?

When it comes to sex education in the public schools, which is what it's coming to as sure as Elizabeth McGonigle is a foot high, I'm a Goldwater reactionary. Let the schools teach the children how to spell.

I'm as horrified as you are.

To be against sex education is distressingly similar to being against the fluoridation of potable water supplies, against the regionalization of government services, against abatement of air and water pollution. But that's whose feet are dragging: mine.

Mrs. Elizabeth McGonigle, a fifth grade teacher in Cape May, is president of the New Jersey Education Association.

"The responsibility [for imparting sex education] is falling on the schools because children are not receiving an adequate sex education at home," she said in an interview at the N.J.E.A. convention in Atlantic City last week, and—you knew it—a panel of experts testified she was right when she predicted that pretty soon now all the public schools in the State will move something over or out and make room in the curriculum for the daily grind about birds, bees, mamas, papas, and the menstrual cycle.

Four of the panelists suggested sex education be initiated in kindergarten, or, to rebabble the owlish idiom, at the kindergarten level.

Who needs it?

And, by the way, what is it?

Both questions are meant seriously, and I suppose the answer to the first is the familiar horror story about the girl who gets married and proceeds to have six or eight babies without ever suspecting the existence of a cause and effect relationship between sex and childbirth. So that's who needs it, Mr. Smartie. And as soon as some advocate of sex education produces the corpus of the heroine in this tribal legend I'll believe her kindergarten teacher should have taken her into the cloakroom after school one day and told her what the United States Government is now telling the maidens of India about the population explosion.

I have faith enough in the competence and authority of nasty little boys and girls in the gutter to believe that no child attains adolescence without a clear understanding of what sex is. And it doesn't seem to me that the most important aspect of the relationship between persons of opposite sex is susceptible of being taught in a public school classroom.

I'm a reactionary. The most important aspect of the deal is love. The subject cannot be discussed without embarrassment in the home, in the classroom, or in a newspaper. Love, honor, cherish until death do us part—how is a teacher to discuss such music with tykes itching to resume throwing bean bags and alphabet blocks at each other? And if the discussion is fixed at any level other than this, what is the child being taught that he can't learn more systematically in a routine biology class?

One of the panelists, the supervisor of health and physical education in the Newark public schools, attributed what he characterized as the breakdown in morality to the children's unsatisfied need for sex education in the home and the school.

The temptation to deny the premise is strong; what breakdown in morality, at a time when young people are involved up to their ears in pitting their strength against war, prejudice, all the dozen kinds of tyranny they're bellyaching about from Russia across Europe and the America to southern Asia?

But let the premise be granted for the sake of the argument, and I move you that morals have broken down not because students haven't been told about sex but because their elders have forgotten all they ever learned in school about honesty. Morals aren't taught. They're learned. The schools might as well have a crack at teaching what's teachable. The world is so full of a number of things, but I suggest spelling.

It's Always Open Season on Scapegoats

Samuel F. B. Morse was a proper Puritan, a pleasantly muscle-bound artist (*The Dying Hercules*), inventor of the electric telegraph, and one of the most mischievous clodpates in United States history. Doing the grand tour of Europe, he stood one day in 1830 watching a papal procession in Rome. As the Pope passed, a soldier—"a poltroon in a soldier's uniform" is the way Morse couched it in his diary—struck Morse's hat from his head.

We shall get to the Halloween solemnities at Westwood and Hillsdale in a moment.

You've heard about the juvenile delinquents' rioting at Westwood and Hillsdale and the consensus among grown-ups that something robust will have to be done?

Samuel F. B. Morse was unable to regard his distressing experience in Rome as an isolated phenomenon—as the peculiar consequence of a sudden and even comprehensible impulse in a pious lout.

Convinced that he had been the victim of base and indiscriminate orders from the papal system itself (to quote his journal

181

again), he hurried home to warn his countrymen that the Pope had insidious designs on the United States. The whole damned anti-Catholic racket in this country dates from that point.

Now let's talk about the teen-agers.

Up there in the Pascack Valley something like fifty or one hundred or maybe 150 teen-agers got into a fight with some exceedingly fine policemen who managed in the end to keep some semblance of the peace and to keep, more importantly, their temper.

The grown-ups are angry, being alarmed, and there's talk of wholesale reprisal—the curfew, antiloitering ordinances, total suppression.

It is going to be difficult to stand forward in defense of the rights of the teen-age citizen—as unpopular as it would have been to speak in extenuation of the Irish Catholic immigrant in Morse's time or any Catholic in Al Smith's, of a Mormon in the 1880s, of a Jew when Henry Ford's *Dearborn Independent* was clobbering the Rothschilds and the Guggenheims, of a Mexican or a Chinese or an American Indian ever. It is not meet that a citizen suggest to his fellowman he may be wrong.

But before we engage in a wholesale terror against teen-agers let's pick up our hat from the sidewalk in Rome and reconsider what really just happened.

In two towns which are really one town but haven't yet gotten around to noticing it, a minute minority of the young people in the county, perhaps as many as one microscopic tenth of 1 per cent, worked themselves into a fury one night.

That's it.

We'd better meditate at some length before we decide on this basis to exile everybody aged from twelve years to twenty.

In the first and fundamental place, it would not be entirely feasible to confine young people to their quarters at the stroke of the sunset bell or at any other hour of day or night. Evidently it is usual and convenient in some of the Eskimo tribes to banish the elderly to the outer darkness when they get so old they're

182

no longer useful around the igloo. The decision having been made that their presence is no longer necessary, the old people just toddle out to die.

I don't think we could make it stick if we tried it, even symbolically, on teen-agers. They'd resist. They'd unquestionably organize for guerrilla warfare. I can't help wondering how long it would be until businessmen in any town afflicted with a curfew would point out that teen-age money is authentic United States currency and that the liquidation of the teen-ager was subverting commerce.

We should have learned by this time that no minority will fit into the tidy matrix in the illiterate or uncaring mind. "Jew" does not equal "international banker," "Catholic" does not equate with the New England Primer's "man of sin, the Pope, worthy of thy hatred." "Juvenile" doesn't mean "delinquent." We should have learned never to mistake a phenomenon for a norm—a poltroon for a Pope.

The Pascack Valley's delinquency problem totals about twenty-five hostile kids, meaning twenty-five hostile homes, and due process can take care of them. Let's forget the witch hunt. Halloween is over.

Integration Problem on Kite Hill

Abroad in the land, despite one man's most conscientious efforts to confute and defeat it, is the proposition that it's proper and beautiful for a man and his son to do things together—always provided, of course, they aren't things like robbing a bank or operating a moonshine still. Said Hal Boyle the other day:

"Few things give us a warmer feeling of the kinship of humanity than the sight of a father and his son flying a kite together on a breezy day."

This is a statement of fact, not about men and boys and kites but about Hal Boyle of the Associated Press. Hal Boyle is reporting on how he feels. There is no way to argue with a man about the organization of his nervous system. But it need not be unseemly to deprecate an attitude, and Mr. Boyle's attitude is the one which led some sardonic old New England Transcendentalist to snarl that a lad is a boy with a man's hand on his head.

Your reporter happens in the first place to be an expert on father-and-son kite flying. In the company of a father we have suffered through many a breezy day as a kite-flying son. In the company of a son we have functioned sullenly as a kite-flying father. God willing, we shall in due time visit our insane aerodynamic theories even unto the third and fourth generation.

From a little way off, Mr. Boyle, from the road at the foot of the hill, it looks charming. High against the wind stands the kite, and here in the clearing are the two, the tall man and the small boy, their heads together over the fat spindle of twine. Human? Obviously. Kin? Yes. Warm? Yes. Step closer, Hal.

"I don't want to seem unpleasant about this, Bill," the father is saying, "but this is the damnedest backlash I ever saw. Can you explain how the string got this badly snarled?"

"No," the boy says.

"What do you mean, no?" says the father. "It's your kite, isn't it?"

"Yes," the boy says, "but you've been winding it in and out; I haven't had my hands on that string all day."

Both are trying to keep the voice low, so as not to disturb the other practitioners of the kinship of humanity, but they are testy, edgy. We know. We have played both roles. A man can fly a kite, and he will fly it well after the fashion of a man. A boy can fly a kite, letting out line enough to extend his personality into the endless four-winded sky, and then he will drive the spindle end into the soft earth deep enough so that it won't tug loose and will then roam about to do such wrestling and shirttail-pulling as there is to be done, but he flies his kite a boy's way.

184

And it is sometimes wondered, not invidiously with respect to either party, whether a boy's way of doing anything has anything substantial to do with a man's way. They are curious about different things. They are asking Nature different questions. They're getting different answers.

No; it's more than that; it goes beyond the difficulty in communication.

At the risk of shocking men we know and like, men whose good intentions we deeply respect, let it be said that perhaps not often enough does it occur to fathers that their sons secretly but desperately wish the old man would go get lost. Boys seem to have scores to settle, pecking orders to establish and solemnize, sudden mass compulsions to put the kites away and hurry over to Charlie's to shoot baskets, which to grownups seem crazy or criminal.

There is no explaining the abrupt impulse to crawl into a drainpipe or stand ankle deep in the mud or sit on a fence and, with a sense of inexpressible sadness, contemplate one's name until it seems to be the name of a stranger and then wonder who the stranger is. There are times, if one remembers matters correctly, when a boy would like to be alone, times—well, out with it!—when one is a little embarrassed by the foolish benevolent presence of this beloved old creature one's father.

He asks so many questions. He tells a boy so many things a boy would as lief not know. He is in such a hurry, as if there were not all eternity to live in. There are so many things he doesn't understand and tries to understand; he is so easily bewildered, so easily hurt, so lonely, so meddlesome. If, in a kindly way, it could be suggested that he go fly a kite!

The Unwashed Influentials

He slouched at the side of Route 28 with a soggy guitar case at his feet and a soggy duffle bag on his back. With strips of white adhesive tape he had spelled "To New York" on the guitar case and "Back to the Pad" on the duffle bag. He needed to hitch a ride with a sucker. He needed also to maintain his detachment from the sucker's world, his noninvolvement; and so, while pleading for a pickup, he had arranged his face in a haughty smirk and stuck a cigarette loosely in one corner of it, and when he resorted to gestures he kept them small and cool—the hand dangled palm outward, and the thumb scarcely waggled. He wore big bugging black sunglasses, a wilted madras jacket, tight black pants, sneakers, and a mystical gray aura of soaplessness. The hair was long and lank.

He had a beard.

He was there again on the next corner, or so you would have sworn except you noticed that the legend on the bag was a little different, the madras jacket a little more pallid or sootier, the sneer—as much a part of the uniform as the clothing—a little more or less sicklied o'er with the pale cast of anxiety.

That one too had a beard.

He was at the crossing beyond that. There were a half dozen of him in Taunton. Providence swarmed with him. The migration was on. Summer was over. It was time to get back to the pad, back to winter ways of indicating one's disgust with the society on which one makes oneself a conspicuous parasite.

They all, to the last man, had a beard.

Of all the ritualistic stigmata wherewith the nonconformists declare their abject conformity, the beard is the one invariable.

When I got home from vacation I helped unpack, and went

upstairs and shaved off my beard. I wept. It had to go. I am willing and prepared to be misunderstood in almost any other respect. I shall not hazard being taken for cool.

And yet I loved that beard. These were the longest vacation and the longest beard of my life, but my feeling for the shrubbery was based not on its establishing records but on its contribution to my personality, which is a small fungoid growth of which I try not to speak or even think ordinarily. I found that, once the beard was well rooted and commencing to flourish, my children actually paused to consider my objections before going ahead with what they were doing. During those weeks I expounded some of the most outrageous opinions I have ever heard from the tongue of mortal man, and people nodded. I instructed ancient sailing men in the art of navigation, explained the Moon's structure to a professional lunar geologist, and straightened out a practicing psychoanalyst on the nicer nuances of the Freudian id. Instead of dragging me down to the beach and drowning me they said there might be much in what I said. In ten days more I would have been as arrogant and mistaken as a prophet.

I cannot bring myself to allege that, despite its transfiguration of my character, the beard was always a bliss. It is difficult to sleep with a beard on one's pillow. It scratches. It rustles. When one turns and squirms in one's guilt-ridden dreaming it catches in the folds of sheets and covers, and one wakes in a nightmare of having been seized by the whiskers in some Bowery saloon or frontier bordello and dragged forth for lynching.

I suppose that when a beard grows ancient and silken like Charles Evans Hughes's or the Smith Brothers' it is not only tolerable but comforting—a scarf against the blasts and chills of winter, at all times a certification of one's manhood and a suggestion of one's authority. But that beard had to go.

It was a mess, but I loved it. It was a problem: I didn't know how to bring it up civilly. I loved it. I might never have been able to make up my mind by myself. The beatniks, the grimy little predators prowling on the road, did that for me. They may be silly or contemptible or insignificant. They did one day make a difference in one life.

Stopping by Woods that Are Not There

Mayor Matthew I. Fox of River Vale read into the record of last week's Township Committee meeting a letter sent to him by a twelve-year-old boy. If the membership lists are still open, there are some people on the rewrite desk out here in the city room who would like to join him as associates in the Douglas Bowen Fan Club.

> I would like to write to you about a woodland problem of River Vale [Douglas Bowen began]. Ten years ago River Vale was full of woods. Today there are few.

The men on rewrite read the letter in a galley proof of a story about it. Afterward on the margin of the proof they wrote the names of the arts and sciences or crafts Douglas dealt with. In the margin alongside this first sentence they wrote "history" and "conservation."

The letter went on:

> As you know, it is because of the population explosion. I know you can't help that. No one can.

The rewrite men's marginal comment: "Sociology. Demography. Biology. Metaphysics. Existential philosophy."

It'll go faster now.

> But I think you could do something. You could make a park. No, not the kind of park as in Woodcliff Lake. That's too touched up.

188

("Esthetics.")

What I mean is a woods. A place where animals could live. Where? Well, take the farm on River Vale Road at Prospect Avenue. There is a little woods behind there. My idea is to buy their property, when they intend to sell it. Then plant trees in the fields and intermix the woods.

("Planning. The stewardship theory of open space preservation. Mapping. Economics. Forestry.")

Cost money? Yes, but what doesn't? If you worry about getting votes, you'll gather the votes of all real people.

("Pragmatism. The art of investing minimal public funds now to ensure maximum public benefits later. The science of calculating the relative risks in alternative lines of conduct. Practical politics. Statesmanship.")

Before you throw this away in the wastebasket, consider about it. Thank you.

So Douglas Bowen concluded. The commentary of his fans along Ulcer Alley concluded:
"Psychology. Salesmanship. The soft sell."
Douglas appears to have made his sale. He wasn't trying to sell the farm and turn its fields into a forest, remember: all he set out to do was to persuade his Mayor to stop and think about it. Mayor Fox said he had stopped and will think about it.
We elders tend to be ham-handed in our appreciation of the young—the treatment tends to afflict the backward with a swelled head and reduce the superior to agonies of embarrassment. There is the danger of patronizing a boy—or a lad, as our excruciating vocabulary of condescension insists on making him —and of enraging a bright young person by whooping and heaving with gratification that he does not appear to be an imbecile. So let's not appear to be paying undue attention to a brief letter that makes no pretensions of its own.

189

But it might repay any adult's study.

Mine, for instance—especially the crisp brevity of the words and sentences, the clarity of the ideas, and the specific recommendations: what to do and where and when and how to do it.

It is a precious gift found only in the young and the highly literate old, and Douglas Bowen and his kind should be solemnly entreated to preserve it no matter how much education they must undergo from now on. In Mayor Fox's mailbox, jam-packed with high-priced junk written by high-priced specialists in promoting a sale or an idea, are not many letters that say fields and trees and animals. They speak, alas, of demography and socioeconomic pragmatism and conservation. They do not touch the busy stranger's heart and make him stop and think. In every fan club there is a trace of honest envy.

A Mild, Satisfying Bog To Stay Out Of

Add things a columnist might never know were funny if somebody didn't open his mail and guffaw:

Dear Mr. Editor: I am fourteen years of age and am entering my first year in —— High School. My father is a policeman. My past record in school is not the best of ones.

As I stated before, my father is a policeman. I want to smoke but my father objects. I ask your opinion. If I get respectable grades, should I not have the privilege to smoke limitly?

Excuse the printing, but my printing is better than my script. Thank you.

Student

The name of the town and school are omitted. The boy might want to be forgetting this one day.

Well, we shall light a cigarette—not because we need or want it but because the slavery has evolved to the point at which we can't even think without twiddling forth one of these idiotic pills—and, setting the cigarette to smolder away its brief existence, let's try this for size:

Why do you want to smoke?

And don't get flip and ask us why we want to smoke, or we'll sick your pop on you. We don't want to smoke. But we're stuck with an addiction that is untidy, expensive, humiliating, and very possibly dangerous. We've tried to lay off, and have managed to stop smoking sometimes for months at a time; but thus far the evidence suggests we can't sustain the effort of abstinence and any other effort in self-discipline simultaneously. Let any other problem supervene, and we backslide. So do other men. We are just about persuaded that, short of doctor's orders or a bad scare, cigarette addiction can't be licked.

It sounds unmanly. It is.

In that light, again, why do you want to smoke?

If you conceive your cigarette as the symbol of your growing up, your manhood, why, we just told you how one deplorably average man feels about that. But it goes farther. If you'll pay a week's serious attention to life as it is in reality, not in television commercials, you'll find the world reserves an especial kind of its respect for the man who doesn't exercise his privilege to smoke.

Listen to man talk as is where men talk man to man—at the bar, at the ball game, at the poker table. A fellow lights up, then proffers the pack to his friends. They mutter thanks, and take a cigarette, all but one.

"I don't smoke," he says, and, Student, you are herewith assured that he couldn't create a greater sensation if he were to say he had just returned from Mars or kidnapped Nikita Khrushchev. Most men who don't smoke owe their abstinence to a wise or priggish parent or, rarely, to a providential allergy or idiosyncrasy. But the effect is the same as if the nonsmoker had overpowered some physical handicap, as did Mr. Roosevelt, or some psychic defect, as did Barney Ross.

191

Let's not get into the question whether cigarette smoking is contributory to the development of lung cancer in people having a predisposition to the disease. Let's pretend that's irrelevant, as it was until Hammond and Horn published their statistics, or let's insist one of the free man's privileges is to decide whether today's smoking is well worth tomorrow's hazard.

Why do you want to smoke?

If, as your note suggests, it is to win a victory over your father, there are better ways than dropping a quarter and a nickel into the slot of a vending machine and pulling the lever. Into every kid's life, we gather, comes soon or late the need to assert that he's his own man.

That's fine. Maybe in a policeman's house it becomes imperative to prove there are kinds of law and order other than the kind the old man works at, just as in a minister's house the kids seem occasionally to be compelled to prove there are kinds of morality which are different but as good as the one which is the family's bread and butter.

But you don't prove yourself by taking to smoking when, as, and if your father says you can smoke. That doesn't establish anything except that he's boss. The way you make the old gent push back his cap and scratch his head and admit, grinning, you're too many for him is to do the things men do when they know they're good. Don't smoke. Don't drink. Don't ever drive too fast. Don't flunk your courses, and for Heaven's sake clean up your script and your spelling. Do what you know you should want to do because you decide that's the way you want it to turn out. Be yourself, not the mirror image of somebody else's taboos.

And if that's preaching, so is a cry of despair at sea in the night.

The Pursuit of Walden

So long, then, the young stranger said, and he went off down the driveway, and his parents said so long and wondered how long that would be. He looked back and waved, then turned into the little dead-end street that runs east by south to the uttermost ends of the world, and after a little while they went back into the house and began stacking the breakfast dishes in the sink and worrying.

He was going to hike—hitchhike, actually walking only between thumbed pickups—north across the border, thence west on the Trans-Canada to the Pacific.

It is an interesting way of being alienated from one's society, his father reflected, being somewhat the way the remora or suckerfish (*Echeneis naucrates*) is alienated from the shark on which it parasitizes. In his worrying his father detected a thin pulse of disapproval or resentment.

"They are so young," said the young stranger's mother, pluralizing him and electing him representative of all his generation—"so young and innocent, vulnerable. Hike across the continent? In canvas sneakers?"

She washed dishes. Her husband wiped and stacked them. They enumerated the hazards in shorthand. Hospitalization and insurance all paid to date. The blood bank coverage, does it cover accident across the border? He's carrying traveler's checks, but does the thief coming on his tent at night know they are not negotiable? It will be bitter cold in the mountains. The police can be abrupt. His back pack must weigh 50 pounds. He has always overestimated his reach in swimming.

They sat down to talk, and found there was nothing left to be talked about except what each knew and neither could say: that they wished they were going too.

They wished they could run and overhaul him and go with him, but they knew they could never catch up, and they knew that, though they matched him step for step down into the surf at the far side of North America, they'd never get to where he was going.

There is one time of life to be moving on, farther into the world, deeper into oneself. Young men have been doing it—thank Heaven, by and large—since the human mind acquired the capacity to differentiate between what it knew and what it dared to dream and hope.

And there is a time to shrug and reflect that one can change one's skies but not one's soul, that there is nothing beyond the horizon except this place by a different name, and that the most revealing and exciting sort of traveling involves not so much knowing where one wishes to be as knowing where one is, not to mention who one is.

The young stranger's parents brewed tea and said little, and wished again that youth were not so often wasted on the young.

This is a footloose generation even when it goes by motorcycle or in a beat-up old VW bus, footloose and irresponsible and, parading its mannerisms in dress and hairdo and music, it is exasperating in a way we never managed to be when we were footloose and irresponsible.

So we elders sip our tea in the kitchen and deprecate a constellation of irrelevancies, and the similarities between these children in search of themselves and the wanderers we reverence tend to escape us. There along the road, back pack on the ground beside them and thumb dangled negligently Utopiaward, are Jack London and Vachel Lindsay and Carl Sandburg, Lawrence and Goethe, Homer and, for God's sake, that pretentious young son of the village butcher who came down from Stratford on Avon to hang around theaters and make fun of his betters. Thomas Wolfe is there. So are James Joyce and, unless I am

194

mistaken, an even dozen unkempt young men, hot-eyed, insisting they have a mission to a world that needs saving.

They live off the land. They solicit food and shelter of a society they affect to repudiate. It is thoroughly irritating. By throwing themselves on the mercy of the passerby they bring him to find that he is merciful. It cannot be said that they are not working toward change within the system.

Still trying to keep it impersonal, I wish he hadn't quit college, but I wish too that college hadn't quit so many decent young people who had been led to put their faith in it. I wish he had a marketable skill, but who's sure anymore what that is and whether the labored perfection of one mightn't be just another prologue to disenchantment and despair?

I wish his ambitions were recognizable to eyes like mine. But I try to bear in mind Bertrand Russell's warning in *The Art of Philosophizing:*

To pursue personal greatness, like Ozymandias king of kings, is a trifle ridiculous, for the greatest power or fame attainable by a human being is still so microscopic as to be scarcely worth even a little effort. But impersonal aims —to try to understand as much of the world as possible, to create beauty, or to add to human happiness—do not seem laughable, since they are the best that we can do. And from the very knowledge of our unimportance it is possible to derive a certain kind of peace, which may make it less difficult to bear good fortune without vainglory and evil fortune without despair.

Each of us goes to seek his fortune in his own way. I never knew of anyone who didn't find it, for better or worse. The road to Xanadu is well marked and diligently policed these days. But it would be irresponsible not to worry—it would be downright unparental.

A Harvest of People

They are students, most of them, and most of them have been through a school year that was physically and emotionally exhausting, and they want to get away from it all, at least for a while.

Up Route 17 they went one morning this week, headed for the farm.

I can't say I understand the details, and one tries not to be too inquisitive, but I approve the principle, I guess. The farm is in upper New York State, and, for all its insufficiency as a mailing address, this is unobjectionable in principle, and it will be a co-operative and a commune. The villagers are said to be restive, as York State villagers have been historically whenever co-operation has emerged from the dictionary and become a physical presence among them, but let's not borrow trouble.

Our house's delegate to the commune took with him sandwiches, a half dozen cans of soup, a baseball, a change of underwear, a sleeping bag, and an idea that if he can get the right camera (Eumig, three lenses) at the right price ($125 second-hand) this might be a marketable documentary film.

I wish I were nineteen years old or maybe twenty.

Not that I yearn to go with them; I have no stomach for that kind of adventure, and besides I suspect the need to build communes is more urgent here in town than it is on any distant countryside; but there's something they need to be told, and they are defensibly indisposed to listen to a voice issuing out of such depressing ruins as they see in me.

They need to be told they are escaping into hardship.

If I said it they'd glance at each other and shrug and smile,

196

and, because I was uneasy and embarrassed by their amusement over my concern, I'd raise my voice. I'd find myself saying that, dammit, for all their classroom drudgery and test-passing, they don't seem to understand how an economic system works.

Indeed they can raise chickens and reap their daily crop of fresh eggs, and if they can buy a cow and keep it alive and fresh they'll have milk and butter. They can plant a kitchen garden and, by keeping everlastingly at the hoeing and spraying and keeping the earth constantly busy between now and black frost, they can have beans and lettuce and tomatoes and corn such as they never tasted before, plus perhaps enough to can against wintertime.

If they're lucky, productive, and persuasive they may be able to barter surplus eggs and butter and produce for necessities they can't produce—salt for the cow, oystershell for the poultry, rations of grain for all the livestock.

Yet barter, payment in kind, has limits, and they have narrowed. For the farm machinery and the gasoline they'll need if they're to produce cash crops, for the electricity they're bringing in from the distant road, for the medicine and the doctor's care they'll inevitably need, for electric light bulbs and books and ball-point pens and beer and perhaps a rasher of bacon once or twice a week they'll need money.

They have contrived a well considered contempt for money, have the children of the affluent society. The contempt is genuine, and as a child of the Depression I envy them, and yet, if they could hear me across the chasm, I should like to say a word in extenuation of money.

Look at it, look for instance at a silver half dollar, not as an end in life but as a magnificent computer mechanism. It is a storage and retrieval device. My half dollar is not merely a certificate that I have done something which my civilization agrees is worth fifty cents: it is the work itself, frozen in time and space, preserved and capable of being performed whenever I take the coin out of my jeans. It says to the tobacconist that I have done fifty cents' worth of work for him and am entitled to demand payment, a pouchful or so of pipe mixture.

I wonder what the commune will do for money to pay the utility bills. Perhaps, like some of the communes that have made a got of it in the Southwest, it will sentence one or two members to go down into town daytimes to swap muscle or skills for currency. I hope this doesn't sound supercilious. I hope it doesn't sound naive.

The hard way may be the only right way to acquire an education. So let there be long talk when the evening chores are done about the way in which a society governs itself and how it devises the ethics that control not only its rhetoric but its behavior. Among a dozen intelligent and like-minded young people there will be agreement as to ends. But means become a problem, even when they involve issues less momentous than how to achieve peace in Vietnam, and when the question is which way is the right way to fence a barnyard, do we put it to referendum? Or is one way the right way? And who says so?

And how do we decide who's working his way as against who's coasting along on a free ride? From each according to his ability, to be sure, but what agency determines what that ability is? When tempers flare, as they will, who'll be the fascist pig that restores the peace and brings the charge, and which man will be the first among equals to sit as judge.

Not so simply as by piling the duffle into the back of the rented truck and moving into the current running north on Route 17 does one get away from it all, I'm afraid. Whatever else an escapist manages to escape, his adhesive self, another interesting storage and retrieval mechanism, always tags along.

Whatever it is, good harvest, men!

What Flavor People Did You Want?

We didn't take down the question, because we had no idea we'd be so oddly troubled by the answers. But this reconstruction of the question will serve:

"Is learning to earn the proper study of the college student?"

It is, of course, a loaded question, a wilted hangdog straw man of a question, and duly it produced the answers it was calculated to produce: no; in college one should not meanly learn to make a living; college is the place-time in which one learns to learn or, in an even more exuberant formula produced in a happy pang of word association by one of the daddies on the panel, college is where one learns to live.

This was Happy Pappy Weekend on the campus. The girls' fathers settle on the town for a couple of days, take their daughters to dinner and dance, talk nervously to the nervous gods of the faculty, get the feel of the place—and come away feeling reassured and significant. Happy Pappy is a sound institution.

The panel discussion had been arranged to let faculty and administrative people talk with fathers about the aims of education. And here was one man disturbed again, not by the students or especially by the trend of the harmless platitudes being exchanged by the faculty educators and the educator fathers who had been selected for the discussion—except in this way:

It is meet and necessary that a school have a clear image of itself. There's a difference between M.I.T. and Sarah Lawrence, between Yale Divinity and the Oklahoma football factory, and somebody in charge had better have a pretty clear idea what the difference is.

But it seems to one man that when educators con themselves into predicting what sort of man or woman will emerge from a quadrennium of any educational process—if education is what we're really talking about—they overestimate themselves and underestimate the people they're discussing.

As, nodding, the educator panelists solemnly jawed away that morning in the time-stained little chapel they created a college that gloomily resembled the clicking, glittering control room of an automated factory.

Click, and the assembly line proceeds to grind out a succession of faceless robots, possibly in smocks, certainly wearing horn-rimmed glasses. These are the worker ants.

Click, and production is switched to philosophers, garbed in toga and sandals and muttering something about per aspera ad astra.

Curiously, these too are faceless.

Click, the well rounded man; click, the literate and responsible citizen; click, the mother who has made religion central to her family's happiness (religion can make any business hum); click . . .

It doesn't work that way, of course. In the long run people, not the institution, decide what it is that happens in any school-room from kindergarten up. Genially they decline to be frac-tionalized. Genially they insist on being economic man enough to make a living and political man enough to run a government and philosopher enough to preserve their sanity in an unpropitious environment. Within a loose tolerance we all of us get to know a lot about one thing and a little about everything. And one of the imperishable miracles in this crazy pilot plant called democ-racy is that, with an illimitable ocean of possible choices before us, we elect to reach so broad an agreement on who and what we are.

So the intellectual assembly line doesn't really work very well that way, and, as long as schools continue despite educators to do their ancient duty of exposing people to infection by curiosity and discontent and the method of inquiry and test, it needn't

200

matter much that teachers sometimes amuse themselves by wondering what kind of universe they have in mind.

The objection is that whenever one of us essays to decide what his fellow man should be and how he should be made that way, one of us is engaging in an exercise that is essentially anti-intellectual. It may be anti-intellectual in the scientific way or the religious way or the political way, but at its heart is a denial of freedom in will and choice. And that, one man thought walking back across the wide square through the snow, is a rum thing to find on a campus.

THE WORLD BEFORE LAST

The World Before Last

We were sitting at the kitchen table latish one night recently, the small boy who lives at our house and I, to unwind for a while before hitting the sack—he had been doing summer session biology homework, and I'd had homework too, and the key was up—and, as men are doomed to do, we were topping each other.

Going down the twisting road to the railroad crossing which the kids call Suicide Hill, he had blown the rear tire of his bike that afternoon.

Blew a gaping tear in it, and a geyser of dank brown water reeked up, but he hauled the bicycle out of its skid, never falling but, by the time he wrestled 'er to a stop, she was facing back the way he came from.

Outside Altoona, I said, the road went down the face of a long steep hill. At the top the trolley tracks ran along the right shoulder of the highway. But halfway down the hill the tracks slanted across to the left side. Where it crossed, along the inner edge of each track had been cut a shallow channel in the concrete for the flanges of the trolley wheels. My fellow schoolboy adventurer was coasting down the hill wide open and didn't see the danger soon enough to veer and hit the tracks at a sharp angle. His wheels meshed into the track channel, and the bike shot off into the brush at the side of the road while the unfortunate pilgrim sailed, kicking and shrieking and surrounded by a blizzard of pots and pans and flashlights and rubbers and underwear, through the air to land with a dreadful clatter far down the road ahead.

The small boy was astounded. This is an effect that invariably pleases a father.

"Do you mean to tell me," he said, "that you had bikes in those days?"

And once more I was aware that the people who I wish would write a book are the ones that don't.

I wish that he would gather himself at his typewriter and, scrupulously avoiding research, write now, using just such information as is in his skull, a book about what it must have been like to be alive when his father was a boy.

He cannot remember a time when there wasn't a television set in the house, and I know that there are moments when he reflects that we didn't have television and wonders what in the world we did. He has learned not to ask. He has learned that a sympathetic inquiry about his elders' moral equivalent of television is to precipitate an avalanche of pious guff about reading a good book, hoeing the potatoes, whitewashing a fence, walking ten miles to school through snow nineteen feet deep, writing letters to dim and often theoretical aunts, knitting, visiting the poor, gathering in the living room to sing hymns.

It was a world without T.V. It was a world in which a boy would go to bed at night and have never a radio of his own to yak him to slumber. Almost nobody had a telephone. Only ten or a dozen people in town had a car. If you wanted to cool off in the summertime you had to take two trolleys and walk four miles for a swim in the bend of the Saddle River behind Scoskie's store in Rochelle Park—air-conditioning wouldn't be invented for forty years yet. If the house got cold in the wintertime you had to trudge down to the cellar and throw a hundred pounds or so of coal, of all queer things to think of, on a fire in a furnace.

The icebox was a box that had ice in it. A man came and put in a block of ice every day.

He is too tactful to say so, but I sometimes think he conceives of his parents' generation as sitting on a sagging porch year after year, gaunt and dressed in tattered overalls, waiting desperately for the wheel to be invented.

I wish he'd write a book about the older generation. It would be exciting to see whether the kids are as far wrong about us as we are about them and the world in which they're the natives and we're the guests and strangers.

206

Shortcake and Bitters

One of the significant yet often unconsidered realities of life in a world threatened with thermonuclear destruction is the fact that strawberries are just about as good as they were when you were a boy.

I don't think this can be said of anything else except perhaps sweet corn, and we had better withhold our judgment on that until the 1963 crop comes in. Since the hybridizers got at it, sweet corn is generally better now than it was when you were a boy, but last year's corn was sorry pickings—some said it wasn't fit for the pigs, and only stubborn loyalists would say it was, remember?

But these strawberries, especially the strawberries being brought down from Saddle River's sun-washed slopes: fat, sleek, clean, juicy, each one embodying some perfect mystical tension of acid and sugar, of tart and sweet . . .

I really deserve to be rebuked for bringing up the subject. So what's new? Strawberries taste like strawberries; big deal; you're writing for a newspaper, and what are you writing this for? Well, I'm writing it because I think it's news when it turns out in the testing process that something tastes like itself.

Salt pork, and I'll tell you what occasions that remark.

On the farm we ate all the varieties of meat we wanted, as long as they were (1) rooster and (2) salt pork. Of the abomination called chicken stew or fricassee, made with the carcass of a fowl born toward the close of the Upper Jurassic, I shall say no more. But my grandmother's salt pork, floured and fried till crisp, then served with boiled potatoes and cream gravy, was the dish with which you would elect to be cast away on a desert island. For breakfast, lunch, dinner, or impromptu after-theater snack, her salt pork knew what was ailing a boy and tranquilized it every time, and the other day in an insane fit of nostalgia I bought a couple of tons of salt pork in the supermarket and took it home and, gathering the family about me to partake in the transmission of a great American heritage, I did with it precisely what Grandma used to do.

Lord, it was ghastly.

The taste of it (rank), the look of it (surgical shock), the feel of it (blubber)—Poe himself could not have conveyed the horror of it, and I was saying to the food editor next day that I must have done something hideously wrong. No, she said wisely out of a long experience with elderly parties' disappointment on revisiting turnip greens and pot likker and red cabbage and the cohen pohen of their youth—no, she said; I had merely forgotten that on the farm we had an ingredient which is not available to the middle-aged gourmet: the appetite of a twelve-year-old boy.

Perhaps that's all there is to it. But I think technology has something to do with our foods' savorlessness. I shall never cease marveling at the miracles of modern food processing and distribution. Whenever I sit down to a plate of frozen beans or instant pompano or corn in January, once more I wonder. But I do not wonder long. Whatever it's called, whatever it looks like, it tastes like technology. We have performed our miracles. We have done away with food.

What I brought home from the supermarket that unlucky day was fried technology.

But I remember the strawberries too. We had a few rows of them in the kitchen garden, but most of the strawberries we got were wild, and wild strawberries are among the commonly conceded excuses for crossing your eyes to indicate ecstasy. Let us be candid. They were all of them small and unconscionably acid, and by the time we got them the birds and bugs and worms had been there first; they tended to be wizened or one-cheeked or hollow-eyed; they would suffice for a shortcake, but, bless you, given Grandmother Caldwell's inexhaustible supply of butter and Jersey cream and crumbly maple sugar you could have made a highly sufficient shortcake out of parsnips or beer-bottle caps.

The strawberries are better this sunny summertime than the last time you ate a quart of them singlehanded. I think it's news. But you'd better see for yourself.

Who Loves a Parade?

The incredible, appalling fact is that the Revolution goes on and on and on.

Choose your century. Here on Main Street you stand in November 1776 watching Washington's tattered army—the bleeding discouraged remnant of an army—stagger out of Howe's clutches. You have a decision to make. Did you march with Washington?

No. The record shows that people like us, landed people, poised and realistic, we played it safe. Let radicals like Tom Paine rant their theory about freedom and the rights of man. We stood along the street and watched the sad and shabby brigades lurch past. We knew better.

The Revolution goes on. In the distance there is the sound of gunfire. Again we stand on Main Street and watch the shabby marchers go by, the white and the black, and it has not occurred to us in these two centuries that the only thing required of us is that we decide which side we're on.

We have tried never to take sides. We have left it for history to take sides. . . . Always?

On the desk beside me is an old history of the county. It lies open at a page which deals with crisis.

The morning after Fort Sumter was fired upon, the Rev. E. T. Corwin, then pastor of the Paramus Church, tied a flag to a pole and thrust it out of

209

the belfry of the old church. When the congregation came to church the following Sunday they found Old Glory waving in the breeze above them. Some of the members objected.

How shall we handle this, padre, dominie, doctor? Some of the members are objecting—in 1776 to taking sides against His Majesty the King, in 1860 to a precipitate commitment to the cause of the Union, in 1915 to a belligerent attitude with respect to foreign entanglements, in 1939 to support of the Allies against the wave of the future, in 1963 to the quarrel of a small contemptible minority. Some of the members object. And now?

I return to my text.

Some of the members objected, telling the pastor it was not right to have the flag there inasmuch as there was a division of opinion in the congregation. They insisted that the flag must come down. Two patriotic members, William Ranlett and John Jacob Zabriskie, approved the pastor's action and declared they would protect him in keeping the flag on the steeple. During the week a committee of the objectors called on Mr. Corwin and demanded the removal of the flag before the next Sabbath's service. Mr. Ranlett, on the other hand, immediately armed and equipped 25 men at his own expense.

On the following Sunday morning, after the congregation had assembled on the church grounds, the committee approached the pastor and told him that, as they had stated before, the flag must come down at once. As they started for the belfry the pastor halted them, and said, "I told you our flag should wave above us until the war is over. I have 25 men who will help me to protect it. The first man who touches that flag to tear it down will be shot!"

That flag lasted, through fair weather and foul, half a year. It was replaced by others until the war was over. The dissident members left the congregation. Many never returned.

How would you have handled that problem, doc, dominie, padre? How, doc et alii, are you handling this problem?

Never has there been a crisis in which the side of the Revolution has been appealing, attractive, glamorous, prestigious. It has always been necessary that when we cast our lot with freedom then we must cast our lot with a rabble which we do not wholly approve. Washington and his tatterdemalion regiments on Main

210

Street. Lincoln and his conscripts from the Northern mills and sweatshops, the silly suffragettes, the loathsome pickets of the '30s —what a wretched lot have always been the fighters of the Revolution! Here they come now, picketing, the Negroes and the paraders against the bomb, the glassy-eyed disarmament fanciers, the waders-in and sitters-down, the Tom Paines and troublemakers, certifying freedom by using it. Where shall we stand—on the curb as usual, surviving but not even knowing what it is we're living through.

The Unlovable Replacement

One of the cold mornings last week when the temperature was two feet below freezing and we were standing at the kitchen door trying to decide whether to wear the blanket to work, the solution of the railroad problem occurred to us.

The sergeant at arms will kindly restore order.

Bring back the steam locomotive. That's the solution. Nothing especially complicated about it (is there?), but we anticipate a dollop of difficulty in explaining the reasoning. This may be one of the things that are more easily done than said.

Perhaps we had better begin with the blanket.

It is a little English car, with the familiar exquisite European workmanship. The doors don't quite close. The window panels don't quite fit. The wind howls through the car the way it howls through Act 1, Sc. 1, *Macbeth*. The British are not stoic or unfeeling. They are nonfeeling. In that car on a cold morning a warm-blooded mammal would be dead of exposure before you could say Route 17 and Race Track Road, unless he wore his blanket.

We come now to irresolution.

Among us slaves to deadlines who sit on the edge of the bed

in the dark unable to tell from how we feel whether we're getting up or going to bed, irresolution is an epidemic disease, painful and chronic but useful. Having determined by examining the face of the clock for the sixth time that one is rising, one gropes through one's ablutions, proceeds to writhe into one's clothes, and at last confronts the rack of neckties.

You now establish what kind of day it'll be.

If you reach out crisply and pluck a tie from the tangle, check its surface against last fortnight's marinara sauce, and don it, the day will be good. It doesn't matter that the tie may be a hideous relic of seven birthdays ago, doesn't go with your shirt or suit, and appears to have been used lately in strangling a sheep. If you select it unhesitatingly you're in shape for any horror the day will produce.

If you find yourself standing there palely wondering which tie to put on, you might as well go back to bed. You're in for a bad day.

It's that way about the blanket.

We were standing there grumbling that the temperature registered on the thermometer in the kitchen window doesn't tell a man how cold he'll be—a thermometer doesn't understand cold the way a man does: wind and wind direction, stage of moon, clammitude, edge, temper.

The 6:01 A.M. train pulled out of the Erie station up the valley.

We now saw what's the matter with the railroads.

This is a little commuter train. It's hauled now, of course, by a diesel engine. It gathered speed on the grade, clattered across the bridge above the pond, nasally honked for the bleachery crossing, and was gone. Full of sound and fury, signifying nothing: on a cold morning one cannot get away from *Macbeth*.

In the old days a man in doubt whether to wear his blanket would have put his ear to the door and listened, and the sturdy 2500-class Pacific would have shouted to him what he needed to know. No matter what the thermometer said, when it was cold

212

outside the steam locomotive would tell you that. Its huff, or choo, would be thin and bronchial, aspirated high in its pipes, uttered with a warning rasp. On warm mornings the 6:01 would come reeling down the grade bellowing German opera from its very guts—lots of diaphragm in it, lots of overtone, the sinus reverberations of an artist with a countryside to startle and his mouth wide open. When it was cold it would say so.

A steam locomotive spoke to you. You trusted it. It liked you. You liked it. It was your brother. You could identify yourself with it when it rushed past muttering incoherently and smelling of sweat and neurotically flailing its piston rods and eccentric valves and crosshead linkings. You could identify yourself with it in its sorrows, and would sit up in bed and heave and grunt with it as it staggered up the grade toting the unspeakable burdens loaded on it by the slave-driving scoundrels in the front office. When, despite the sand on the rails, the wheels would slip and spin and the locomotive exhaust would set up a great decrescendo howl of frustration, you'd fall back in bed and beat your pillow and wish you could go out there and help the poor devil. It was an inefficient old bum. But we loved it, and loved to go places with it.

It is impossible to like a diesel engine. You could no more be affectionate to a diesel engine than tiptoe into the kitchen and chuck an electric can opener under the chin. We didn't desert the railroads. We deserted diesels.

If the railroads want to bring back people let them bring back old 2500. That's what.

The Potbelly Revisited

The morning after this latest of the snows we judged it might be shrewd to get in to work early. So to catch the 5:23 out of

Midland Park the compleat neurotic got up at 4:15, and floundered over to the queer little station with time to spare for making the acquaintance of the potbellied stove. Before the other 5:23 commuter came in we had a precious few minutes alone with the stove. Our boyhood on the farm came back to us. Only a moment; a moment of strength, of romance, of glamour—of youth! (Conrad) And the best we can say for boyhood on a farm is, you can have it. (Caldwell)

Lord, it was cold!

The Susquehanna's potbellied stove is an Estate Hot Blast Smoke-Consuming. Across its cast-iron top is graven the legend: "If You Like Me Tell Others About it." It is whitewashed, about the size of a small fiend; it burns bituminous coal; it stands on a square of zinc over near the wall of the station agent's office, which has a heavily barred opening down at floor level. That's how the agent keeps warm. It looks like an ingenious way to let people goggle at alligators in a zoo.

Keeps warm?

The potbellied stove at the farm was, as we remember it, more elegant than the Susquehanna's. It was lower—no bigger than a well born hobgoblin—and heavier in the paunch. It was glossy black, had brilliant brass ornaments like a 1912 Ford, burned hard coal, and had isinglass windows, delicately crazed. This was so that our sainted grandmother could peer over her spectacles into its depths 179 times a day and say humph.

But that icy morning in the Susquehanna station we took judicial notice of one thing in common between the two potbellied stoves in our life. Each emitted about as much heat as would an adult mouse.

For all one commuter knows, the Susquehanna potbelly does duly heat up later in the day, and if this is the case it is herewith granted a severance from the following generalization, which will be stated in the form of a law: that the charm of ancient institutions varies in geometric proportion to one's distance from them in space and time.

We'd drag in the stove from the barn in the fall and attach its pipe to a hole in the wall and stoke it up, and, since the flue was choked with swifts' nests or leaves or the remains of feeble-minded guinea hens, the house would be filled with smoke and spectral figures and humphs. But after a while the obstruction in the chimney would burn out with a hollow roar. Then we'd open the doors and windows to disperse the fumes, the water in the bedroom bowls and pitchers would freeze over, we'd close the doors and windows, the water would stay frozen, and we'd settle down miserably for another old-fashioned winter.

Out in the kitchen was a vast gray grease-bespattered stove that was always warm because, humph, the victuals had to be cooked and there was no known way of convincing a slab of salt pork that it was warmed through if it wasn't. The kitchen was comfortable. But it took a later culture, which doesn't have to live in the kitchen, to establish that living in the kitchen is gracious. On the farm, one lived in the room where the pot-bellied stove was. Manners, the old minesweeper used to say, was manners, humph, and she wouldn't have you boys sitting out there in the dark a-tittering.

So into the room where the potbellied stove was she'd take the only operational kerosene lamp in the house, and she'd pull a chair up close to its bleak flanks and peer under her spectacles at day before yesterday's issue of the Elmira *Star-Gazette*. Every once in a while she would lower the paper and impart culture. It said here that a man she called that sniveling hypocrite Wilson had made another speech. We could take a hint. We would say humph and try not to titter, and after an hour or so of this we'd ask if we might be excused and go to bed.

The best room in the house was not, of course, the room where the potbellied stove was. In the parlor were kept the Bible, the sofa, the platform rocker, the Victrola and records (to be played only on feast days), the hams and apples and honey and sides of bacon. It was the freezer. Through it we'd run barefooted to the stairs, then up them to our room, and then we'd commit ourselves to the icy sheets, in agony, with a sob. She often heard us in our anguish, and would call up through the grilled register in the floor that we were just as warm up here as she was down there. This was nothing but the truth. As we were saying of boyhood on the farm, you can have it.

Notes at Quarter Past Fifty

In certain clandestine ways the most interesting item we shall never see under "It Was Today" is as follows:

"William Anthony Caldwell, uh, was born, 1906."

Almost everybody must have a sort of ex-officio concern, even enthusiasm, over the fact that he was born, and a man should be excused getting almost fanatically sentimental over his fiftieth birthday. We are aware, now that our second half-century is upon us, that a decent regard for the opinion of mankind dictates a slight rhapsody or a cry of bitterness. At his fiftieth birthday a man should produce an ode, a tear, at least a creak—he might at the very least say something astringent, carefully avoiding self pity, about the fact that the people who make "It Was Today" get there on the record of the years he'll never see again.

Can't.

Ten is the year of discovery, twenty is the year of high-hearted adventure, thirty is the year of fulfillment, forty is the year of desperation; but at fifty a man finds he has made his settlements with himself, and he finds that himself scarcely gives a damn.

You must not misunderstand this. Settlement needn't mean adjustment, and a part of settlement may be thanking whatever gods there be for his unconquerable soul—his contract with himself may stipulate that he is a rebel, angry, not a bit enchanted with the world he helped to botch.

But even the angry rebel is not sure at fifty that his anger matters much, even to himself. This is the way things are, and this is the way things will remain as long as the human race is a swine, and, while a man is content that there are truths and that they are good enough to die and live for, he knows his dying for them wouldn't even for him be a thing which would validate them.

He is not sure of anything, including this statement. From the grotesquely limited evidence available to him he gathers that time—in this gulf of the universe, at any rate—flows in one direction. It appears to him that growth, being conditioned by time, goes on. Evidently whatever now is, better or worse, will be past tomorrow. From time to time he regrets that he is involved in this process and is probably among the things which too must pass, but he is able to acknowledge that time and growth are wise to make no exceptions. If there were dispensations for him, so might there be for cancer and overpopulation and bishops who bless their nation's artillery in the name of the Almighty who is the father of us all.

He finds tears in his eyes more often—at the sight of a flag snapping, at the look of young people marching, at the sound of music, at being confronted with anything in the earth or sea or sky that is innocent. He finds it more difficult to harden himself against the tears—and yet more difficult than this to understand them.

"Swine," he says, but he knows men aren't swine on purpose: sometimes they know not what they do, but they do it for a decent purpose, reverently even when what they do is the ultimate irreverence which is death—even the killer is sick, and the name of his sickness is humanity, and he is not to be hated for it any more than is the cripple to be hated for his deformities.

He wishes he were young, but he no longer entertains the hallucination that matters would have turned out much differently, say, better; he knows that he is the product of such potentialities as wouldn't be altered the width of a chromosome by a swig of the elixir; and, in the next breath, he utters his thanks that he need not go again through the childbirth horror of any adolescence.

He has learned, he thinks, to value his own friendship; he needs his own good opinion, and sometime recently he thinks he found that of all the people he knows the hardest to deceive is himself. To his chagrin at first, later reassuringly, he found himself an indulgent friend, willing to accept his shortcomings— provided he does not lie about them.

There are nights when he's tired, but he's glad to be tired, because he's glad to be alive. There are times when he gets as far as knowing what happiness must be like. There are whole days when his faith—in time, in growth—gets the better of his doubt. He knows the cosmos, which will still be here a billion years from now, doesn't notice which are the faith days and which are the doubt ones. He's getting old, and all this reminds him is that he'd better—the day he stops, he'll really be in a jam.

The Nourishment in Rationed Water

He cannot now be sure he will be ready for it, after all these years of midnight shower baths and johns that flush at 3 A.M., but a boy who did a stretch of his growing-up rap on a hilltop farm will know how it is if water rationing should come—he will sigh and say doggone but know how it goes.

The cistern pump in the sooty little kitchen would run dry first when a drought was on the countryside. But that was no harm done. The cistern was a big stone-lined catch basin under the house. Its contents would be rainwater that had fallen on the roofs and had come to the cistern by way of eaves and downspouts, and it took no Koch or Pasteur to tell a farming family that the stuff was dynamite.

One was forbidden to drink it. Cistern water was for washing

218

up before meals, doing dishes, mopping, scrubbing. It didn't count as water. When the rusty little pump on the drainboard of the sink gasped and went dry it was not missed. When the smell of frying chicken was in the air a boy could dare to hope he might not be required to wash up before dinner. On a farm one lives on hope. A drought was not unwelcome up to this point.

On the farm were two other wells—really three, counting the half-sunken barrel into which some deep-lying spring had been tapped, but we were not to drink from this or indeed jump into the barrel to cool off, because the cows and horses watered themselves at its icy brim. I think I perceived the non sequitur in this line of reasoning when I was four years old. The prohibition stood.

The well outside the kitchen door produced what the management conceded was water. I have wished I could have loved that pump, and sometimes I wonder why I didn't. It seems to have been an efficient pump, having a high-pitched shriek when used, and it was tall and willowy for an iron pump and kept painted bright red, and Heaven knows it served us faithfully within its limitations. We just didn't get along.

Perhaps I associated it with hard and meaningless labor, as this is associated by some men with a demanding or hypochondriac wife. Once the cistern went dry we'd have to bring in water by the pailful from the kitchen pump not only for drinks and cooking and sterilizing the DeLaval cream separator morning and evening but even for those wretched ablutions. I try to remember it now, and the image shimmers and drifts and fails me; so I know I want to forget, and I know why, I think: because the kitchen pump was a symbol of slavery. It went dry only once that I remember.

At this point rationing began.

The third pump was away off beyond the barnyard, and I don't know why; I suppose because some swindling old dowser with a willow-withe divining rod instructed my grandfather to put it there. It never did go dry, for a fact, but the round trip to the north well for a pail of water must have totaled a good quarter mile. We learned to get along on pow'ful short rations, and, now that I am rummaging in these cerebral folds, I remember a subsidiary reason. The water was cold and clear, but it did have a strange bouquet—wild.

The pump stood on a rickety wooden platform. Its stone foundation had crumbled here and there, so that there were big breaches through which a boy could stick his head and stare down into the darkness and shout to hear the echoes. The guinea hen is an uncommonly stupid beast even among poultry. Guinea hens do not flock. They scuttle about in single file. If the lead guinea hen had walked through one of those holes in the foundation . . .

We were instructed not to find out. Water rationing is a nuisance. It might be more inconvenient yet if there were no water to ration.

In the fall, after the rains had filled the other wells, the hired man took the north well apart and removed all that was mortal of that year's guinea hens. Still, on a farm there was water to be rationed, and we shall have to see whether as much can be said for a great industrial society.

The Dragon in the Hills

In North Branch a girl, young, tiptoed delicately along the mud of the road shoulder, carrying a baby, leading a three- or four-year-old by the hand. In Hortonville church was letting out. The girls and the stout farm women let the old men go first along the road to the parked cars, each cradling his head behind a shoulder raised against the wind-driven shower of sleet. Down by the shallow brook that brawls alongside Brag Hollow Road a collie wandered.

The dairying countryside that soars across the sky from Monticello west to the Delaware is a world stripped of its young men.

It is as if a monstrous dragon had crept up the hills the way the mists do and had left the land bereft of its youth.

The figure of speech is invidious. One by one, the able-bodied young have gone off to war.

But the cows must be milked twice a day or they sicken, and the forage crops must be harvested in accordance with an ancient schedule which is not subject to negotiation or abandonment.

So the young man who lives at our house said he thought he'd go up into New York State and see whether he could get a summer job on a farm, and he said I could come too, and one of the phenomena we noticed after we'd pulled off 17B and started climbing into the folded hills was that people seeing the young face in the window of the car would stop and smile and wave.

Perhaps they surmised a good omen. Perhaps they supposed the boys were coming home.

I shan't allege that I understand the farm bit. For a while I thought a peculiar nostalgia was driving the boy who lives at our house. I think I have talked too much to the children about the farm in the Finger Lakes hills where I did some of my growing up. Experience does not deteriorate in old men's retelling, and I am a careful editor—the only memories left among my preserves are magic.

So he would ask at Goshen whether this country was like the farm at Sugar Hill, then at Wurtsboro, then at Calicoon.

No, nothing like that; we were driving on 17 in a storm, and the mountaintops were drowned in a boiling surf of clouds, whereas at Sugar Hill all the days were warm and fragrant of buckwheat, drowsing in the murmur of bees, and always the galleon fleets of flat-bottomed golden clouds went sailing down the sky toward a sea a boy could only dream.

I talk too much. A child might go searching for a father's lost childhood.

It wasn't quite that. He never did say why he wants to work on a farm. After a long time, after we'd talked about the strip slums and the megalopolis and the war, Harlem and school and prejudice and girls, he wondered out loud how often people these days do things for no better reason than thinking the things had better be done.

Below the road the rocky fields fell away sharply to a stony stream, at the other side of which a meadow stood canted on its edge. Beyond, in the mist, the glacier-rounded mountains marched back, dogwood-pied range after range, into the clouds.

This is what it was like, I said.

He said this was where we were going.

The farmer he'd come to see was in the barnyard loading manure into a spreader. They shook hands and laughed about something, and went into a shed to talk for half an hour or so. The sleet turned to snow, and an old man wearing tan waders armpit high came tottering around a bend in the stream, fishing downstream, wet fly, for trout.

The universe didn't seem to have changed much, except that the only young man in all those hills was the one who came back to the car.

The hours will be from sunup to maybe 8:30 P.M. or until the work is done, whichever comes later. He can handle the tractor. Most of the milking is done by machine. But three or four cows a day must be milked by hand. That he'll have to learn. With the family he'll get all the meat and potatoes he can eat. He had never heard the phrase used seriously, and the farmer was surprised that he had smiled. He said he's not doing it for the money. That was made to sound final.

A scallop of manure had adhered to his sneakers. He bent with a wisp of tissue, but decided not to clean it off.

Just Time for a Few
Extemporaneous Remarks

One of the legends—the one of them which had been the more trying to men who must not only wonder at what he said but wonder at the way he said it—was that he dashed off his text on the back of an envelope during the long train ride from Washington to Gettysburg.

He didn't. Two drafts of the Gettysburg Address are preserved in the Library of Congress. He may have improvised one detail. "That this nation shall have a new birth of freedom," he had written in Washington. When he stood forward at the battlefield, gaunt and shawled, to say his small poem which lives, like Pericles's over the Athenian dead, so much more vividly as confusion swallows up the cause for which the last full measure of devotion was given—when he stood up to speak, he amended the line: "That this nation, under God, shall have a new birth of freedom."

The speech was wrought and reworked. It had to be. The sense of it is a statesman's sense. But the music is measured mathematics: see how the fugal scurry of "conceived in liberty and dedicated to the proposition" abruptly resolves itself into the horn call that still echoes in a billion skulls: "that all men are created equal." He was a genius. Geniuses work at their trade.

The other legend was that the speech was ignored by the crowd and overlooked or disparaged by the press.

Going on at Gettysburg College is a three-day centennial observance of a man's getting up and saying a few words of which his personal bodyguard, Ward Hill Lamon, remarked only, "I am sorry to say it did not impress me as one of his great speeches."

After it was over a Philadelphia newspaperman sought out the President. "Is that all?" he asked. That was all. Today, the 100th anniversary, the Soldiers National Cemetery, where the address was uttered into the custody of the ages, will be rededicated.

It has been said the crowd was merely bewildered. Alexander Woollcott once argued that it had been tired and deafened by Edward Everett's two-hour foreword, that it needed time, as does an audience in the theater, to accustom itself to a new sound level. Lincoln was finished almost (3 minutes) before people were adjusted to his high Midwestern twang. By some accounts, it applauded just about courteously. By some, it was silent.

The press? A Harrisburg newspaper whose name appears to have been disremembered:

> We pass over the silly remarks of the President; for the credit of the nation we are willing that the veil of oblivion shall be dropped over them and that they shall no more be repeated or thought of.

They just don't make newspapermen anymore the way they used to. The London *Times* reported as a fact that the occasion was made ludicrous by some sallies of the poor President's. "Anything more dull and commonplace it wouldn't be easy to produce." That, folks, was *The Times* of London.

Yet the *Chicago Tribune* recognized the speech for what it was, classic, and the *Washington Star* carried the text in full and scarcely mentioned the fact that Everett also spoke. The Springfield (Mass.) *Republican* formulated a text for generations of English teachers:

> Turn back and read it over. It will repay study as a model speech. Strong feelings and a large brain were its parents—a little painstaking, its accoucheur.

Lincoln was a proper poet; and so he was dissatisfied with his results. He had managed to purge out of his language even a trace element of animosity toward the South or self-righteousness. He had managed to clarify the historic function of the

224

war as a test and a vindication of self-government by and for and of the people—there is no way to say it other than his. He had managed to relate in a single electrifying passage the glamour and horror and bitterness of the battle with the serenity of the pure central idea.

"It didn't scour," he said. Later he reproached himself again: "It fell on the audience like a wet blanket. . . . I ought to have prepared it with more care."

Not What She Does But Is

Some of my best friends are mothers. With no sense of uneasiness on either side I mingle with them daily. As a tad I played with many persons who turned out eventually to be mothers. Except when reckless agitators who do not understand our way of life incite them to these distressing demonstrations in clamor for their so-called rights I consider them valuable citizens of this great republic. I can see no reason why in due time they should not achieve equality.

But Mother's Day seems to me an unnecessary embarrassment.

We shouldn't celebrate motherhood. This is not to say I shan't celebrate it. Of course I shall, as conformably and unhappily as I celebrate Brotherhood Sunday and Be Kind to Animals Week— I shall obey some meddler's order to stand forth and do in public the reverence I'd more enjoy doing in other seasons for better reasons. I'll fetch myrrh and frankincense and do the cooking and dishwashing. But it's going to be about as much fun for both parties to the transaction as it is when I sprint across a room to shake hands with a Negro because people are looking.

I'd better explain that. I know a lot of Negroes who don't want to shake hands with me. They consider me a parlor sociologist who doesn't know what time it is—or, worse, the kind of arrogant meliorist that makes a hobby of welcoming the Negro into the white man's world, title to which remains in the white man's possession. They don't want to talk to me about the race problem and the gathering storm; they would prefer to bring their elephant jokes up to date, talk about Hemingway, or listen to Bach records. Here I come beaming, hand outstretched, ugh.

It gets complicated. They don't want to waste time on this bore. They'd prefer I didn't gallop up in fraternal greeting. But if I didn't cross the room to say howdy they'd know people would expect them to feel hurt. For my own part, I consider quite a few Negroes to be a thundering bore and would willingly forgo the ceremonies. But I know that people expect them to expect me to expect them to expect me to kick up a convivial fuss. There we are pump-handling each other sweatily and wishing the day might dawn when we'd dare just to wave and say hi.

Again our choice making is the mirror image of the conformity we affect to despise—is the nonconformity of the atheist or the beatnik or the adolescent who finds out what one just doesn't do and then proceeds to do it.

Where did Mother go?

The day always turns out less excruciating than in prospect it seems to me. Good mothers, who are not so rare as you might suppose from watching people in supermarkets and at vacation resorts, have a knack of setting at ease all their children, including their husband. But I cannot shake off the feeling that we're celebrating the wrong thing in the wrong way for wrong excuses.

The act of motherhood, while difficult, can be done by almost any human being of the correct sex. Billions of people, many of them having no especial talent for the job or any flaming ambition to do it, have been mothers—indeed, in certain circumstances motherhood is about as distinguished as corns or pimples.

The mothers we writhe and whoop around tomorrow are getting honored not because they're mothers but because they're mothers of us. She's not the point. We are. We celebrate ourselves.

226

There'll come a time, some other time, when a man might try to say that a mother is reverend because for a certain time in certain ways and with respect to certain human beings, her children, she managed to be what is best, being most human, in any of us. She managed to love unquestioningly, absolutely, and no need to ask for your definitions. You did not have to prove anything or deserve anything. You were you. All you had to do, all she had to do, was to be.

I'll try to remember Mom day.

A Man Must Say It His Way

It appears that freedom speaks no tongue but its own yet what it says is unmistakable and unforgettable. There's Hanukkah. Again, there's Nehemiah Mark.

Hanukkah is the Jewish festival—the Festival of Lights, and the word means "rededication"—that starts at sundown Saturday and goes on through the next eight days.

Nehemiah Mark is an artist and a bit of a legend. He's to be at the Bergen County Y.M.H.A. Sunday at 8 P.M., when it opens its celebration of Hanukkah by opening a remarkable show of Jewish art by Jewish artists.

At Hanukkah men remember Mattathias and his five sons the Maccabees. They led the resistance of the Judeans against the Syrians 2,100 years ago, and took back to be purified the temple Antiochus had polluted. So remembered is one of man's first recorded struggles to be free in his own way.

In any language the meaning is always clear.

Nehemiah Mark was a great and honored scholar in Hebrew letters. The son of a renowned European rabbi, he was a teacher too, and then—at the age of fifty-seven—he gave way to anger. His people were being systematically murdered, and his big powerful hands drew off his vestments and groped about to do the things that had to be done.

He became a wood carver.

Since then he has been pouring all his horror and love, anger and learning and pity, into wood carvings. People look at them, and see things they had never known before—they aren't pretty, but they say freedom is a knowing that must be acquired and a doing that no one can do for you.

A serious old man who does not suffer fools gladly, Mark will be there at the Y.M.H.A. at 211 Essex Street, Hackensack, through the three-day show. Not there but represented by works conceded to be among the world's finest, even behind the Iron Curtain, will be names you may recognize: Jack Levine, Chaim Gross, Alexander Dobkin, Moses and Raphael Soyer, Abraham Rattner, A. Raymond Katz, Saul Raskin. These are a few.

And there are very great artists who won't be there and won't be represented. We'll just take down what Sam Kadison said when we checked back a couple of the spellings:

Strange names? Not to those of us who thrill to any lonely man's effort to say his way what has to be said. What do they say? That the world is filled with tragedy and disappointment but it's a beautiful world all the same—that before the Assyrians and since them there've been self-appointed gods who wanted people to lead their lives according to these gods' filthy billboards. . . . Some of these men carried their brushes through concentration camps, and declared them at customs in their new world.

Some didn't make it. They're the ones that won't be on the Y's walls.

We asked tall, pipe-smoking Sam Kadison how the Y show was assembled, and he said, "Man to man, one-to-one contact." He's a camp director by trade, and talks about art in a gusty bass that makes the subject sound somehow manlier than varsity football. How come the Y directors decided on an art show—why not something, well, else? The Y is an educational institution among other things, he said; the subject of the festival is freedom; how can the subject be discussed in more immediate terms than painting and sculpture? Moreover, he said, people at the Y are sometimes concerned about the ego images that are placed before young people. What is the ideal we give them to live toward? If we lead them to conceive freedom in terms of freedom to drive the biggest car in town, own the biggest house, give the biggest parties, we're leading them to miss the point. The point is that a man must be free to feel things his way, see them his way, say them his way. "Sometimes," said Mr. Kadison, "he must be angry, and you can't be angry at the right things unless you're free to know what they are."

Once Nehemiah Mark was a poor and obscure struggler, but a certain rich man saw that his work was good, and offered him the kind of money that means success, arrival, reputation. That was the turning point. Gladly Mark chose freedom. He chose to afford to do it his way, say it his way. Such money would give a man security, leisure, inward peace and contentment.

"No," he said.

At Such a Time, Where's Father?

There are moments of embarrassment so painful, as when one finds one has usurped another's place in the electric chair, that they can be borne only by calling to mind the only immutable truth in the universe: this too shall pass. On such a moment, men, are we met today. It is Father's Day. We are about to be subjected to organized adulation. Smile—inscrutably, if you know how. Bear up. If all goes well, tomorrow will be Monday. If it isn't, we'll have one hell of a story breaking. In either case, we can slide down this pedestal and duck back into being ourselves as against being statuary.

This too shall pass, but in the meantime we're stuck with another undeserved responsibility—to play the game, play the role, on Father's Day just for a change to be a Father.

Who dat?

I have here a remonstrance from the venerable John W. Terhune of Park Ridge, a naturalist whose love of all things great and small is broad enough to include fathers. He doesn't approve *The Record's* traditional editorial on Father's Day: "At this particular time, when respect has sunk to its lowest ebb in this century and permissiveness has replaced it with arrogance [the editorial] is belittling and humiliating. . . . Who in good conscience (editors included) would speak of their father as The Old Man and address him as Pop?"

If the question is not rhetorical, then the answer is that incalculable millions of persons do both these things. No offense is implied, none is inferred, but let's stipulate that it may be one form of extremism. Let's stipulate that Father is not Pop or The Old Man.

Then who is he?

Mr. Terhune suggests that an apt alternative to the Pop editorial would be "A Father's Day Prayer," by Virginia A. Keck, which begins by thanking our Father in Heaven for the good Fathers on Earth . . .

Created in your image and likeness, they bear within them the spark of divinity.
We thank thee for their steadfastness and courage;
For their steadfast devotion in providing for their families;
For their wisdom in combining discipline with love in guiding their children.
We thank thee for the many sacrifices they make willingly
To create a happy, harmonious home;
For quiet understanding that strengthens their children
In facing the problems the day brings.
We thank thee for these men
Whose greatness lies in living unobtrusively but effectively . . .

This happens to be my first exposure to the poesy of Virginia A. Keck, but it suffices to persuade me she is engaged in another form of extremism.

230

Who is Father? The more diligently we try to define him, the foggier he gets.

Without fathers, what would the race of Man be? Scarce, sir, almighty scarce, growled Mark Twain. The subject is sensitive, but in etiological terms—in terms of phenomena's causation—fathers are responsible for their children the way ragweed pollen is responsible for hay fever, period. No especial credit attaches. It's the other way around. Name any problem—any, from air pollution and automobile design to zwieback but especially including overpopulation—and you'll find fathers at the bottom of it.

Fathers abandon families, abuse children, declare wars or protract wars undeclared, extort rents from slum families, swindle widows, mislabel as food cans of imitation additives, rob banks, flunk students who get the better of them in classroom disputation, bomb churches, corrupt politicians and government or are corrupted. If on Father's Day they got the just deserts which are as much as any minority is entitled to expect, there'd be a lynching.

But we are not so much interested in what a father is as in who he is in the eyes of his worshipers for a day, and for clear focus on this image I turn to the Father's Day advertisements. Business knows what the family wants to think of Father, and last week's ads were merciless in their depiction of an ideal no man can live up to.

He is twenty-three years old but affects maturity by growing an Anthony Eden mustache, is flat-bellied, and has hair or professes to (wigs, washable, $5 up). He drinks heavily, plays golf and tennis and spends most of his time swimming in the backyard pool or else sailing his yacht, and stays up all night watching color TV. He is itching to paint the house ($4.99 a gallon, down from $6.99 this day only), and would finish and panel the attic if he just had $697.98 worth of power tools, but what he has been waiting for is that ten-horsepower, eight-speed tractor ($699) to haul the lawn mower around his 0.4 acre of crab grass.

He rides a motorcycle to work, wears river-scenery shirts, sleeps on a water bed in a seven by seven umbrella tent, mixes drinks in a power cocktail shaker, and takes 35-millimeter color pictures of the reclining chair he's too high on sacramental whisky to recline in.

I don't know whose image or likeness he's created in, but to me he looks like Pop. Hang in there, men. By tomorrow he'll be gone and forgotten.

In Tribute to Martyrs

About tomorrow's Memorial Day embarrassments there's not much that can be said coherently. In Harrington Park the Girl Scout cadets will be suffered to march in the parade now that they've taken the peace symbol off their float. In Teaneck the veterans and the peace walkers will have separate but equal ceremonies. In Fair Lawn quite a batch of organizations are out of the parade because the Committee for Peace is in. In Leonia the Citizens for Peace, forbidden to parade, will convene a forum on the war. So what's new?

Year after year we go through this self-righteous squabbling over the question who is fit to honor the dead.

What is left except to say again that our vanities are beside the point?

There is no way of mourning adequately for all the dead who ever died in war for us, and I remember thinking something like this last year and the year before: they died for us all. They died for us all, and they seem to have left no record attesting that they died for the right people only—they had but one life each to give for their country, and they never said they were dying for me but not for you.

"The purpose of their fighting was to establish order and peace and justice," I seem to have said two years ago today, and I apologize for having found no other way to say it. "Their wars seem not to have produced these things. But to this they may be indifferent. They had their dream. They died for it. . . . And if they can look down perhaps they can be forgiving enough to smile over the small safe wars we fight now over their bones."

"How can advocating peace be construed as a slur on their memory?" a girl named Sharon Hughes asked in a letter to me a year later. "However, this is not what I am writing for."

What she was writing for was to synopsize for me a scene in Kurt Vonnegut's novel *Cat's Cradle* (Dell). It's about some old established institutions, such as war, and in the passage Sharon Hughes considered relevant a United States diplomat is about to make a speech commemorating a small Central American country's 100 Martyrs for Democracy. The 100 were soldiers who signed up for World War II but were drowned in their home port.

Ambassador Minton discards his prepared speech, which was probably "fustian and bombast" [wrote Sharon Hughes]. He said: "I am about to do a very un-ambassadorial thing. I am about to tell you what I really feel. . . . We are gathered here, friends, to honor the 100 Martyrs, children dead, all dead, murdered in war. It is customary on days like this to call such children men. I am unable to call them men for this simple reason: that in the same war in which they died my own son died. My soul insists that I mourn not a man but a child. . . .

"I do not say that children at war do not die like men if they have to die. To their everlasting honor and our everlasting shame they do die like men, thus making possible the manly jubilation of patriotic holidays. But they are murdered children all the same. And I propose to you that if we are to pay our sincere respects to the 100 lost children of San Lorenzo we might spend the day despising what killed them, which is to say, the stupidity and viciousness of all mankind."

He had brought with him a wreath spanned by a cream-colored silk ribbon bearing the legend "Pro Patria," and he was moved to recall a passage in Edgar Lee Masters's *Spoon River Anthology*:

I was the first fruits of the battle of Missionary Ridge.
When I felt the bullet enter my heart
I wished I had stayed home and gone to jail
For stealing the hogs of Carl Trinary,
Instead of running away and joining the army.
Rather a thousand times the county jail
Than to be under this marble figure with wings
And this granite pedestal
Bearing the words "Pro Patria."
What do they mean, anyway?

What do they mean, anyway? [the ambassador repeated] They mean for one country. . . . Any country at all.

This wreath I bring is a gift from the people of one country to the people of another. Never mind which country. Think of people. . . .

And children murdered in war.

And any country at all.

Think of peace.

Think of brotherly love.

Think of plenty.

Think of what paradise the world would be if men were kind and wise.

Stupid and vicious as men are, said the ambassador in Kurt Vonnegut's novel, it was a lovely day. He was almost done. "I, in my own heart," he said, "and as representative of the peace-loving people of the United States of America, pity the 100 Martyrs for being dead on this fine day."

He sailed the wreath off the parapet.

This is a curious piece of copy: poetry within a novel within a letter within a column.

But what's new? What's left to say? Maybe only this, with which Sharon Hughes ended her letter:

"I think it is a good, fine speech. I wish we had heard it this Memorial Day. Perhaps someday we shall. Maybe even in Bergen County."

Now let's quarrel over who has the better right to parade his reverence.

234

Beyond Thanks

Some of the Thanksgiving exhortations, begging your pardon, seem to be based on the difficult proposition that Providence is either feebleminded or inattentive.

People keep recommending that other people give thanks for all the blessings we're floundering in, and, while this department doesn't deprecate gratitude, still it cannot bring itself to accept the assumption that the Almighty is surprised and pleased by a sudden torrent of trumped-up testimonials. Indeed, we are reverent enough to suppose that the Almighty isn't surprised by anything.

It may be impious to attribute human sentiments to the cosmos, but if the righteous can insist that pressure-group thanksgiving makes a difference in our favor, we shall have to insist on the possibility the cosmos resents being treated as if it were a low-voltage Congressman, susceptible to goose grease and flummery.

Providence has been around. It knows whether or not we're grateful. It knows what we're grateful for. So do we. Let's come off it.

We believe there's a case for thanksgiving—for Thanksgiving —and we believe this consists in its compelling us to say in specific terms what it is we're thankful for.

Now, what would that be? And, again, we'd better try to avoid enumerating the victuals on the table the way a back-country ecclesiastic says grace—shouting the names of the dishes as if we were ordering the meal and the Lord were the waiter, hard of hearing, and we were thundering the order into his ear trumpet.

We'd better leave out the grub on the festive board, since there

235

is no evidence that in our virtue we earned it and since up there the implication that favorites are being played might be resented.

We'd better not emphasize the lavishness of the living standard at all. In the good book are several broad hints that the only use of a lavish living standard is to share it—not a little bit off the edges but radially, like a pie, equally.

We can't possibly discuss the 1958 model cars, color T.V., the bank balance, the smooth low-cost ride on the Parkway, air-conditioning, fur coats—if we start calling attention to these we may remind the audience of some of the unpleasant aspects of Nineveh, Tyre, Babylon, et seq.

We should be thankful for our freedom. We'd better not bellow. There are questions on which we might be cross-examined. Freedom for whom? What kind of freedom? Freedom to do what? What are we doing, besides giving it favorable mention from time to time, to keep deserving this freedom?

This is nothing frivolous. One by one you must strip away the things for which a man can utter thanks and then be stricken in his conscience or convicted of thanklessness. Soon or late, if we are serious, we must come down to a handful of small blessings that don't get named very often in urbane society.

We can see, taste, smell, eat, relish. We don't often do these things well. But in a pinch we'd have that capacity. We'd have the capacity to live gladly.

We can hope, and in defining what we hope for we can define what can come true—whether this be in very humble terms, like the hope we express when we sow seeds in the earth, or in ultimate terms, as when we work as well as we can to cultivate a brotherhood of man in the supposition that the ultimate kingdom must be something like that.

We can be faithful, and a reason for thanks is that we have been given the power to formulate the values whose sum is our faith.

We can live, not very long but passionately enough so that we can be sure we've made a difference—since each of us is all mankind, and what we choose to become is what we choose the world to be.

Each in his maimed way, within the limits of our handicaps, we can obey the commandment that we love one another. And it may be useful to observe that every man of our time who has reached the uttermost limit of science and there stored away into the abyss—every Einstein, Eddington, Jeans, Oppenheimer—has turned to us white-faced and told us that to love, God help us, is all we can do.

When we mean what we say we can be careful what we say, even in such terms as thanks, because in no vulgar sense or mystical sense either we can be sure that the universe is what we say it is.

HAIL BROTHERHOOD,
WHATEVER THAT IS

Hail Brotherhood, Whatever That Is

This being Brotherhood Week, the soft touch for a writer before he can duck out and take an infidel for lunch, on toast, is to say something forthright in favor of brotherhood, and I'd do it and duck if I knew what brotherhood means.

What's brotherhood?

At one level of meaning, I'm brother to one brother and two sisters. We preserve a sort of dogged residual affection in spite of having been brought up in the same family. If one of them telephoned me and chirruped happy Brotherhood Week, William, I'd wonder what they were so sore about.

At a second level of meaning, I'm a white Anglo-Saxon Protestant. I am immodest enough to think I have friends of all the creeds and colors there are, perhaps excluding the Eskimo Indian. If I were to call one of them and assure him that I seize this opportunity to consider him my brother, I'd know what he was sore about.

He'd be offended at my condescending to grant him a favor which it is not within my power or competence to bestow.

I have great faith in brotherhood, for somewhat the same reasons I have great faith in Darwin's doctrine as to the adaptation of species. As early as now in the twentieth century biologists must hurry to examine the disease-prone or resistant characteristics of primitive people because mankind is becoming homogenized so rapidy that the idiosyncrasies are dissolving. One of these centuries we shall all of us look pretty much alike, speak a common language, speculate in the same way about Man's ultimate relationship to the same universe, call it what you like. Brotherhood will be along presently.

But in the meantime it is easier done than said.

241

For to put brotherhood into words is divisive.

Except in a formal paper on comparative religion or the arts how can Jewishness be discussed without drawing a line whose purpose is to separate? How will any one reduce to words a man's state or condition of being a Negro or a Chinese without notifying him that he is not a brother to the W.A.S.P. and never will be? I may be oversensitive, and I don't know what noun or adjective to substitute for it in our eternal yak about the subject, but it seems to me that "Negro" itself is headed for the same embarrassing uselessness as has swallowed up "colored" and "darky" and the deliberately pejorative words. Among young people, especially boys who respect and admire Negro athletes and artists for their intelligence and virtuosity, color is not mentioned except by the colored.

But my point remains intact. Any word is divisive. We are to each other what we do with each other. Fighting for the rebound under the basket, where the action is, everybody's color-blind and the Brotherhood Week services are functional and interesting.

Brotherhood Week is not devoid of value, since it compels us in company to confess certain ideals and thus afflicts us with the hell of uneasy conscience when during the other 51 weeks we fall short of the stated standards.

It is useful principally, though, in confronting us with the idiocy of such irrelevant prejudice as pens the Negro in his ghetto because his skin is pigmented and condemns him to a life of dependency at idiots' expense. It is useful in confronting us with the idiocy of the school election vote in Wayne Township, where a majority of voters rejected board candidates because they're Jews but the same voters couldn't tell you at pistol point what a Jew is.

Someday, if a just divinity can contain its rage and disgust long enough to let us find this for ourselves, we may learn that we are all of us guests in the household of mankind, brothers because, God help us, we can be no other. We shall have no more reason to exclaim over our equal brotherhood than to celebrate with hymns the marrow in our bones.

The Ceremonies of Innocence

On the bulletin board outside the door of the church is thumb-tacked this sheet of paper, and the citizen stops, thrusting his jaw forward in the pugnacious tilt that indicates he's using the lower lens of his bifocals, and reads it under his breath.

> We have created parishes that are in practice privileged sanctuaries serving to further suburban white segregation. . . . We have done little to equalize educational opportunities. . . . We have . . .

The document distributed to Protestant Episcopal parishes in this countryside by the Episcopal Society for Cultural and Racial Unity in the Diocese of Newark is described as a declaration and petition.

It is in fact a confession.

Addressed to the General Convention of the Episcopal Church, it confesses:

> The result of this racism at the very heart of the church's life is an inability to address its mission to the crucial issues in the life of the country.

Many Episcopalians signed it Sunday. Many didn't. The little man wearing bifocals grumbles a little, but signs, and his willingness to confess a weakness in himself and indict one in his church says something important about human nobility and aspiration.

Yet I wonder what is said about human comprehension of reality when a suburban petitioner takes forth his pen and signs his name to a statement that he hasn't done enough to equalize

243

educational opportunities. Are all of us sure we know what we're saying? Do we know what in fact ought to be done to equalize educational opportunity?

The question must be raised just as tactlessly as this because, the very Sunday the Episcopal rectors were confronting their parishioners with this confession, another commentator was suggesting people in the privileged suburban sanctuaries should do more to equalize educational opportunities—and was saying what he means.

Dr. Kenneth B. Clark, a great psychologist, a member of the New York State Board of Education, and a Negro, recommended that all of the schools in the nation's great old crowded cities be done away with and that the city children commute to school in the suburbs.

"What I think is needed is a bold, new, total, crash, imaginative approach to public school reorganization," he said. He happened to have just such an approach in his pocket.

By taking the schools and the children altogether out of the inner city, he said, we'd break the pattern now developing: city schools for the poor, suburban public schools for the middle class, parochial schools for segregated education. "One advantage of this [plan to move city children into the suburbs] would be that there would be no particular haven for middleclass whites to flee to," he said.

Dr. Clark is a careful scholar. He is capable of saying what he means.

Respectfully it will have to be asked whether he knows what he means.

The proposition that children can be educated to cope with their environment by bringing them up in a radically different environment has been around. I have never seen a responsible study indicating how the school districts—the privileged sanctuaries—of Nassau or Westchester or Rockland County would be persuaded to build the schools for the commuters from Harlem.

244

I have never seen how their people would be persuaded to vote yes on school budgets swollen by the cost of plant and personnel for the commuters.

And I have never heard a convincing demonstration that the educational problem of the ghetto child would be solved by sentencing him to spend two or three hours a day riding to the country and back in a bus. Busing is an adequate short-range solution for a problem here, a tension there, but it is not a pedagogical device. The cure for what ails the schools will not be found in confessions, indictments, or magnificent either-ors. It will have to be found in there where the children are, where they develop a sublanguage and a subculture of their own which they are compelled to develop outside the system rather than in classrooms planned and manned for other centuries and other peoples.

Journey into Hope

I have a sensitive Jewish friend who goes a curious pilgrimage from time to time—perhaps as often as once a month. When he wearies of the smell of blood and sweat, the idiot reiterations of existence, the pallid bitter razzmatazz of the struggle for survival, when he is almost sure there is no possible further excuse for the existence of the human race—that is to say, perhaps as often as once a month—he goes over to Holy Name Hospital in Teaneck and talks to the sisters.

"Then by and large you deal with the rejects, the losers," I said to Sister Mary Rosarii.

She nodded. She is small and bright, and wears rimless glasses, and has been dealing with the world's rejects for twenty-three years, and she said, "There are the bad days and good days and then terrible days, but no one is a reject until he has been rejected." Here it doesn't happen.

My friend had found me in the bruise-colored state of doubt that always comes before Christmas. I'd spent too much of an afternoon talking to a man in naval intelligence about the horror in Vietnam. He had asked his admiral how long the war will last. "If you mean this skirmish in South Vietnam, 10 years," the admiral had said contentedly. "If you mean the war for the heartland, make it 150 years." In southeast Asia my agents, scarcely more than innocent kids themselves, were killing innocent kids, and here on the highway people were killing each other in the stampede to spend money in the biggest spree an affluent society ever saw.

So he let me go a pilgrimage with him. Here we sat, the Jew and the Presbyterian, asking Sister Mary Rosarii how it is, knowing the things she knows, that she can be so sure tomorrow will be better.

"Faith" is the word she used. But I am not sure she ever did answer the question in words. To say faith, it seemed to me, merely defers the problem or transfers it to a different venue. The sisters are wonderfully articulate. But this kind of verbalization doesn't seem to enchant them. They have work to do.

Sister Mary Rosarii is director of the Hospital's department of social service. She deals, I said again, with the losers. An alcoholic son steals his waitress mother's pay check, drinks it up, then to get that off his mind thrusts her out of his speeding car. She is found three days later caked with mud and blood and frozen. "I fell," she says. Rejection? Here are the unmarried mothers, pale and defiant, the lip trembling, hated by family, disavowed by lover, spilling over in talk of abortion or suicide.

Here come the rejects wasted to bones and self-hatred by their addiction, the rejects wasted by want and malnutrition, the old, the babies born hopelessly deformed or hopelessly retarded. For too many of the unwanted babies—the illegitimate and the congenitally defective—there's no place to go. Sister Mary Rosarii and her little staff go find a place.

On the back of the door to her office is a big framed panel of pictures: beautiful children, all of them laughing now. Sometimes it turns out all right.

Once a baby was born in a cave in a dusty little town named Bethlehem, and he was one of the rejects, I guess. His father was an elderly woodworker, and his mother was young, perhaps 16, and from the accounting that lies outside the canon you take it that in Nazareth they were aware her pregnancy had given rise to insinuations. They had come down to Bethlehem for the census and tax, and they stayed, and the baby was born in a feed trough gouged in the floor.

For there was no room at the inn. And afterward the paranoid Herod would command the massacre of every male nurseling in Bethlehem aged two or less, and the baby's first memory would be of the desperate flight into Egypt, would be a memory of hardship and irrational violence and bewilderment and exile.

And specifically because he lived and died the way he did there is room at the inn here in Teaneck, of all exotic places, and there is a thing whose only name is faith but no such thing on Earth as rejection. Because of that, this; because of one life, these lives; I still don't know what faith means, but when the stars come out there is a sort of passionate intuition, and this may be as far as one pilgrimage can get.

Love It or Leave It, as Who Doesn't?

"America—Love It or Leave It!" snarled the bumper sticker on the Cadillac I was tailgating up the Turnpike, and bless me if it didn't mind me of Jack Benny's dilemma.

The holdup man brandished a pistol under Jack's nose and said, "Money or your life!"

Silence.

The holdup man said it again. Again no answer. Next time the thug said it the menace was harsh and unmistakable. "Money. Or. Your. Life."

Irritably Benny said, "Shut up. I'm thinking it over."

"America—Love It or Leave It!"—and I wonder how many more than 98 per cent of the sanctimonious dimwits lugging this ultimatum across the countryside do indeed love their country. I wonder indeed whether they know what their country consists of. I wonder, to get back to Jack Benny's dilemma, whether the kind of America they have in mind wouldn't be a pretty good place to get out of.

One would want to think it over.

As the sticker "Support Your Local Police!" is a coded warning to Negroes, "Love It or Leave It!" is a cryptogram notifying dissidents there's no room in the sign luggers' America for hippies, Yippies, campus rebels, argumentative intellectuals, draft resisters, or indeed dissent itself.

Let's see. An America without dissent would be an America without a Bill of Rights or a Supreme Court or, come to think of it, elections.

It would be a fascist America.

Love it or leave it?

One would want to think it over.

I don't know which America they're talking about. The only one of which I am aware is a country in which more than 20 per cent of the people are black and more than 50 per cent are young. It is a country which encourages disagreement and progresses by taking its choices between raucously differing propositions advanced by candidates many of whom are (cf. Norman Thomas, Eugene V. Debs, Borah, LaFollette) un-American today and laureled patriots day after tomorrow.

Now tactfully let's ask how many of the gentlefolk who wear their patriotism on their bumper really love and trust the country whose name they use.

See whether a statistic disturbs you. Early this year the United States Public Health Service reported that the United States birth rate continued in 1968 an 11-year decline, to a record low of 17.4 live births per thousand of population. The total came to 3,470,000 more or less, but the rate had dropped almost 8 percentage points in a decade, from the record 25.3 in 1957.

The Population Reference Bureau, which is research and non-government, had gathered that somebody was trying to tell us something. It had looked upon the decline of the birth rate early in 1968 and had decided that it could be attributed to the increase in the cost of living and the intensified competition in education.

That has to be a guess. So does this, which is my guess: that a certain impressive number of young people are reluctant to bring children into a world of Vietnams and antiballistic missile systems and crime and violence and pollution.

They have looked at the casualty lists from Saigon and the superhighways. They have seen the countryside vanish under a creeping tide of sleazy housing developments. They have contemplated the oil-smeared beaches of Santa Barbara and the garbage-choked streets of New York and the chains of puddles which are the rivers of August, hideous with dead fish, and the young couples have made a decision.

It is that this has become no safe place for a child.

The young distrust the country, and are told to shut up or get out.

Love is what we say. But what we act out is something like contempt. We rip down the woodlands and supplant them with reeking factories. Wherever Nature's creatures run wild in the land bequeathed to us we destroy them and not because we're hungry. Where we found majesty we put a motel. Where He leadeth us beside the still waters we leave a midden of beer cans and automobile tire carcasses and used facial tissues.

Then we go far away for a precious vacationtime respite from the horror we have made, and where we go we build hot dog stands, dams, concrete hotels, and marinas whose fleets are capable of befouling the sea itself. To escape from awareness of this insanity we take two tranquilizer pills and half a bottle of gin. Love it? Who doesn't? Leave it?

Who doesn't?

The Unfinished Pursuit

Against July 4 we've treasured up the extraordinary phenomenon —it occurs in Englewood—which is people who believe that Thomas Jefferson and the representatives of the United States of America, in General Congress assembled, knew what they meant when they said:

> We hold these truths to be self-evident: that all men are created equal: that they are endowed by their Creator with certain unalienable rights; that among these are life, liberty, and the pursuit of happiness. . . .

A lot of ingenuity and passion have been invested in trying to prove that "equal" is a figure of speech. And one is tempted to be appalled at our desperate search for metaphor in the words we live by—in holy writ and the Declaration and Constitution. When meanings are clear they annoy us, but let's get down to Englewood.

Last time the Board of Education met, the Superintendent of Schools, Harry L. Stearns, was asked if he thinks Negro children are inferior to whites. He said no. He was then asked if the teaching in the Lincoln School is inferior to teaching in other elementary schools. He said no.

A Board member shut off the cross-examination at that point. But enough had been said by then to make it clear we've an integration problem every bit as nasty, in its gemlike way, as anything in the South. And we'll not make it go away by coldly ignoring it or calling it something else.

Englewood, which used to be a city of big houses needing

250

plenty of domestic help, has a relatively high Negro population, about 25 per cent—the unassimilated leftover in the Fourth Ward of the old man-power pool.

So it has an integration problem. Districting for schools the way other towns do gave it an almost all-Negro elementary and junior high school. The State said that kind of districting must go; so new lines were set up. The colored children in the old Lincoln Junior High were sent to the Engle Street school; segregation was ended, at least until the movement of population in the town gives it another Negro school; but here came another problem. . . .

People seem to have discovered that the Negroes moved into the Engle Street schools are integrated into classes generally. There's a way to set up a school so that the bright kids are in one class, moving at its own rate; the less bright go into another class, and so on down, until you get to the least bright class. It's called homogeneous grouping.

One takes it that homogeneous grouping would have created in their new school a class grouping in which colored children would in effect have been segregated. Bluntly, they're not all of them brilliant. And in Englewood there's bitter and growing resentment because the nonbrilliant are being integrated the way the Supreme Court and the State Department of Education command they must be.

There's a case for the people who resent it. The division of children into bright and dumb classes is the pattern in Europe, and it works; educators here don't have to be told we may yet pay a grievous price for a kind of integration that tends to slow a class to the pace of its tragic gropers.

But in a town like Englewood the contrast is sharp and irritating. Englewood's not the only one, but there it shows. The bright kids in these schools of ours are the children of the nation's business and intellectual elite. The man who's picked by a corporation to be shifted from a branch office in Dubuque or a laboratory in Georgia to run the home-office operation in New York is pretty likely to be brilliant, realistic, and tough. And the genes of his breed are very rarely polluted with tolerance.

What he sees is that his dainty daughter sits in class next to a boy who looks to him uncouth, that her development—into, let's say, a Madame Curie—must wait, day after day, while the teacher tries again to explain to the colored boy what the other kids got first time around last week.

How do you tell him that integration is right and must be done now, even before such other things are done as trying through new techniques to get the most out of the gifted kids in the same classroom with the ungifted? How do you tell him that our generation must do for the Negro child—but three generations out of slavery, but five generations out of the jungle, a twinkling—what our metaphor-fancying parents refused to do? How do you tell him that there are no inferior races once any race's people are given their chance? How do you tell him Jefferson didn't mean a metaphor and freedom isn't a figure of speech and those old guys in their hour of darkness and peril and need didn't pledge their lives, their fortunes, and their sacred honor to a quibble or a pun?

The Liar Inside the Skull

Intolerance is abject foolishness, to be sure; but the Anti-Defamation League of B'nai B'rith has devised a dazzling way to let intolerant people catch themselves making fools of themselves.

In the film strip it uses at its rumor-clinic sessions is a somewhat crude drawing of a subway-car interior. There are a lot of details for watchers to notice and remember and transmit. And among these details are a squat white man with a straight razor in his hand and a tall Negro, well dressed, evidently a professional fellow.

Zvi Sobel, program director of the B'nai B'rith regional office, was telling—at the New Milford B'nai B'rith women's Brotherhood Month meeting the other night—about the characteristic switch that occurs when tangled people try to report what this picture shows.

You remember Demosthenes:

"Nothing is so easy as to deceive one's self, for what we wish we readily believe; but such expectations are often inconsistent with the reality of things."

But people keep finding it hard to believe what they do to themselves at the rumor clinics. The film strip being finished, they set out soberly and seriously to describe what the picture showed them. There's this white chap, and there's this big Negro, and the Negro has a razor in his hand. The witness saw not what's there but what he intended to see. One night Zvi Sobel clicked the film back to the original picture, showing the white man holding the razor.

"That's what I said," a woman crowed. "The colored man has the razor."

Mr. Sobel went over to the picture, and pointed at the razor in the white man's hand.

"The colored man has the razor," she repeated. She is not insane, blind, or ill meaning. That is what she saw.

Every lawyer is familiar with the six earnest eyewitnesses who at the identical time and the identical place saw six different automobile accidents, totaling one in all. That's a trick we make our memory play us. What Zvi Sobel was talking about is the trick we make our very eyeballs play, our sense receptors, our sacred cortex itself.

In September 1950 a man named Fred Goodell, Jr., killed his baby, a querulous six-month-old named Nancy, and put the body in a paper bag and stuffed it under a rock on Garret Mountain. Then he reported her kidnapped. Next morning the police started talking to the neighbors about Nancy. One of them, a kindly oldish woman, said she'd been past the Goodell house on her way to the store just a few minutes ago, and there was Nancy as usual in her carriage, gurgling away cute as pie. The baby had been dead at least twelve hours. The witness had just seen her—not an empty baby carriage; the baby. She took a lie-detector test, and passed. That's what she saw.

When as a Deputy Attorney-General in charge of the State's enforcement office Nelson F. Stamler at last got a line on the guy who had been running a dice game in Lakewood a while before, he took no chances on a sour identification. With infinite craft he got pictures of the man at work—a slight twisted citizen with a hooked nose and an oddly hooked little finger.

Mr. Stamler rounded up witnesses by the dozen, and they swore Mr. Stamler's pictures were pictures of the very Harry Goldsmith who had run the games in the hotel at Lakewood. The hotel manager took his oath. Policemen took their oath. The case was airtight.

Stamler sent for Harry Goldsmith, to confront him with the charge and his accusers.

It was quite a pursuit story, but Nelson finally got the man he wanted for operating the game at Lakewood. Ran him down in prison at Montreal. Harry Goldsmith had been in a cell there for the last ten years, and had never been within 100 miles of Lakewood in his life.

In that case people were not only insisting they had seen something that was never there but insisting the camera saw it too.

Perhaps the shocking and incommunicable gift of the poet and the scientist is to see what's there, no more, no less; perhaps that's the difference between them and clucks like us, who are doomed—physically, in fact, not metaphor—to see the lie inside our mind, to run over and over through the falsehood we're stuck with. The first and worst of frauds is to cheat oneself, snarled the abolitionist Gamaliel Bailey; after that all sin is easy; but you ought to put yourself through the rumor clinic and see.

And Sometimes the Luck Runs Out

We are fortunate, Fred Morrow had said at lunch.

The road back to the shop from Petrullo's, where the Rotary Club meets, runs through the Negro district—the old Negro district.

It was a windy day, bright and sharp and cold. On the sidewalk in front of the saloon the shabby men were standing, as they always do, winter, summer, rain or shine. They aren't going anywhere. They aren't doing anything. They stand there and just be.

To the Hackensack Rotary Club had said brilliant young E. Frederic Morrow, vice-president for public affairs of the African-American Institute:

> We are fortunate to have among us a race of people who can put our system to its test. . . . The Negro is the acid test of democracy. If it cannot work for him here and now it cannot work for anybody else anywhere else.

He said much more than that, did this distinguished son of a distinguished family that grew up in the old-block district. He said much more.

He said there is no longer room in this country or this world for detached islands, be they persons or ghettos or States or continents.

He said the colored people of the world, whom he knows as well as does any man in the country, understand the stark reality: if the dignity of man is true at all it has to be true entirely, it has to be true for the least of these the brethren of us all.

He said a nation, like a man, must have an inner peace if it is to be healthy.

Out of his experience in the field for the National Association

255

for the Advancement of Colored People, in broadcasting, in the office next to Dwight D. Eisenhower's in the White House, in the mansions of the Presidents and prime ministers of the emerging countries, Fred Morrow reminded us we're guilty and we know it and we're not the only ones who know it.

Listening to him, you couldn't help recalling Lincoln's warning:

"Those who deny freedom to others deserve it not for themselves, and, under a just God, cannot long retain it."

But Mr. Morrow had said we are fortunate that we have the Negro there to function, just by being there, as a test of us. Yet, going past the saloon on any shabby street where the men stand waiting—for what?—how often does any of us in the world's dwindling white minority reflect on how miraculously fortunate we are?

After Little Rock mused John Steinbeck:

I am constantly amazed at the qualities we expect in Negroes. No race has ever offered another such high regard. We expect Negroes to be wiser than we are, more tolerant than we, braver, more dignified than we, more self-controlled and self-disciplined. We even demand more talent from them than from ourselves. A Negro must be 10 times as gifted as a white to receive equal recognition. We expect Negroes . . . to be more courteous, more gallant, more proud, more steadfast. In a word, while maintaining that Negroes are inferior to us, by our unquestioning faith in them we prove our conviction that they are superior. . . .

We are astounded, as some of the Rotarians were, when we find that a Negro remembers bitterly the way he was treated, as Nkrumah of Ghana remembers what happened to him when he was a student in this country. We are appalled when a Negro remembers and says, after Shylock, "Why, revenge! The villainy you teach me, I will execute, and it shall go hard, but I will better the instruction." We wonder why Nkrumah does not believe us when we tell him about democracy. We have been taught by gentle men who love us deeply, like Fred Morrow, that if on

Route 40 in Maryland a Negro stopping on his way from the White House to the United Nations and asking for a glass of water is hurt and turned away by a white swine he will be compassionate enough not to notice.

We are fortunate in the Negro's patience and his pity and his willingness to think well of us, and the universality of that willingness supports the possibility there is such a thing as a race instinct.

We are fortunate that the Negro runs the test by reporting at the school, asking for the job, going into the restaurant, taking a seat in the bus or the train. Like the shabby men in the street, last to be hired and first to be fired, he makes the tests, and he waits, and it never occurs to him to do unto us as he has been done by.

A just God might not be so patient.

The Invisible Man Who Does the Talking

If you think "gallant" is too jaunty a word for the job the people in Temple Beth Sholom did on prejudice the other night, go thou and do likewise.

It may be the hardest work in the world. It may be impossible.

They're having a series of what they call introspective panel discussions. That night as Jews they tackled the subject "The Prejudices of, Not against, the Jew"—and be it entered to their immediate credit that they acknowledged there's a bizarre lot of anti-Semitism among Jews.

Not far from where they were meeting in New City is the Village of New Square, which enjoys a relatively high incidence of highly orthodox Jews.

Said panelist Judd Goldgeier:

"Some of us are embarrassed because the people in New

Square, with their wide-brimmed hats and long hair, don't conform to the Ivy League image."

And the introspectors courageously speculated whether Jewish attitudes are imposed on the Jew by the community or are imposed by the Jew on himself in anticipation of what might otherwise be imposed. They examined the hierarchy of Jewish elites, the way in which each successive wave of immigration produces its low man for the totem pole. "Gallant" is not too jaunty a word for it.

What's astonishing in the Temple community's doing this thing at all is that a respectable collegium of scholars will tell you it's impossible to detect prejudice from the inside. A culture can't criticize itself—it takes an anthropologist, examining it from the outside and subjecting it to comparison with other cultures, to comment coherently on a society. There's another analogy. You can't psychoanalyze yourself—in the very process of trying, you drive your problems into hiding.

Run your own experiment. What are your prejudices? I have here one doughnut that says you'll find on careful examination that you have no prejudices at all.

You do, to be sure, entertain a few well developed opinions, all of which are corroborated by scientific evidence and the testimony of history, horse sense, and human nature. But prejudice? I have yet to meet the man who began a dissertation with the acknowledgment that he was prejudiced.

Prejudice? Every man born under the United States flag knows he can look any other man in the eye and tell him to go to hell, and yet I have noticed that nobody laughs immoderately at the bad jokes of the poor. We none of us judge a man by his appearance, which accounts not only for interracial-neighborhood blockbusting but for the difference between the way the doorkeeper treats the man who gets out of the back seat of a Rolls-Royce and the way he deals with the man who parks his own 1956 Dodge. Our respect and love for wise old age is such that by overwhelming national consensus we characterize it as a social problem, and so wide and warm is our affection for our children that "teen-ager" has become a synonym of "delinquent."

I am trying to talk about the ways in which prejudice sings its wry little songs without words.

We consent that people who can trace the family tree back to the *Mayflower* or the Revolution are the betters of people whose family came over in 1910 or last week, and we are shocked when some irreverent outsider points out that the better part of the old family tree is the part that's underground. We revere the law, despise policemen, consider all lawyers crooked, and regard judges as mere lawyers who've banked enough cabbage to take a cut in pay. We reverence women and make sex the dirtiest and most popular of all subject matter. The second most popular is politics, at which each of us is an expert until he becomes expert enough to be a professional, at which point he becomes a numskull and a swindler.

Our prejudices speak for themselves because there's nobody to talk for them. There is more in the success of the blond Texan pianist Van Cliburn than can be accounted for in his piano playing, and even in the desegregated professional sports something about prejudice may be trying to mutter itself in the fact that, brilliant and intelligent as are Negro backfield men, not one plays T-formation quarterback.

A prejudice, which is nothing but a vagrant opinion without visible means of support, does happen to be a self-curing ailment once it is diagnosed. Merely to ask yourself why you have it is enough to make you realize you don't want it. But from inside a man's own skin his prejudices are undetectable.

My own prejudices? I have no more of them than you—about 210 all told. I wish I knew what they are.

Nothing to Lose but Your Symbols

If your town has its Negro ghetto, don't be ashamed of it; enjoy it while you can; the ghetto is a status symbol for whites.

At a conference in Chicago so says Dr. Kenneth B. Clark, professor of psychology at the City College of New York. The theme of the conference, called by the National Committee against Discrimination in Housing, was "A Thousand Harlems." Its objective was to define ways of breaking up the ghetto.

Dr. Clark is a national figure with a couple of local angles. He gets around a lot out our way. Of the thousand Harlems he has seen we've one each in Englewood, Hackensack, and Teaneck; a big and growing one in Paterson; a scattering in Rockland County.

The ghetto helps whites take their mind off their own problems [he said]. They talk about all those terrible illegitimate kids in the central city, and they forget all about the abortions in their own gilded ghettos.

He is a Negro, tall and very literate (his study of segregation and its effect on children was one of the Supreme Court's guides toward the 1954 decision), and he tends to talk with the Clark tongue tucked snug in the Clark cheek.

He went to school in Harlem.

"I thank the Lord my teachers didn't know I was culturally deprived," he told Teaneck teachers at a workshop in human relations just two years ago. "If they had, I might never have learned a damned thing."

And he could tell you what he meant: educators have no time for educating children in ghettos because they're too busy thinking up labels for them ("culturally deprived" or "disadvantaged") and explaining to each other why such children cannot

260

be taught (poor environment, broken home, illiteracy in the home environment). So by the time ghetto children get to third grade 30 per cent of them are below their grade level in reading and by the time they've had the advantage of six grades of prejudice disguised as sociology or sympathy 80 per cent of them can't make grade level.

He wondered out loud whether the children might be better off if they didn't go to school. Even away back in 1963 it was a startling view of the dropout problem. He specializes in startling views. "The school people make sure that very few of their prisoners escape the schools unscathed," he said at Chicago.

He deals in paradox, and surprise is an element of any paradox, but is there anything novel in what he reports, is there anything we didn't know?

What is a Negro ghetto? "An involuntary prisonlike confinement that destroys and dehumanizes powerless people."

How does the ghetto happen? Ghettos are not accidental, he says, but are planned and maintained by the use of the power of government.

The white man's government? "Negro politicians are as much a part of the conspiracy as white politicians—in fact, they often work in concert to exploit the ghettos economically."

He said it, and it made headlines in Chicago, but what in it is news—how much of it can't you confirm out of your own experience, however limited?

In a thousand Harlems the prisoners stand on street corners staring out at nothing, dehumanized and powerless. That's the way it is. That's the way it's wanted. Dr. Clark is bitter. Isn't that just like them?

He and the other specialists summoned to the conference said something can be done. The Los Angeles County Commission on Human Relations is moving Negro families into areas only a few blocks from the periphery of the ghetto so as to overcome a characteristic hesitancy to go first into an all-white neighborhood. Apartments can be opened in places where private housing can't. Picket lines sometimes work. When they don't sometimes prayer does.

But the key, said Dr. Clark, is to convince the nervous white man who owns a little house that he won't lose status if the ghetto in his town is broken up.

All he'd lose would be a status symbol. What's surprising is the number of culturally undeprived people who'd feel lost without it.

Walls, Sprawls, and the Old Refrain

Governor Hoff was speaking now of the wall that makes a ghetto of the world outside it.

In the end [he said], the solutions of the problems of megalopolis are going to have to emanate from private interests—in particular, from the private citizen.

And you wondered again how often we shall have to go through the stately old ritual. How often must we rise and chant it?

> The status quo is brutality;
>   We must change it; to arms; let's start!
> But we can't legislate morality—
>   It'll have to come from your heart.

Year after year we intone it. We name the evil du jour. We agree it must be eliminated. We decide it cannot be eliminated by law. We then adjourn the meeting. This is a mistake.

Governor Philip M. Hoff of Vermont was addressing the National Housing Conference at Washington on the injustices that are brought about in the name of home rule.

Here's the megalopolis, a vast blob of a city sprawled across the face of the Earth from Boston to Washington. Within it are

262

a half dozen States, hundreds of counties, thousands of municipalities. Some are rich. More are poor. Some solve their problems in education and public service—health, safety, law enforcement. More don't. By a powerful federal government we are compelled to provide for the common defense against external enemies. But against the internal enemies whose names are crime and delinquency, illiteracy, blight, sprawl, and the meaninglessness of life, each town is pretty much on its own. That's home rule.

Mr. Hoff had just paid a visit to what he described as a better community in New York State. He didn't give its name. Its people, he said, work in New York City, get their culture in New York City, yet want no part in the problems of New York City. Governor Hoff said:

> They build nice walls around their community, and will fight the world to maintain [the walls]. . . . Such practice leads to provincialism, which is not fair financially, and the solution will not come about until we have broken down the political lines that make the provincial attitudes possible.

He said that, and three horizon-rattling cheers for it, but then he said the solutions can come only from the heart of the individual citizen. And it becomes necessary to point out that no walls ever came tumbling down at the sound of this uncertain trumpet.

For more scores of years than it is pleasant to remember, every effort to write into law the Negro's right to decent treatment was frustrated by that pious irrelevancy. Only now, after 100 years, are we learning to blurt out the truth of the matter, which is that it doesn't make a particle of difference how your heart is disposed toward the Negro. The state of your morality isn't even interesting. What matters and what can be written into law is that no one may legally translate into overt action his prejudices or his primitive hostilities and fears.

The law doesn't forbid prejudice or hatred. It forbids kicking people around.

263

And the news is that the crazy thing works. With the help of the law and despite the mysteries of the human heart, the Negro is making it.

Someday the United States Supreme Court will find a way of construing the language of the Constitution to mean people cannot be deprived of equality in access to good education, to safety in the streets, to stability in the character of their community, by an accident of geography. A child must not be penalized for life because his folks settled in a town that hates schools or can't afford them rather than in the town next door that's proud of its schools.

Justice to people requires that as great regional entities we zone for land use, impose taxes fairly on all the people in the region, and distribute them in such a way as to equalize the conditions under which we live. We have come at last to the point at which we admit all this. We have even come to the point of sighing that line about morality and the heart. I guess that means the war is over, settled in our favor, but there are a lot of bloody battles left to fight.

The Revolution of the Meatballs

The thrust of the Supreme Court decisions leading from Gideon through Escobedo to Miranda has been grievously misunderstood. Police officials, persons dedicated to the support of their local police and ridding Rutgers of Reds, and impeachers of Earl Warren insist on construing these limpid clarifications of the Amendments as decisions favoring the criminal element, the dregs of society, as against our kind of folks.

They may be a little capricious politically in the way such socialists as Henry Ford III, George Romney, and Laurance Rockefeller are. But they are our kind of folks. It is time to suggest the possibility they are writing the decisions for our kind of folks.

They are well aware of the disadvantages that have been inflicted on their kind of folks by 6,000 or so years of the Judeo-Greek-Christian ethic. They know how wretchedly a lifetime of self-disciplined good citizenship can wither a man's survival instinct.

They know, for instance, that at some magic moment during the summer you'll be lying on some beach groping to re-establish your relationship with your mother the sea. Along will come a brawling teen-ager who will kick sand on your sandwiches, bounce a nine-pound beach ball off your cranium, shatter a bottle of beer at a place where it will not fail in due time to amputate one of your toes, snatch your towel to dry himself, and sit down under your umbrella to play rock music as a decibel threshold over which to carry on conversation in a shout.

Your impulse, which will be correct, will be to go steal a baseball bat from another teen-ager and return and beat your teen-ager's roof in.

Throughout your life you have been resisting such impulses, partly because you have equated nonviolence with the state of being civilized but mainly because you've been afraid you'd be caught. Gideon-Escobedo-Miranda opens a breathtaking news vista to folks like us. Duly we proceed to knock all the meat off the little fiend's bones. Along come the johns. They ask whether we are responsible for all these bones and entrails. Resist the damnable middleclass itch to say yes and lug in the extenuating circumstances. Instead, ask the policeman whether he has taken care to safeguard your rights under the Fourth, Fifth, and Sixth Amendments, not to mention peripherally the Fourteenth. With a little practice you may find that by offering the man a cigarette coolly and pausing before you ask whether he has called your lawyer—you may find you can suggest to him that unless he pulls up his socks he might be placed under citizen's arrest for criminal neglect of duty.

Don't wince or wilt when he asks whether you don't want to help the police. The correct answer is:

"I'm trying to help you stay out of trouble, my friend. Have you arranged for my bail, or shall we just forget the whole of your unfortunate behavior?"

The middle class has been victimized by professional criminals occupying the socioeconomic strata both below it and above because the sense of guilt is built into middleclass people. The average man submits to muggings by his social and physical inferiors because he's afraid he might hurt his assailant. We let ourselves be bullied by hitchhikers, shoplifters, hotel employees, burglars, theater ushers, and dope addicts so sick they could not vanquish a chipmunk in hand to hand encounter.

The Supreme Court has stricken from the wrists of a whole people the shackles of a priori guilt by bringing into the open the central question:

Guilty of what? How are they going to prove it?

Your defense of your person and sanity against the evils converging on you is to shatter and remake your image of yourself. Face the world uncowed. Think of yourself as a criminal.

The Monster that Cleared the Slums

One of these days, when the oil wells gurgle dry and we're all cut back to one-lung motor bikes running on banana squeezings and fried eels, people are going to be wonderfully nostalgic about the automobile.

They affect now to hate everything related to the internal-combustion engine, from strabismic four-eyed headlights to tail fins and exhaust smog, but then they'll sit on the porch of the motel—converted into a rest home for the thirty-five-up elderly —and talk about high old times in the family car.

Your reporter would just like to have it remembered that, in a peculiarly complicated way, he got sentimental first about the automobile.

"Remember?" people will begin; and the things they remember will be the homely little things—the time Pa was waltzing down to Hoboken for a cigar and ran over the old lady, the kids' running up to Rockland County of a summer evening to get stoned on German beer, the drag races on the toll roads at 2 A.M., the picnics on the highway islands in faraway Paramus.

It is petitioned some one try to recall we pointed out that the automobile came very close to doing what could not be done by all the forces and techniques of government and private enterprise, what could perhaps not be done by any other agency short of a nuclear bomb.

It came close to clearing central cities of their slums.

Jouncing in a bus across midtown New York the other afternoon, we began to see things we didn't know were there: whole blocks away, there'd be great sleek strange buildings in stone of many colors; and, having grown unashamed of our indomitable ignorance, we'd keep asking people questions.

Finally a man said:

"Most of the buildings have been here for years. What hasn't been here is the parking space. Last time you were here there was a slum between you and that view of the town. They took the slum down."

We said we suppose a high-turnover parking lot actually yields a higher cash return to the owner than even a cold-water tenement.

"About that I wouldn't know," the man said. "I do know they had to find some place to put the cars."

And he repeated the dictum—goes all the way back to the last report of the Metropolitan Rapid Transit Commission, we believe—to the effect that if the railroads keep killing themselves off and everybody coming into town by rail has to commute by car New York will need to convert into parking space the

267

equivalent of all the land between the Battery and Forty-second Street.

Oddly, this rather violent idea seemed attractive. One would like to salvage City Hall, parts of Greenwich Village, the Metropolitan Opera, and the Circle in the Square on condition it revive "The Iceman Cometh."

Look around your own town. Hackensack had to get off the street shoppers' cars—didn't somebody tell us once they'd total 125,000 any 24 hours of a big week-end?—and so it has dug into the middle of its midtown blocks, swept out the mountains of packing crates and rats and mud, and put the parking plazas there. Ridgewood did the same, and so did Westwood and the Twin Boroughs. You can now look across what—sentimentally —can be called vistas, and there are slants of light and rain or mist in which what you see is not too far from beautiful.

Let's not deceive ourselves about the slums and junk that had to give way to metered parking stalls. You can kill off a slum. You don't kill off the people who lived in it. And making room for a car where people used to sleep eight in a room doesn't necessarily improve the people's earning capacity or social assimilability. All you've ever done is to kick the slum out of that part of town and made it go settle down in another part or another town.

But that seems to have become a constant in any kind of clearance. It may be that the slum problem—or call it the ghetto problem—is so inextricably tangled in all other problems of government, city management, finance, overpopulation, stupidity, and beastliness that we'll never get it solved.

All we're arguing now is that the automobile, for all its arrogance and inefficiency, for all its shouldering and blustering and like bad manners, did open the heart of the city and let us see that it was not so bad as we'd thought. Would it be shocking to say thanks?

Settlement of a Wager

Martin Luther King, Jr., bet his life that the Negro could make his way into the mainstream of life in the United States by means of nonviolence, and he lost.

So a just cause has its martyr duly crucified, and it remains to be seen whether his truth goes marching on—or whether the doctrine of love and hope and gentleness which he preached and died for was ever the truth at all.

We had better not lapse into any such orgy of self-laceration as distorted the reality and trivialized the event when John F. Kennedy was murdered in Dallas.

Mea culpa, then cried tens of millions who had nothing on their conscience except the comprehension that not enough had been done to make the world conform to the bright young dream Kennedy had enunciated. It was not the truth. Kennedy had died the victim of our hate, we said, luxuriating in our confession, and everything we did from then on made liars of us.

The ultimate proof came forward instantly. Kennedy had been loved. We had not repudiated his dream. The stutter of the funeral drums had scarcely stopped echoing when the new President and the Congress proceeded to write into law all—but all—of the social legislation Kennedy had planned for the rest of his eight years in the White House.

In his death he had triumphed.

The analogy should not be pressed. But it should be borne in mind. The difference between the contexts of the two assassinations is wide, and the difference has been made clear by the report from the President's Commission on Civil Disorder.

At the time of Dallas the crisis was years away. Now it is at hand. At the time of Dallas the thing most to be feared was callous repudiation of the white's contract with the Negro, signed 100 years before in the blood of the Civil War. The thing most to be feared now is the cleavage of the country into two societies, one white and one black, one having unlimited access to the good life and one herded into its dismal warrens and kept in repression under the guns of the superrace's police, both irreconcilably hostile. The danger is civil war. In a nation that affords any man with the price of a gun access to his private arsenal, the danger is sudden death. Nobody is immune.

Against such a hardening of hostilities Dr. King had bet his life.

There will be a time when, collecting and absorbing the totality of his work and works, we shall be able to appreciate more passionately the immense grandeur of this simple man. He was a prophet, and he knew it, and alone among the statesmen of his time he dared to utter his vision in the unabashed language of poetry. He had become a legend in his time. In the years to come he will come to tower over his time. It is a way martyrs have when their cause is just.

Unless!

Dr. King will be immortal, unless the justice of his cause requires that memory of him be suppressed in a society which cannot afford to acknowledge that he was right.

Legally, the black is the equal of the white; socially and economically, he is inferior, not by reason of personal worth or genetics or traceable reason but by reason of an idiotic habit.

Idiotic habit pulled the trigger in Memphis. Let's not generalize the responsibility for any murder. Whenever blood is shed, in a kitchen brawl or on a battlefield, our hands are stained to some extent, but we cannot accept individualized blame for all human villainy.

Yet the death of Dr. King cannot be extricated from involvement in the cause he led. And the cause—the development of the struggle from reform to peaceful revolution—is intertwined in the life of each of us, white and black.

270

In the name of all the martyrs let no man yet say the assassination has proved that nonviolence will not work. Give Dr. King a chance to prove his case.

The black power he sought was a simple thing, so naive and innocent, so naked that it embarrasses most men and women to say its name. Its name is, for God's sake, love.

He bet his life.

Before we give way to rage and bitter tears let us beseech ourselves to consider the possibility that we won his bet.

WHO LET THIS BUM INTO THE HOUSE?

Who Let This Bum into the House?

It's embarrassing, and I suppose the lapse is attributable to my bad habit of having birthdays so often, but doggoned if I would ever have recognized this barrel-chested, bullet-headed, bemedaled goon that's lumbering around introducing himself as my government.

He's a government that has interests separate from mine, as in southeast Asia, which—for reasons he is not disposed to divulge—he will not explain. He is the law. For my own good he will sick his spies on me, tap my telephone, arrest me without a warrant, lock me in preventive custody, and charge me if I squawk with doing irreparable damage to the national security.

His powers are hereditary, like crown jewels, and so are the mistakes which he has established as loyalty tests. If you would die in defense of the mistakes made by this government's great-great-granddaddy you're loyal. If not you are engaged in treason.

He is stupid. In the suppression proceedings against the *New York Times* and the *Washington Post* the government said its classification of secret documents is absolute and final, the ultimate wisdom, and when Judge Gurfein looked at the documents and said fiddlesticks the government said that naturally the classifications will be reviewed and revised. He is vain. When the appeals judges asked what injury has been done by the publication of the Pentagon papers so far the United States Attorney in New York replied that the government's rights as author of a literary work had been infringed.

Who the blazes is this blubbery impostor? Even now that he has introduced himself I do not recognize him.

Lay the mistake to an unsystematic upbringing among wild-eyed Middle Western conservatives, and it still seems to me that the concept of government as a person having rights and privileges arrogated to itself for private reasons of its own is a novel and ominous concept. As I was given to understand the relationship, government was the creature of a contract between you and me. It was what we agreed it was. Its powers were limited and transient.

And its capacity to do harm was carefully divided among three jealous and competing branches having built-in incentives to keep each other sawed down to size.

Get a scholar to tell you when that tripartite system fell apart —maybe in the thirties and forties, when F.D.R. made the judicial branch an annex of the executive department, maybe in the sixties, when L.B.J. went to war without asking the legislative for a declaration or even telling Congress and the people what he was doing and they were paying for in blood and money.

But perish it did, and in its place here's the Big Brother government, the jealous author government, the keyhole-peeping government, this parvenu monarch that said in two circuit courts last week he'd be glad to sit down with the press and renegotiate its freedom under the First Amendment.

I do not love this stranger.

The multiplying cases of de facto censorship are important not only because they involve the freedom to know on which the purity of democracy depends but because they test the competence of this new government to control the flow of information for reasons of its own on mere allegation, not proof, of clear and present danger.

No matter how the Supreme Court decides the cases, even if the *Times* and the *Washington Post* and umpteen other defendant newspapers prevail, the First Amendment has been badly damaged as of now, and—worse—the government has established its power to stalk into the newspaper shop and stop the presses.

Where does that end?

They're saying in some of the cities that this is likely to be another long, hot summer. Unemployment, which the Detroit 1967 riot investigations found to be the detonator in any explosive situation, is up in the cities—to 40 per cent among black teen-agers. Dope addiction is up. Hope is down.

So much can be reported safely. But go one more step, and listen for the footfall on the stairs.

Now suppose some busybody newspaper team finds the city —the state, government—is buying gas and Mace, tanks, field artillery. And suppose that in good conscience, toward the prevention of bloodshed and havoc or toward the investment of tax money in humane and efficacious ways of reducing tension— suppose the newspaper writes the story and prepares to publish it.

There's the footfall, and here's the chief of police with a temporary restraining order forbidding publication of the copy and the supporting documents such as bonding ordinances and city council resolutions. Publication of this inflammatory stuff would endanger relations, prevent the deployment of forces according to secret plan, in a word confront the government with irreparable demage to its interests.

Farfetched? I wish it were. I wish it were melodramatic and fanciful to suppose the day might come, once we grant this monster standing and a soul of its own, when government could prevent the publication of contract awards and no-show job appointments and shakedown and graft and the other absolute corruptions to which absolute power is subject. But unless we toss that swaggering bum out of here it may be later than you think.

A Hollow at the Heart

It may be as some fear: that freedom, grown old and tired and being blinded by the storm, is staggering toward its Valley Forge. It may be that its champions are dwindling away by reason of death or desertion or sheer exhaustion.

Probable? No.

But possible—that, beset by predatory Communism to its Left and by indigenous illiterates and fascists to its Right, freedom might one day need a plan for surviving a bitter winter of siege and training before it could emerge and fight? It is possible.

This appears to be the possibility that was uneasily contemplated by a task force of educators and legal specialists at a 3-day seminar in Warrenton, Va., ending November 18, and I should like to interpolate that I use the term "task force" under protest. In less than twenty fleeting years we have reduced this once useful device to junk. See "decimate," "internecine," "psychological moment," "protagonist," "hectic," "dilemma," and "to the Nth degree." Oh, well, the task force—sponsored by the Civil Liberties Educational Foundation and chaired by Supreme Court Justice William O. Douglas—decided that the public schools are falling far short of their basic responsibility to teach the meaning of the Bill of Rights.

I also object to the verb "chair." I wish some one would appoint a task force to improve the education of educators. But this is no time for hobbies.

The question, which is serious, is whether, once we ever let the Bill of Rights wither away—now the unpopular Fifth, next the inconvenient First, then in turn the integrationist Fourteenth or the criminal-coddling Fourth—the rights could ever be reconstituted.

The Warrenton seminarians found two indictments.

I.

Surveys of secondary-school curricula leave us in no doubt that education in the principles of a free democracy is a backwater, both in terms of time committed to it and [in terms of] the care and thought devoted to its method. . . .

II.

Other surveys of student and adult opinion disclose a lamentable ignorance of both the content and the history of the Bill of Rights and a dangerous indifference to its application to current issues.

Startlingly but properly this grand jury refused to vote a bill against teachers and administrators. The schools are an organ of the whole community, it said, reflecting the climate of the community and the disposition of the citizenry as a whole. With this latter party it dealt severely:

The root of the present shortcomings seems to lie in a fear of controversy. From an educational standpoint this is especially unfortunate. Nothing is more closely attuned to the educational process than the probing of controversial public questions, for nothing serves better to demonstrate the immediate relation between the classroom and the world outside its walls.

Once more is raised the interesting and offensive question that sometimes troubles the sleep of judges and law-school professors: If we had the Constitution to do all over again, would it ever be ratified in the twentieth century United States?

Over its vast uneven surface the Bill of Rights is exciting, and the subject should excite people themselves living through the crises of Mississippi, of Government seizure of the news as a propaganda agency, of the witch hunters' howling that men must be made to incriminate themselves, of Bobby Kennedy's insistence that the Fourth is all right as long as it doesn't interfere with his wiretapping. I should think it would be impossible to discuss the subject without setting a classroom afire.

But at the heart of the Bill of Rights is a matter even more controversial.

279

As T. V. Smith has said, the Constitution is about the things men do, about their right to do. The Bill of Rights concerns itself with the right to be. Again and again, in Amendment after Amendment, it insists that a man is more than a citizen, a soldier, a trader, a judge, a consumer. It insists that within himself he is private, individual, and absolute. "[The Bill of Rights] conferred as against government the right to be let alone—the most comprehensive of rights and the right most valued by civilized men," said Justice Brandeis.

We importune the children that they prepare to acquit themselves like free men.

And we neglect to tell them what a free man is. We forget to tell them the name of the right we expect them to cherish and defend at any Valley Forge.

Don't blame the school. The school is you.

Eavesdropper's Invasion of His Own Privacy

When brawny Jack Ackerson (American Legion card C752429) shows me in the March issue of *The American Legion Magazine* an advertisement for a parabolic microphone that amplifies sound 1 million times, retails at $18.95, and bears the trade name The Snooper, why, I share Jack Ackerson's sense of shock and anger.

Scarcely three hours later I wonder what I'm laughing about.

Eavesdropping is a nasty business. The very archness in the text of the ad intensifies the nastiness.

World's only private listening device; aim it at a group of friends a block away and hear every word. . . . Just think of the ways you can use this. . . . The best part—a regular tape recorder can be plugged into the back to take everything down. Have fun!

And eavesdropping is the fastest growing nasty business in the country:

Microphones in the martini olives, government tracers on your mail, laser devices that throw a picture of you and what you're doing on a television screen blocks away, experts whose assignment is to pick over your garbage and wastebasket, tape recorders hooked into your sweetie's telephone, oldfangled mikes under your bed, bugs in your walls—and on the market this month are two books telling you how to plug in on what other people are thinking. Aim your sixth sense at a group of friends 500 miles away and hear every word. Have fun!

Intellectually you are convinced that the national passion for snooping is repellent.

But there's a mystic line of cleavage at which the whole menace shatters into silliness. Yes, the advertisements in magazines and newspapers for reflector mikes and wire taps are alarming enough to warrant the Commerce Department's present speculation whether it shouldn't recommend legislation prohibiting inter-State shipment of privacy-invading gadgets. But the evil is self-limiting, isn't it?

We are approaching a saturation point. When we get to it, everybody will be bugging everybody else. I wonder, three hours after the flush of anger subsides, what's new. I wonder whether we may not be conferring more attention than it's worth on a not unfamiliar civilized activity called scandal-mongering.

The danger created by the proliferation of electronic bugging devices is not that some excitable Legionnaire will find out something about me which in a less favored century I could have kept secret. Long ago I adjusted myself to the grim fact that what people say about me is true. It is based on an immoral certainty. What could a man deduce from my mail or my telephone conversation that he wouldn't have gathered from my behavior? No; the danger in snooping's becoming fashionable is that we'll all get so busy impersonating counterespionage that we'll never get any work done. The day is dawning: 180 million people glued to their

281

earplugs, sitting there in the cellar hour after hour, listening to each other breathe. The search for subversives will destroy the national economy.

To what purpose is all the snooping? In the oceanic mass of any day's private affairs there's scarcely an atom of useful information. Through the kindness of an engineer now dead and presumably roasting, I was permitted once to listen to a tapped conversation between a distinguished criminal wintering in Florida and his resident agent in New York. They talked about horses. Now and then they'd ask each other if that fella ever did anything about that there. It was the dullest morning I ever spent outside a hospital. I had to labor hours overtime to catch up on work neglected. I felt like a heel. I resented being seduced into the glum adventure. My eavesdropping was an invasion of my rights. The eavesdropper himself is the most pathetic victim of eavesdropping. Have what fun?

I don't want to wreck a burgeoning industry, but eavesdropping is a damnable bore. I overhear conversations all the time, and so do you, and what would you pay for an electronic device that would make the clatter absolutely inaudible?

The Angry Young Men

One morning the foreman was found shot to death in the parking lot.

"You know, Joe," said the police detective, "it isn't a young man's fault that he does what you did here. From my own experience I know that a lot of people ask to get shot."

Joe was a seventeen-year-old. He worked the 4-to-12 shift. Max, the stiff, had been foreman on that shift. Joe and Max had been yakking at each other for months. Joe was the suspect. But until this detective came on to the job Joe had just sat there denying any part of the murder.

The detective could see how it was. Max was riding Joe, trying to get him fired, as he'd done before to dozens of other teen-agers. But Joe was no mouse.

"Just tell me he forced you to do it," the detective said, "because that's a lot different from shooting him just for the hell of it. That's what happened, isn't it; he forced you into it, didn't he?"

Joe was no mouse. He confessed the murder.

The story is told in the June 1960 issue of *The Prosecutor's Digest,* which is published for policemen by the Bergen County Prosecutor's Office but which is a work of social criticism that deserves the respectful attention of philosophers and statesmen. This time, in a digest of a piece out of the journal *Law and Order,* it is telling policemen how to interrogate juvenile suspects—but it could be telling a much broader audience what goes on in the juvenile mind.

Bear in mind that *The Prosecutor's Digest* is talking about mechanics, not psychological or sociological doctrine:

> Whether adults are ready to admit it or not, . . . many youths resent their elders because they feel that the older persons have not accomplished anything in this world and are not capable of controlling their own emotions. Furthermore, youths believe that adults are not able to understand and guide young people.

So in one of the case studies the detective puts it to his suspect this way:

> I agree with you that most older people are not right and usually do not know what they're talking about. Most adults can't even think for themselves, and certainly they can't think for others. But . . .

But, the detective says—putting the problem on a brisk workmanlike basis of pure self-interest—the kid he's questioning, Jerry, is in a jam, and the detective wants to help him out of his jam, and if Jerry doesn't accept the offer he'll wind up a couple of weeks or months hence in prison or a morgue.

Jerry didn't want to talk. But he gathered that he and the detective had so much in common—their hatred of adults—that he could trust the man. He confessed.

Is the detective a wretched hypocrite? "When they pay you peanuts for all the work you're doing here, it's only natural for a normal person to make it up taking, right?" So the detective began with Ralph. "Ralph, that's just what you were doing, just making up for your poor pay, wasn't it?" It was.

Says the *Digest*:

> The high cost of cars and spare parts, the desire for clothes, and the need for money for dates are the most common reasons why youths steal, whether it be from their place of employment or by committing crimes such as robbery or burglary. Understanding the youth's need for money and continually discussing this with the suspect will usually cause him to confess.

Tom was suspected of stealing systematically from lockers and desks in his school. A rookie was sent in plain clothes to question him—the assignment is unpopular—and, face to face with the kid, was so embarrassed he started talking desperately about handball and baseball and games. The two gassed away animatedly for an hour or so. Then the detective remembered what he was there for.

"Tommy," he said, "did you take that wallet?"

Answer:

"Yes, but I was just going to spend the money on food for home."

His father had skipped two years before. His mother had been ill since Christmas. Well, society, which hadn't cared much, got the welfare department on the job, the family pulled itself together, and Tommy wasn't arrested but went on to college and a career in one of the learned professions.

It's a good workmanlike study, not only of juveniles but of the society they live in. Maybe crime is the only honest form of criticism that's left.

How To Write a Test Paper

If (1) your fate had been so fickle as to make you the mayor of your town and if (2) you had been so improvident as to put off until now writing the speech you must read to people on your inauguration New Year's Day, a suggestion could be made:

Forget the wonderful persons who get up early and come, dragging their January 1 hangover behind them, to inauguration ceremonies. Banish them, friend and foe, from your mind; write them out of the script; resolve to talk about the town as if the people in it did not, as individuals, exist.

Heartless?

It sounds cold-blooded. It isn't. The mayor who has persons by name in mind when he undertakes to discuss a town's problems is doomed to a series of misunderstandings and misstatements. Persons die or move away or get caught and sent to jail. Individual persons are the mere cells, now flowing and now forever gone; the town, the collective people of the town, are the living tissue.

So much—and too much—for preamble, and the principle must go without saying; and yet on New Year's Day there'll be mayors reading their prospectus for 1965 and glancing sidewise to see whether the president of the taxpayers' penny-pinching association is applauding what was just said about keeping stern control on the costs of public education.

Too many mayors will write their inauguration address and shape their policy to serve persons, not people.

The suggestion is that they draft the paper for the audience which won't be in town hall that day.

Any mayor sufficiently determined can please a dozen or so powerful persons in town by hammering educational programs down to the three Rs and holding school expenses to what they were ten years ago. The saving might be a few hundred thousand dollars a year and 10 points on a tax rate. The cost?

An inadequate school program might cost the children a few million dollars—the cash difference between the income of well educated citizens and functional illiterates.

It might cost the intangible difference between a full and happy life and a life of frustrate misery.

Insufficient schools might account for the need this afternoon for a big and expensive police force, the need years from now for an expensive welfare program.

They might cost the town its economic future. The kind of business or industry a town yearns to attract, the kind that builds and keeps a tidy shop and pays lavish taxes and furnishes its own services, is precisely the kind that finds out before it makes its move what kind of schools it's getting its people into. The town that saves money at the expense of its children and teachers is the town avoided by what's called desirable industry.

That, a onetime mayor might say a quarter century from now, was a hell of a price to pay for pleasing a dozen monomaniacs.

The fanatics mayors often have in mind are always few in number, and they are unreliable. They shuffle on or off. The fabric of the town and its problems remain constant. If housing is needed now, it will be needed tomorrow no matter what curses are uttered by whom on the homeless and the poor. If parks are needed this year they'll not be less needed next year. If the slums are intolerable they'll not improve, and if the people living in slums are miserable they will not be rendered happy by reflecting that in the opinion of the mayor's best friends they could escape their infelicity by changing the color of their skin or hustling out and making a million dollars. Rats in the cellars, raw sewage in backyards, the illnesses and loneliness and the terminal hopelessness of old age—the things that matter don't come to New Year's Day meetings or listen to inaugural addresses.

To these, the constants, I'd like to hear the mayor speak. It's a suggestion.

286

That'll Teach Them What?

There is, of course, no such thing as a good theory that won't work in practice. There are good theories. These work when put to the pragmatic test. There are bad theories. These don't. We come now to the Blair theory.

This is the theory of deterrent severity. It postulates that if you belt a teen-ager hard enough it will loosen his second cousin's teeth, rattle his grandmother's piano all out of tune, and drive the entire population in his age bracket into holy orders.

Before Magistrate Stanley J. Blair of Laurelton came two eighteen-year-olds. On a charge of possessing a can of beer he sentenced them to one year in jail. They had the can in the car.

The ferocity of the sentence made news of it. So it got a good play in the papers. So did Magistrate Blair's theory, as popularized by Police Chief William C. Poole of Lakewood:

"I think it's high time judges stopped babying these kids and started getting tough with them. If we had more of the same type of punishment we would have less delinquency."

Now let's put the Blair theory to the pragmatic test.

He pronounced the one-year sentence Thursday. Friday he had to reduce the sentence on the possession count to thirty days, the maximum under the law; so the story got another go-round that day too. But Friday night some kids aged fourteen to seventeen, male and female both, congregated in the woods behind the Susquehanna Railroad's little old Campgaw station to roast wienies and beer it up, and it took a detail of six policemen to break up the bacchanal.

We are not applauding these young ruffians, and for the record will here and now disparage their desperate behavior. They are present simply to serve as experimental animals. Using them, we have just tested whether the Blair theory works.

It doesn't.

But Magistrate Blair should be felicitated for proposing the theory. He has brought into the open the whole of what may be called the sentimental view of human affairs.

The unsentimental view is that of the experienced and disenchanted criminal-court judge, the experienced Prosecutor and probation officer and reporter and indeed criminal. These people know and sometimes say that any crime has a certain fixed worth in terms of imprisonment or fine, that justice is done only when the punishment is hand-tooled to fit that crime precisely, and that no good is done by affixing to one crime the punishment for another.

Mr. Blair seems to have visited on his two teen-agers his society's vengeance for some things these teen-agers didn't do but some other teen-agers did. And he seems to have a substantial part of his society's opinion supporting him. Said Mrs. L. J. Dalton:

"This might be a good way to start cracking down on these teen-agers."

"I think under the circumstances one can of beer to an eighteen-year-old can be very dangerous," said Mrs. M. F. Davenport.

But these are sentimental statements, expressing not a set of facts but a complicated emotion. Sacco and Vanzetti were punished sentimentally, by reason not of anything they had done but because their society was simply overflowing with a generous compulsion to punish somebody. In Delaware we resolve deliberately, in the form of legislation, to flog people; in Mississippi we sentimentally hang them; in New Jersey time after time we have heard sentimentalists plead for the castration of sexual deviates —not that this barbaric surgery would alter the balance of forces in certain human bodies and personalities which produce sex aberrations, but it would make a lot of us feel better.

288

One decade we're admiring the Russians and the Chinese and our admiration is sentimental—it has only casual points of contact with the realities of that decade. Now we're hating the Russians and Chinese; and this too is as sentimental, being as far from a particular critical judgment, as the mass-distribution birthday card.

Teen-agers' drinking is not a consequence of law or public policy; for the cause of it and the cure we shall have to go beyond that. Delinquency is not the result of children's being unafraid of punishment. To punish any specimen for the sins of his kind is as futile as to kill an ant for its antness and expect that to teach ants in Africa a lesson.

The kids in Franklin Lakes had beer with their hot dogs. Let them go for the time being; if any lynch party is to be organized, it has its business with others. Let's see whom, unsentimentally.

Seminar at the State Line

Out of all the hundreds of stops they've made at the Rockland County roadblocks the police have plucked forth one teen-ager for driving while drunk and one for beer running. The purpose of the roadblocks is not to make arrests but to organize a body of statistics, of course—and I cannot for the life of me understand the statistical significance of measuring the flow of mountain rills but ignoring the torrent of teen-age traffic that ebbs and flows across the George Washington Bridge. Yet it had better be acknowledged that on the showing to date the teen-ager totes his grog with greater grace and competence than does his old man.

Or else he runs out of money sooner.

But, inefficient as the up-County roadblocks may be as a crime-detecting device, hadn't we better start worrying about their efficiency as an educational institution?

289

If his teachers have been diligent the teen-ager understands long before he is old enough to know he's thirsty that the law is a majestic edifice—the ultimate result of human wisdom acting upon human experience for the benefit of all the people, as old Johnson said it. If his teachers have told him to memorize the theories of law it is proper for him to know, he may remember more complements to the law than does any lawyer.

"There are two, and only two, foundations of law: equity and utility." That's Edmund Burke.

"The absolute justice of the state, enlightened by the perfect reason of the state: that is law." And that is Rufus Choate.

"Reason is the life of the law, . . . which is the perfection of reason." That's Coke.

"Law is the crystallization of the habit and thought of society." That's Woodrow Wilson.

Briefly, the law is uniform, it is general, it is based on certain common concepts of morality, it is equitable, and above all it states for us the standards of behavior which we approve most enthusiastically when we find ourselves adhering to them, as all of us do from time to time.

But at the State line the teen-age drinker discovers that what's illegal on this side of the street is approved by the law on that side. He finds that what New Jersey deems to be contrary to the peace and dignity of the State is considered in New York to be absolutely essential to them. He learns for himself by doing—in the best tradition of John Dewey—that whether or not you're a criminal depends not on what you do but on where you are, which on the whole seems a seedy way of studying relativity. On his way home from the latest refinement of the child-labor sweatshop he is stopped at the roadblock by the kindly policeman.

The policeman inquires, not necessarily in these words:

Did you go over into New York State and do that which New Jersey forbids you to do?

"Yes," says the driver, hiccuping fragrantly. "Why?"

290

"I just thought I'd ask," says the blue-coated student of probabilities and statistics.

No matter how earnestly young people yearn to admire and respect their society, how can they escape coming to the conclusion that the law is a giggling old fool if not downright insane?

And how can they escape noticing that the New York age limit is fixed at eighteen years precisely because it sets up an apparatus for the exploitation of a class, i.e., themselves? By this time there remains no latitude for doubt that the liquor lobby in Albany wants the eighteen-year law left as it is, no matter how vehemently decent. State-line saloonkeepers protest they don't want teen-agers' allowance money—or any piece of the paltry wage earned by a kid who has gone out of school to work at that stage of immaturity.

And there remains no doubt that the sovereign State of New York has a vested interest in what Marx (among other commentators on the law) called the conversion of immature human beings into mere machines for the consumption of goods. New York is calculated to have a $13-million tax stake in the teen-age traffic. As long as it's dragging the house cut from that sweatshop it is not likely to turn suddenly starry-eyed about equity, utility, and perfect reason.

That's another lesson a bright kid is not apt to forget.

All, Alas, According to Plan

Under a mangy sycamore tree on a sidewalk in Harlem a little old woman was shrilly discussing municipal planning.

"Why," she said, "these kids don't want sprinklers down there by the river. Down there by the river"—she stabbed the air with her umbrella, pointing east on 126th Street—"there's a river to duck into, a day like this. We want the sprinklers here."

Her three-housewife audience muttered: yeah, yeah, up here. The traffic light changed. The eavesdropper had to move along.

Heading across the County, then across Harlem on the way to the airport, he had been wondering who is consulted when the planners make their plans.

Here along the highway is a tidy park with nobody in it—clean green baseball field, benches, fences, swings, basketball goals. It stands deserted. In the middle of town two dozen clamoring kids are playing a strange and dangerous game. On opposite sidewalks they form jostling teams. As the traffic flows past, they bounce a biggish rubber ball on the hardtops. "Catch a fly you're out," they squabble, and lunge for the twisting ball.

I suppose purists would object that it would be a recklessly unscientific land use if we were to put the village park in the center of town, supplanting the present parking plaza, and were to make the merchants park at the edge of town—where normally the Little League baseball field is now located—and walk to and from their place of business.

So this will not be proposed. But a question may be risked. For years the foremost mystery of life in the United States has been the identity of the respondents in public-opinion polls. Who are the people who constitute that scientifically randomized cross section of the population which decides whether we should go ahead with the Atlas program or reduce the dollar limit on tax-exempt reserves in savings and loan associations? But the phantom poll respondent has a rival. Who tells the planners what to plan?

I have heard that sometimes questionnaires are circulated. During the Commission campaign in Ridgewood last month the candidates recalled that along in 1958 people were asked what kind of town they'd like Ridgewood to be and most of them—eighty-five per cent or so—said, "Residential." I do not mean to minimize the value of such research. I just don't know what it means.

At a planning conference in 1955 Dr. Leonard J. Duhl, a psychiatrist on the staff of the National Institute of Mental Health, suggested that a lot of planning is done not only by planners but for other planners. He told the planners to go talk to other people. Specifically, at one magic moment he told them to go see a psychiatrist. Mayor Farnsley of Louisville did, and the doctor was able to help—not just in the design of park benches, street signs, traffic control, and so forth, but in concentrating the municipal government's attention on the needs of people.

But Dr. Duhl went on:

> In making use of people in planning who are not planners, let me put in a plug for the ordinary guy. Getting his advice has two values: in terms of the advice itself (since as products of the middle class ourselves we usually know only the needs of the typical middle-class American although this doesn't reflect the needs of all people) and also in the opportunity for the process of active participation by the individual concerned. Helping people to help themselves has become an important byword in many programs. It is more than just a trite slogan. The meaning of the participation process does much for man's need to belong, create, and play a part in the society he lives in.

He said there is a substantial danger that, even when planning accurately represents the articulate opinion of a community, it won't meet the community's needs:

> In many instances the power structure [of a town] is such that a small few, usually of the middle class, hold . . . the memberships in all the organizations. Too, many groups organize but have limited power to really act and be felt. We must not be afraid to involve both the organized and the unorganized in planning. . . . This must be true participation, not just that of participants in a questionnaire.

Not often enough is it remembered that planning per se is nothing sacred, that every last one of the horrors that surround us had to be planned.

Dr. Duhl was talking about mental health.

And the old lady was right about those sprinklers.

Pilot Project in Resurrection

Notice is taken herewith that we've gotten down to the point in the campaigning at which people are described in public as isolationists, scabs, socialists, crooks, and fascists.

Your reporter has a suggestion to make.

It is that we evolve a method of ascertaining, by objective and if possible scientific means, whether the candidates for office who are accused of being isolationists, scabs, socialists, crooks, and fascists are in fact isolationists, scabs, socialists, crooks, and fascists.

The findings would be tested and tabulated and in due time published.

That's all. The truth would not become available in time to affect this November's election results—the reports could not possibly be worked up and made public much before the April or May of any year after the election involved. We have long since triumphed over any hallucination that we or anybody else can reform politics in the United States. We aren't interested in reform. It interferes with the benign processes of Nature and natural selection. If people can persuade themselves that the issues in this campaign are bimetallism and the Dred Scott decision, if by reason of their consenting to behave like boobs they enfeeble the republic and accelerate its downfall, well, vox populi vox dei, and who are we to meddle?

But it does seem to your correspondent that we might be getting a better quality of men to run for office if we could give people this guarantee:

No matter how a candidate might be fouled in the autumn

campaigning, by the time the dogwoods next bloomed we'd have him cleaned off and good as new.

Perhaps the mayor of your town is the best man available for the job. On averages, chances are he isn't. On averages, somewhere in town tonight, reading a book or pawing over some work he brought home from the office or making a string of phone calls for some institution or church or college or charity that has engaged his attention, is a better man. Go now and ask this better man to run for the mayoralty.

1. He'll point out to you what's happening to Nelson Rockefeller and Averell Harriman in New York, what happened to Cliff Case in New Jersey, and he'll ask you why he should subject himself to being thus beslimed.

2. He'll point out that he has a family.

3. He'll point out he has a job, meaning an employer and business associates to whom his integrity is some high percentage of his total worth.

4. He'll point out that in politics people play for keeps, meaning to win at any cost, meaning to kill.

5. He'll point out that to campaign in the only way he could do it, seriously and effectively, he'd have to talk about bread-and-butter things—garbage contracts, paving contracts, purchasing methods, certain curious lacunae in law enforcement, certain infestations of nephews in civil office.

6. He'll point out that to attack the establishment at the only points where it's vulnerable to legitimate attack he'd necessarily threaten to take from greedy and ruthless men their power and their money, millions of dollars, cash.

7. Finally, he'll point out that these men would undertake to ruin him.

And he'd ask you why he should go out of his way to seek his destruction.

The argument against running for public office is almost impregnable, although it must be noted that, by and large, we keep getting candidates and they keep proving out an extraordinarily fine assay. But suppose some great clearing house could be established, perhaps by one of the foundations, to publish annual reports covering the entire nation. Robinson, James E., candidate for Council in East Wheeze, N.J.: it is not true that this man was an isolationist before World War II; research team No. 651 finds that he did in fact boo Henry Wallace at a meeting in July 1939, but he was booing the farm program, not the transfer of destroyers to Britain. Fustian, Gerald F., mayor, Grunton, Mass.: did not have an affair with his secretary; indeed, never had a secretary. You see what we have in mind. The report could be published, of course, as an appendix of the political parties' established magazines or reports or even, to avoid libel complications, inserted in the Congressional Record. It would do no immediate good except to rehabilitate the reputations of innocents. If it demonstrated to voters that they're being swindled in nine campaigns out of ten it might, of course, eventually effect a reform, but that would not be its primary purpose.

Cash Registers Don't Care Who's Running Them

The sound of breathing never stopped. Longie Zwillman stopped. A lot of people resumed.

Zwillman can't talk. We're told the Federal Bureau of Investigation people had asked him some questions he couldn't answer. Your reporter does not know what this phrase means: maybe the way the poor little devils he bullied on witness stands and juries couldn't talk. So Zwillman went down to the cellar and anesthetized himself with a half-bottle of bourbon and, ever fastidious, hanged himself in the closet.

So he'll not be telling the F.B.I. or the McClellan committee investigators swarming over the State what there is to know about jukebox money and where it was invested in New Jersey politics and business, industry, crime, vice. A lot of people are breathing easier.

But the system didn't hang itself.

The jukeboxes play on, hoeing in teen-agers' dimes to be mixed with bookie money and racket money and then cooled off in legit-looking factories or laundries or golf clubs. The garbage trucks rumble through the streets. The statesmen still buy their votes in the rotting wards where people can't read and can't think except with their glands. The system—the invisible republic that sits with society's jugular between its first two fingers and sucks at it as if it were a soda straw—isn't going anywhere. Longie didn't make that much difference.

We're told it is naive and futile or merely romantic to talk like this.

We're told the system, the international supergovernment whose cabinet met at Apalachin, is a fact of life—you accept it, the way you accept pollution, automobile accidents, Khrushchev, brutality, ignorance.

We're told—from the witness stand—that if you want to sell jukeboxes, write a best-seller popular song, produce a hit, open a saloon, run for office, ship a cargo, you deal with the system.

Yet it is impossible to believe this is true. Sometimes it looks true. Sometimes it looks as if, at a moment when our attention may have been on other things like a war, the government of the United States and its States and counties and towns split in two like an amoeba. It looks as if one government is the one you see, the one you elect, the one that sends you a tax bill and maintains armies and goes through its stately rigadoons with Hitlers and Tojos and depressions and Khrushchevs. It looks as if the other government is one utterly separate from this but complete with its own constitution and laws, its bureaucracy, its legislative and executive branches, its department of defense and police and courts. That is how it looks when, say, a Willie Moretti becomes dead, not by reason of anger but to maintain the peace and dignity of the superstate.

It looks as if, over on the hither side of the dividing line, are people like us—the unorganized, unsophisticated, unknowing, the tender-minded, the obedient, with our trusts and dreams and political-science textbooks and letters to the editor.

It looks as if, away on that side, are the realists and doers—the tough-minded, hard-handed, utterly undeceived: the gangsters and racketeers and their agents in public office, some of the unions though not all, some of business but by no means all, some of industry and, the Almighty help them, the arts.

No use complaining: if that's the way things are, we shall not alter it much by denouncing it. If the mobs have taken over to the extent they seem to have done, if they have made their arrangement with any part of labor to keep their mutual affairs separate from the affairs of society, if we are being governed and pillaged by an instrumentality we cannot confront or control, then this state of affairs isn't going to be annihilated by any man's disparaging it. Society has found it must deal with such things in other ways, ranging from revolution to the invention of special ethics and special agencies dispensing ruthlessness. Lincoln had to do it for a while. We shall have to see how society in the United States decides to deal with interstate conspiracy that has hired away legislatures and police into its private service. That'll take time.

All we set out to say was that Longie's stopping breathing is just another failure, because he stopped before he could be made to answer the questions. But it's a large enterprise, and the proprietor's absence will hardly be noticed by the cash registers. There'll be others to ask.

The Y.R. and the Rage to Live

We were warned Young Republicans take themselves much too seriously.

"As a matter of fact," an old Republican told us on the way to the midwinter convention of the Young Republicans of New Jersey Inc., "Young Republicans are required to surrender their sense of humor as a condition of their acceptance into the organization."

This is not quite true.

George M. Gillette, Jr., of Norwood, the Y.R.'s national committeeman, was making a serious point, but judge for yourself:

One cold midnight in October 1952 he was called to the phone by a Young Republican potentate in New York and told to have six New Jersey Young Republicans report for compaign duty at the George Washington Bridge plaza at 6 A.M. sharp next day. George said bitterly no New Jersey Young Republican has been up at 6 A.M. since the morning he was born, and what was this all about.

Bikes for Ike, said the New York thinker. Young Republicans were riding bikes for Ike from Maine to Florida, and the Bergen County Young Republicans were to seize the steaming velocipedes from the New York members of the relay team there at the Bridge, and were to ride them to Cape May, where they'd hand over the bikes for Ike to a Delaware team.

George said he had a constructive suggestion.

If the New York bike-for-Ikers would take the ferry to Staten Island, he said, they could pedal across the island and find along its southern edge a fine beach. Let them don water wings, said George, and paddle south by west, and pretty soon they'd fetch up on the Delaware shore, where they could deliver the bikes for the continuation of this spectacular irrelevancy.

But, said Mr. Gillette, in a word, New Jersey Republicans would not be riding bikes for Ike.

Matter of fact, while one noticed a certain stuffiness in some of the debate going on throughout the day at the Suburban, up there on Route 4 in Paramus, the verdict here is that Young Republicans are at least as well fixed for a sense of humor as old Republicans, Democrats of all ages except the ones who were brought up to believe they stood for decentralization of government and the federal republic after Jefferson, Socialists, Communists, and Prohibitionists.

Republicans maybe don't have much to be humorous about. "The question," said Senator Dumont (R., Warren), "is whether the party is to go forward, stand still, or slip back." A frown darkened his handsome face. "Although," he added, "I can't see that we're in any position to afford any further slipping." And it is conceivable that the same fortitude of spirit that would make a young citizen choose being a Republican these days—it's like being a Democrat in Ridgewood—requires a certain craggy solemnity of spirit.

They disagree. "It's discouraging," said Dr. Charles R. Erdman, the Princeton history professor who is now as state chairman presiding over the party and is sometimes mistaken for a wholesale junk collector—"it's discouraging to be in a situation where you've got to fight Republicans rather than Democrats. The basis of our quarrels troubles me most, whether the quarreling goes to the roots of our political beliefs or is a grab for political power." His handsome face clouded over too. "Although why any one would be grabbing for power with things in this condition," he said, "I cannot see." They do disagree.

Mr. Gillette was saying he happens to be a conservative Republican. . . .

"George is Pandora," said a Young Republican sitting next to us, taking notes on a yellow pad. "And that conservative-liberal-modern stuff is the box."

300

Mr. Gillette had finished and sat down. A tall young man at the end of the table got up.

"About that conservative Republicanism of George's," he began.

The man sitting next to us whispered:

"Morris County man. Ran Frelinghuysen's campaign. A bit of an egghead, but very bright at that."

Over in the corner of the room a man was saying this phony liberalism of Case's (R., N.J.) is, for his money, not Republicanism. Another man quoted a line of Dr. Erdman's: "I believe in taking a lesson from history." "We should look to the future, even if we are Young Republicans," said the other man. It seemed to one stranger that the quality of the humor was not inferior. Must be something else that's the matter.

How Not to Do It Yourself

You're President. Or—if you don't mind slumming in your day-dreams—you're Governor or mayor or Chairman of the Joint Appropriations Committee.

The Treasury has collected $1 in taxes. You are confronted by three shrill completing claims on the $1—from, let's say, education, warfare, and highways.

How do you make the choice?

Easy, roared Dr. Paul N. Ylvisaker of Cranbury, director of Public Affairs for the Ford Foundation.

1. Raise $2 more, but that's not cricket, isn't safe except the first year after election, and suffices mainly to fetch six more claims.

2. Analyze the three claims before you. What party do these people belong to, did they contribute to your party's last campaign, and how loud can they holler?

3. Create two new tax-collecting units of government, on the theory that taxpayers, like crows, can't count past three how many hunters are after them.

4. Decide that two of the claims involve maintenance charges that can be deferred.

5. Borrow the other $2, and let the next administration figure how to pay it back. . . .

The author of this good-natured synopsis of sin used to be a City Hall working stiff himself (executive secretary and consultant to the Mayor of Philadelphia) and an identifiable egghead (faculty, Swarthmore, Minnesota, Harvard, Pennsylvania), and he was telling the State planning conference in Trenton that governments, like doctors, have specialized so intensively that nobody—federal, State, local—has noticed the patient's in pretty rocky shape.

But it's easy to choose who'll get that $1.

6. Refer two of the claimants to some other level of government, and do not fail to tell them their problem is the other guy's responsibility and has been too long shamefully neglected.

7. Or explain angrily you could finance all three programs if the other level of government weren't short-changing you in taxes and grants.

8. Recommend handing the whole job over to private industry. Private dollars go three times as far as public dollars, as every one knows.

9. Set yourself up as a special district or authority, lend the money, and charge 7 per cent interest.

10. Set yourself up as a suburb, and zone two of the claims out of your jurisdiction.

11. Get rid of this nuisance of people as constituents, and go out and get yourself some uncomplaining industry.

12. Appoint a commission, to report as soon as you've gotten yourself a better job.

13. Put the mess to referendum vote.

14. Spread the claims over three years, and hope an election doesn't intervene.

302

15. Make the expenditure that will be most highly visible (freshly painted fire plugs) and comes closest to preserving such traditional values as motherhood and the American way of life.

16. Be moralistic. Say the two claims you reject are outrageous raids on the public treasury, are socialistic, or contravene the master plan.

17. Underestimate your revenues, and at the end of the year parcel out the unexpected surplus.

18. Keep the tax rate where it is, and pray hard for the economy and the tax base to produce $3 where only $1 grew before.

19. Be Solomon. Cut the $1 into three parts, and forget the question of who deserved the whole of it.

20. Spend fifty cents, and consult tomorrow's editorials as to how you'd better spend the rest. . . .

23. Hire an economist to calculate the marginal utility of each of the three optional ways of spending the $1, first making sure he is an economist whose:

a. Findings will agree with your prejudices and political calculations, also whose

b. Computations will be so complicated that any taxpayer will give up and concede they may be fair.

You must have seen familiar little faces peering out of some of these gnarled lines—your mayor's from No. 13, Governor Meyner's from No. 18. Dr. Ylvisaker made no bones about the dramatis personae of No. 23. It's he:

"Face it; it's a losing game," he told the haggard officials in his audience. "Quit the public service, and join the rest of us who are doing the claiming. It's more fun. You can spend more money. And, as long as it's on a private account, nobody's asking any hard questions."

Right to Privacy: Do We Want One?

Absolute personal privacy is that which every one demands and doesn't know what to do with when he gets it. There is no such thing. Under the conditions of the world we live in there cannot be such a thing as privacy—civilization would collapse within 10 minutes if the courts ever devised a way of making people let other people severely alone.

But privacy is very big this year. The country was outraged when the Passport Office in the State Department sicked its embassy dicks abroad on a Harvard history professor, H. Stuart Hughes, on the theory that somebody guessed he might be unsound in his political opinions. It was shocked when General Motors hired a private eye to turn Ralph Nader inside out ("See what makes him tick—his politics, his marital status, his women, boys, etc.") because Mr. Nader had written a book suggesting the automobile industry may not be paying sufficient attention to safety factors in car design.

So privacy is big, and a couple of recent Supreme Court decisions anchor the right to privacy in the Constitution itself. To be sure, the Constitution does not enumerate privacy among the specific rights, but in Griswold v. Connecticut, the Planned Parenthood birth control case, Justice Douglas laid the groundwork for a luxuriant growth of case law:

> Specific guarantees in the Bill of Rights have penumbras, formed by emanations from those guarantees that help give them life and substance. . . . Various guarantees create zones of privacy.

So there is indeed such a thing as privacy comma it says here. Now, how do you go about getting it?

Before ever the baby emerges from the womb, he is a record and a number in half a dozen filing cabinets. His parents have testified. The innocent unborn has sat upside down for an X-ray portrait. His blood type is established. By the time a competent obstetrician has ordered his mother to the delivery room, more is known about that baby than the world knows in such unimpeachable form about William Shakespeare or the late Socrates.

And from the moment he is footprinted at the point of delivery to the moment when the doctor sighs, puts the pennies on his eyelids, and signs the death certificate scarcely a day goes by but his privacy is assaulted again. Behind him as he staggers through the world he leaves a great snowdrift of confessions; medical histories, school records some of which drag his innermost psyche twitching onto the paper, report cards, college entrance examinations, intelligence and psychological tests, job records, experience résumés, employment interviews, credit rating examinations, and questionnaires by multiples of a thousand.

The right to privacy didn't even exist as a concept until 1890, when Louis D. Brandeis wrote an article under that very name in the Harvard Law Review. Now that we know we have it, eagerly we disclose to any jackass who asks information about ourselves of a kind pre-1890 people considered a matter of confidence between themselves and God—nobody else's business.

The trend is in the right direction. Invasion of privacy has become a richly profitable racket, a hobby for troublemakers, and in business and industry a competitive device infuriatingly cheap and unfair.

But privacy? How useful to a man whose integrity has just been invaded by the shriek of a jetplane, the stutter of a pneumatic hammer in the street below, or the idiot yowl of a fight next door—how useful to him would be an assurance that nobody can legally install a bug under his desk or his bed?

And to the millions who scrawl their dirty words to lovelorn columnists and ex-parte marriage advisers and fan-magazine psychiatrists, would privacy be a prize or a prison? A nation that has made a religion of letting its hair down and crying on each other's shoulder may not want to be alone.

Should a State Demand or Deserve?

When the New Jersey Senate abruptly, almost furtively, enacted the other day a bill requiring that schoolchildren salute the flag and recite the pledge of allegiance, in that hushed moment the State was not a commanding figure but a pathetic one.

There stood the poor old shrew yearning to be loved but saying, "Whether or not you love me, tell me that you do!"

The bill's specific purpose is to coerce statements and gestures of conformity out of little Black Muslims, who allege a religious scruple against this harmless classroom ritual and who are allowed by the Commissioner of Education to stand mute while their classmates go through the motions. This is the specific purpose. But it seems to me the Senate's neurotic invasion of the private conscience raises questions broader than Black Muslims do.

To an extent, subject to veto by the Governor, the Senate speaks for a State, and a State is its people, and people are society; and there is something miserably unfunny in society's pleading that it be told it is revered and loved.

One of these days some child—he may be a Black Muslim, at that—is likely to pipe up in his dreadful innocence and ask society and its Senate why, if they want to be loved, they don't try a little harder to make themselves lovable.

It's the only society we have, and so it is good or will have to suffice, of course, and yet it has been behaving lately in ways that arouse a wonder whether it's going through some paroxysmal change of life. Society is law and order, it is security, and yet I wonder how much love Miss Genovese would have thought she owed, if she had survived, to the society that sat in its window and watched the stabbing.

"One nation under God, indivisible, with liberty and justice for all": with how much feeling will Jose Manguan, twenty-six, repeat the pledge next time he gets a chance? There he stood, alone and workless and despairing, poised at the rail above the river. And the crowd on Brooklyn Bridge shouted jump. "Jump," society had cried to the 19-year-old fidgeting on the 11th-story ledge of that Albany hotel. "Oh, if he doesn't jump soon I'll miss my bus," a girl complained to her date. The police talked the boy in from the ledge (and they were society too, a piece of it), but what he'll remember are the grinning faces and the taunts and the groans when he decided to commit survival.

The normally reverent *Hudson Dispatch* was cogitating the other day on a County Judge's warning that we are threatened by something like anarchy. It too reflected on the divisibility that supervenes so often:

"Last week a young woman was raped in New York in broad daylight. Forty persons at least were in the vicinity, all of whom could have offered some assistance. But nay, they preferred not to become involved. A couple of days later an elderly man was robbed of his meager $19 pension check as he walked along a street of Trenton with his wife at 11 o'clock in the morning. Fifteen bystanders or passersby made no attempt to help the victims or alert police. . . . They too did not want to be involved. Does man no longer consider himself his brother's keeper?"

How lovable really is this wolf-pack society that turns and rends the laggard, the sick, the stranger? A civilization day by day is the sum total of billions of separate decisions. Among us we have made some intricate arrangements which depend on highly abstract, sophisticated acts of faith or consent. Money is a fiction once we see that a dollar is a piece of dirty paper, nothing more. Property is a fiction. Brotherhood is a living reality on this street but on that one is a ghastly joke. How can we command loyalty in a child who has known since he was three years

307

old that his only world is a conspiracy against his body and soul?

A little pledge of allegiance can't really hurt a child, but let no one say such legislation as Senator Stamler's (R., Union) will make no difference. The State that must rant and plead for outward show of reverence is not the State that is revered in its merely being. It, if not the child, can never be the same again.